Robert
A. Parks

D1308315

GEORGE WASHINGTON
The Pictorial Biography

The bronze Washington equestrian statue in Union Square, New York, where Washington was received by citizens of New York following the British evacuation of the city, Nov. 25, 1783. One of the earliest noteworthy equestrian statues in America. Figure designed by Henry Kirke-Brown; base designed by John Quincy Adams Ward. Dedicated July 4, 1856.

For Matthew William, Carol Ann,
Clark II, Leslie Elizabeth, Brian,
Victoria Ellen, Bruce and other
descendants of men he led.

*"Let his countrymen consecrate
the memory of the heroic General, the patriotic Statesman and
the virtuous Sage. Let them
teach these children never to
forget that the fruit of his
labors and his example are
their inheritance."*
— SAMUEL DEXTER,
in the U.S. Senate, 1799.

Banner of the Commander-in-Chief's Guard, commonly called The Washington
Life Guard. The personnel were purposely drawn from all thirteen colonies. It was organized in 1776, when the army was based on Manhattan Island.
During that period Thomas Hickey plotted an abduction of General Washington
for the purpose of turning him over to the British. (Hickey was exposed and
hanged.) The Guard continued in existence until the army was disbanded in 1783.

Signature in book-plate (*right*) is definitely not that of its owner, who never spelled
out the George in his signature any time after his youth, though he did write his full
name occasionally in legal documents. This is one of the several different designs of
book-plates Washington used for volumes he chose to keep.

George Washington

The Pictorial Biography

by Clark Kinnaird

EXITUS ACTA PROBAT

George Washington

Bonanza Books · New York

Washington's Address Card

INTRODUCTORY NOTE

The prevalent popular image of George Washington in his lifetime, and at least a half century afterward, naturally was shaped substantially by the pictures of him that the public saw. The scores of paintings, drawings, sculptures, made from life by accomplished artists, became private possessions of individuals or were exhibited in buildings accessible only to a relative few in the United States or in Europe (where admiration of this American arose spontaneously among kings and commoners — including commoners in England). Visualizations of Washington's features and mien in the public mind generally took form originally from the contemporary woodcuts in the press or cheap prints of engravings that were circulated — many of them crude in artistry or inaccurate in portraiture and background. One result: perpetuation of the mythological scene of the boy George beside a fallen cherry tree, hatchet in hand.

In choices for this pictorial biography, preference was given purposely to those eighteenth- and nineteenth-century illustrations (other than cherry tree scene conceptions) that were circumstantially influential in molding conceptions of Washington's character and environment prevalent for decades before inventions of photo-engraving and printing processes brought readers of newspapers, magazines and books close reproductions of Washington portraiture and photographs of surviving structures and scenes associated with his career. Changes wrought in those structures and scenes in intervening decades have made some illustrations herein more accurate representations of Washington's era than modern photographs.

Necessarily, a number of significant events in Washington's career are not given attention in the pictorial chapters. They are included in the detailed chronology preceding the index.

C. K.

CONTENTS

Above: Obverse and reverse designs of the medal voted by Congress for Washington on March 25, 1776, in recognition of his having driven the British from Boston. It was the first medal voted by Congress for anyone. The war delayed its execution (it was struck in France from a die cut by Duvivier) and the medal was not presented to Washington until 1786. (From B. J. Lossing's *Pictorial Field-Book of Revolution.*)

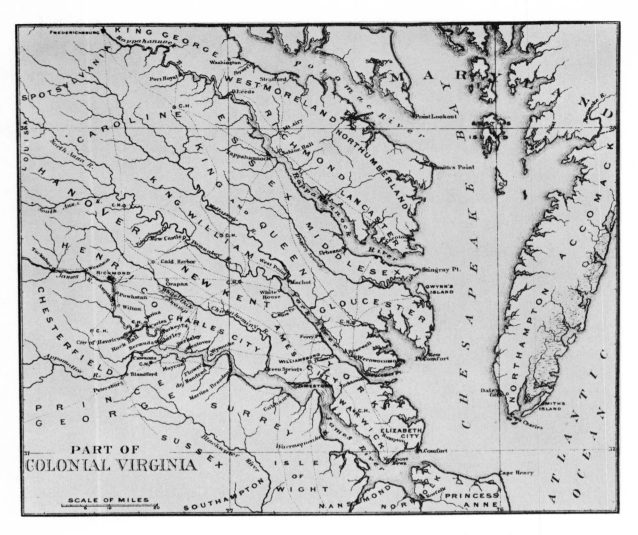

Colonial Virginia, reproduced from *Virginia, A History of the People*,
by John Eston Cooke, 1883.

VIRGINIA, when George Washington was born, had been undergoing settlement and subjugation for 125 years. The Washington family had been established there for almost a century.

The estimated population of the English colonies in America in 1740 was 894,000. Virginia was the most populous colony, with 200,000; Maryland was next, with 105,000. Negro slaves constituted a large portion of these totals; it is calculated that 75,000 Africans were brought into the various Colonies before 1725. There also were numerous white persons in condition of servitude, under indenture or other form of legal bondage.

The wealth in goods and credits that the tobacco ships returned to Virginia collected in relatively few hands. As was discovered quickly, tobacco could not be grown profitably in the same fields year after year. Planters reached out for larger and larger tracts; small farmers were squeezed out or subordinated.

The planters along the James, the Potomac, the Rappahannock and the York created an aristocratic pattern that the South was to follow until the middle of the nineteenth century. They asserted practically all the authority as well as all the economic power in the Colony. They were the principal county officers, judges, colonels of militia, the revenue officers, the majority of the membership of the House of Burgesses, the vestrymen in the churches. George Washington was born into this caste.

I

FORMATIVE YEARS

"Associate yourself with men of good quality if you esteem your own reputation; for 'tis better to be alone than in bad company."

— "Rules of Civility," in Washington's boyhood copybook, before 1748

The earliest characterization at length of George Washington is the impression he made on Captain George Mercer, an officer in the Virginia Regiment in the campaign against the French. Mercer, who served under Washington as company commander and aide-de-camp, wrote in 1760:

"He may be described as being as straight as an Indian, measuring six feet two inches in his stockings, and weighing 175 pounds, when he took his seat in the House of Burgesses in 1759. His frame is padded with well-developed muscles, indicating great strength. His bones and joints are large, as are his feet and hands. He is wide shouldered, but has not a deep or round chest; is neat waisted, but is broad across the hips, and has rather long legs and arms.

"His head is well shaped though not large, but is gracefully poised on a superb neck. A large and straight rather than prominent nose; blue-gray penetrating eyes, which are widely separated and overhung by a heavy brow. His face is long rather than broad, with high round cheek bones, and terminates in a good firm chin.

"He has a clear though rather colorless pale skin, which burns with the sun. A pleasing, benev-olent, though a commanding countenance, dark brown hair, which he wears in a cue. His mouth is large and generally firmly closed, but which from time to time discloses some defective teeth. His features are regular and placid, with all the muscles of his face under perfect control, though flexible and expressive of deep feeling when moved by emotion. In conversation he looks you full in the face, is deliberate, deferential and engaging. His voice is agreeable and rather strong. His demeanor at all times composed and dignified. His movements and gestures are graceful, his walk majestic, and he is a splendid horseman."

This is a portrait drawn by a subordinate officer, one close to Washington in age. Washington had made a similarly strong impression upon his superiors, older men. Robert Dinwiddie, the royal governor of Virginia, wrote to General James Abercrombie, the British second-in-command in North America, in 1756: "Sir: Give me leave to pray your attention with his Lordship in favor of Col. George Washington, who I will venture to say is a very deserving gentleman, and has from the first commanded the forces of this dominion. Gen. Braddock thought so highly of him he made him his aid, and if he [Braddock] had survived, I believe would have provided handsomely for him in the Regulars. He is a person much beloved here, and has undergone many hardships in the service, and I really think he has just merit."

A short time before Braddock was killed, in 1755, he penned in a letter: "Is Mr. Washington among your acquaintances? If not, I recommend you to embrace the first opportunity to form his friendship. He is about twenty-three years of age; with a countenance both mild and pleasant, promising both wit and judgment. He is of comely and dignified demeanor, at the same time displays much self reliance and decision. He strikes me as being a young man of extraordinary and exalted character, and is destined to make no inconsiderable figure in our country."

Whence came the remarkable characteristics and talents Washington evidenced so early — from heredity? from environment? We shall see.

Washington said that he resembled his father in appearance and character. An acquaintance of Augustine Washington described the father: "Six feet in height he was, of noble appearance and manly proportions, with the most extraordinary muscular power. Over at Principa Iron Works where he acted as agent, he used to lift up and place in a wagon a mass that two ordinary men could hardly have raised from the ground." Augustine was florid in complexion, with brown hair and gray eyes, of genial nature, and called "Gus" affectionately by his friends.

Aside from the mention of him in quotation of the fatuous anecdote about the cherry tree, Gus Washington usually is a forgotten man in popular accounts of his son George's life. The tendency is to cater to the American matriarchal sentiment and thank Mother Washington for George's character. Paradoxically, more attention usually is paid to the subject of George's paternal progenitors in England than to his maternal forebears — a tacit concession that he may possibly have inherited some of his noble attributes from his father's side.

Washington wrote in 1792 that the history of his ancestors was, in his opinion, "of very little moment, and a subject to which I confess I have paid very little attention." He understood that the first Washingtons in this country arrived about 1657. He did not know "from whom they descended" or from what part of England they came.

It was established later that the first Washington arrivals in America were John and Lawrence, two of the six children of the Reverend Lawrence Washington, onetime rector of Purleigh. The rector was the great-grandson of Lawrence Washington, a mayor of Northampton who, as a partisan of Henry VIII, was enabled to purchase one of the priories seized during Henry's appropriation of Church properties. It stood at the village of Sulgrave, in Northamptonshire. Washingtons retained the property less than three generations; it was given up, under pressure of debt collectors, by the Reverend Lawrence Washington's uncle in 1619.

Detrimentally to his own later fortunes, the clergyman was a supporter of the royal Stuarts. Under Cromwell's government, he was forced out of his good living at Purleigh. It was charged he was "a common frequenter of ale-houses, not only himself sitting dayly tippling there, but also encouraging others in that beastily vice." Partisans of the Reverend Washington declared this to be nefarious slander and subterfuge; they characterized him as a rector of rectitude, "pious, modest, sober." The best they succeeded in doing for him was to secure permission for the Reverend Washington to preach at the small chapel at Brixted Parva, where his poverty matched that of his parishioners.

John, the rector's eldest son (born about 1632) escaped this poverty by going to sea. After voyages to Scandinavia and the German states, John Washington reached Virginia in 1657 as mate of the *Sea Horse*. The ketch, while heavily laden with an outbound cargo of tobacco in hogsheads, dragged bottom upon a Potomac bar. Before she could be refloated, a storm swept up the river and capsized the *Sea Horse*. Instead of abandoning the wreck, the captain set the crew to work raising the ship. During the ensuing weeks of labor, John Washington met and cultivated the acquaintanceship of a neighboring plantation owner, Nathaniel Pope, and of the latter's young daughter Anne.

HERE·LIETH·THE·BODI·OF·LAVRENCE
WASHINGTON·SONNE·&·HEIRE·OF
ROBERT·WASHINGTON· OF·SOVLGRAE
IN· THE·COVNTIE·OF·NORTHAMTON
ESQVIER·WHO·MARIED·MARGARET
THE·ELDEST·DAVGHTER·OF·WILLIAM
BVTLER·OF·TEES·IN·THE·COVNTIE
OF·SVSSEXE·ESQVIER·WHO·HAD·ISSV
BY·HER·8·SONNS·&·9·DAVGHTERS
WHICH·LAVRENCE·DECESSED·THE·13
OF· DECEMBER·A: DÑI: 1616

THOV·THAT·BY·CHANCE·OR·CHOYCE
OF·THIS·HAST·SIGHT
KNOW· LIFE·TO·DEATH· RESIGNES
AS·DAYE·TO·NIGHT
BVT·AS·THE·SVNNS· RETORNE
REVIVES·THE· DAYE
SO·CHRIST·SHALL·VS
THOVGH·TVRNDE·TO·DVST·&·CLAY

Woodcut of Washington family arms as represented in a stained-glass panel removed from Sulgrave Manor to the parish church, where there are five such panels. Two similar panels from Sulgrave Manor, commemorating marriages of two sixteenth-century Washingtons, are at the Corning, N.Y. Museum of Glass. Note the stars and stripes, suggestive of the origin of the American flag. *Below:* Half-penny token of an earlier English Washington.

Arms of Lawrence Washington (died 1616) and his wife, Margaret Butler, upon a slab at St. Mary's Church, Great Brington. They were grandparents of the Lawrence Washington who settled in Virginia in 1657 (the latter the grandfather of George).

Left: Watermark in paper made for the general's personal correspondence in his later years, and the encased pen he used when traveling (*above*).

John Washington wangled a release from the articles that bound him to the ship and married Anne Pope. Anne's father must have approved: He gave the couple seven hundred acres of land and took John's note for enough money to get the new plantation going. When Pope died, his will canceled his son-in-law's unpaid note.

No attempt will be made here to follow the fortunes of John's brother, Lawrence, and the latter's descendants. "In truth not having enquired much into the names or connection of the lateral branches of the family, I am unable to give satisfactory account of them," George Washington also recorded in 1792.

John Washington did well for himself quickly. Within two decades, he owned considerable acreage in Westmoreland County (acquired by various means), had a mill and other enterprises going for him, and enjoyed the standing of gentleman. His great-grandson, George, wrote that John "was employed as General against the Indians in Maryland, and as a reward for his services he was made a Colonel; and the parish wherein he lived was called after him." He was a burgess, a vestryman.

Colonel John had two sons, Lawrence and John, and one daughter, Ann. Lawrence was the grandfather of George. Lawrence was sixteen when Colonel John died in 1677 at the age of forty-three. Lawrence's life was shorter.

Lawrence married, in his twenties, Mildred Warner, daughter of Augustine Warner of Gloucester County, by whom he had two sons, John and Augustine, and one daughter named Mildred. He died in 1697 and was interred in the family graveyard at Pope's Creek. The widow went to England with her three children and there married one George Gale. She died in childbirth. Gale kept his foster children in England, attending to their upbringing and education, for twelve years. Then he went out to Maryland as agent for the Principa iron company. The young Washingtons accompanied him, or followed soon, and, going to Virginia, claimed the inheritance Colonel John had bequeathed to them through their mother — some 5000 acres of land and his working enterprises. Augustine took on another interest: he became agent in Virginia for the Principia company. He also added to his property

when, marrying as soon as he was twenty-one, he collected a substantial dowry.

George Washington wrote: "Augustine, son of Lawrence and Mildred Washington, married Jane Butler, the daughter of Caleb Butler of Westmoreland, April 20, 1715, by whom he had three sons: Butler (who died young), Lawrence, and Augustine, and one daughter, Jane, who died when a child. Augustine then married Mary Ball, March 6, 1730. . . ."

Augustine described his marriages as his "several Ventures" in his will.

By coincidence, the family line of Mary Ball was established in America the same year her husband's was, i.e., 1657. The circumstances of her grandfather, William Ball, were somewhat different from those of John Washington on the latter's arrival that year. William Ball had inherited property in England. He was a former officer in the royal army and the son of a highly placed attorney in London. Ball brought along his wife, several children, and a number of servants to attend him on the plantation he acquired at the mouth of Corotoman Creek, in Lancaster County. His antecedents, his substance and his quality admitted him to Virginia's ruling caste without delay. He became justice of the peace, burgess, vestryman.

When William Ball died, about 1680, the youngest of his children, Joseph, went to England to look after the father's estate for the heirs. Joseph married there, remained some years, and brought five or six children with his wife when he returned to Virginia. Joseph Ball spent the remainder of his life on a plantation called Epping Forest, on the left bank of the Rappahanock River.

Ball's first wife died a few years after arriving in this country. At the age of fifty-eight the widower married again. The bride, much his junior in years, was distinctly his social inferior, an almost illiterate widow named Mary Johnson. She had a son, John, and a daughter, Elizabeth, by her first husband when she moved into the Epping Forest mansion. Possibly intentionally, the date she bore Joseph Ball a daughter, Mary, does not

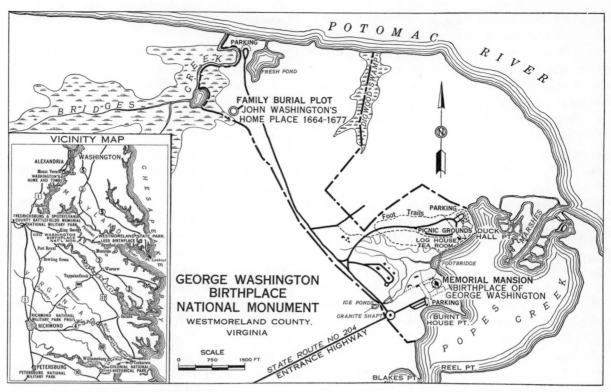

[↑] George Washington Birthplace National Monument, created 1930, prepared by the National Park Service and published in a pamphlet issued for visitors (Govt. Ptg. Off. 16-20707).

[↓] Washington ancestral plantation region, from the same pamphlet. John D. Rockefeller, Jr., assisted the Wakefield National Memorial Association to acquire title to Augustine Washington farm.

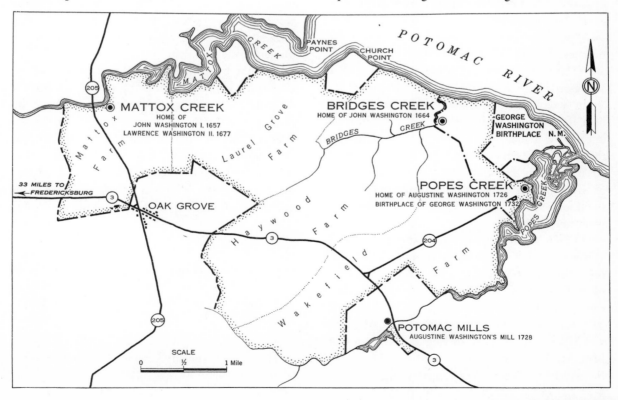

appear in any known records. Consequently, no one was ever sure of the age of George Washington's mother. She was probably about three when her father died in 1710. After taking care of his older children, his will left Mary 400 acres of land, three slaves and fifteen cattle.

Mary Ball soon had a stepfather, Richard Hewes of Northumberland County. Presumably, she was in his household with her mother until the latter died in 1721. Mrs. Hewes bequeathed most of her property to Mary, and designated George Eskridge, a well-to-do lawyer in Westmoreland County as the girl's guardian during minority. Mary divided her time the next few years in the homes of Eskridge, her half sister Elizabeth and members of the Ball family.

Augustine Washington probably became acquainted with Mary while she was a young miss. She attended the parish church to which he went with his first wife and their sons.

Following Jane Butler Washington's death in 1728, Augustine took the two sons to England and put them into Appleby Charter School, where he himself had been entered years before by George Gale. Injuries he suffered in a carriage accident prolonged his stay in the Old Country. This occasioned his becoming acquainted anew with Mary Ball, who had grown up since he had last seen her. She was in England visiting her half brother, Joseph, Jr.

The earliest existing letter of hers was one addressed to Joseph, Jr. in 1723, when she was about seventeen. It said, among other things: "We have not had a schoolmaster in our neighborhood until now in nearly four years." In Virginia in that day, the education of girls was given less attention than the schooling of boys. Mary Ball's handwriting remained stiff and cramped and her spelling bad. In comparison, her husband was well educated.

While the date of her wedding to Augustine Washington is recorded as March 6, 1730, there is no certainty of where it took place. The author of the sketch of Mary Ball Washington's life in the *National Cyclopedia of American Biography* gave some credence to a statement that Augustine and Mary were married in England, and quoted a Mrs. Morer, daughter of a woman who claimed to have been George Washington's nurse, as saying George was born in England. An old wives' tale, indeed!

The place of George's birth is not stated in the record of the event in Mary Ball Washington's Bible: "George Washington, son to Augustine Washington, and Mary, his wife, was born ye 11th day of February 1731/32, about 10 in the morning, and was baptized ye 3rd day of April following. Mr. Beverly Whiting and Captain Christopher Brooks, godfathers, and Mrs. Mildred Gregory, godmother."

Mildred Gregory was George's paternal aunt. She married thrice, the last time to Colonel Henry Willis of Fredericksburg.

Presumably, George's birthplace was his father's house near the Potomac, probably on Pope's Creek. The exact location of the house and its appearance have been matters of dispute among authorities. There is persuasive evidence it was a simple dwelling built by Augustine Washington about 1726 at a cost of 5000 pounds of tobacco (the prevailing currency). Persons who claimed they saw it remembered the building as hip-roofed, with dormer windows and a one-story wing in the back. The latter was a bedchamber and in it Mary Ball is supposed to have borne her first child, George. The long side of the house fronted the Potomac which was about 350 feet distant. Around the house were the fields of the owner's broad domain.

What happened to the house is a mystery. One story is that in the spring of 1735, while the servants were preparing ground for tillage by burning the "trash" of the preceding year's crops, fire got out of control and swept through the Washington dwelling. For this or some other reason, Augustine moved his family in 1735 to a second property lying on Hunting Creek — the present Mount Vernon. The dwelling on Pope's

OPPOSITE PAGE—*Above:* George Washington's assumed birthplace on Pope's Creek, as pictured in Washington Irving's biography (five volumes, 1855-59), from some existent descriptions.

•

Below: The Colonial-type mansion erected at the site by the Wakefield National Memorial Association. Dedicated in 1932.

Augustine Washington and Mary Ball was Married the
Sixth of March, 17 30/31

George Washington Son to Augustine & Mary his Wife was Born
y.e 11.th Day of February 1731/2 about 10 in the Morning & was Baptized the 5.th of April
following, M.r Beverley Whiting & Capt. Christopher Brooks Godfathers and
M.rs Mildred Gregory Godmother

Betty Washington was Born the 20.th of June 1733 about 6 in y.e Morning
Departed this life, the 31.st of March 1797 at 4 Oclock
Samuel Washington, was Born y.e 16.th of Nov.r 1734 about 3 in y.e Morning

Jane Washington Daughter of Augustine and Jane Washington
Departed this Life Jan.y 17.th 1734/5

John Augustine Washington was Born y.e 13.th of Jan.y about 2 in y.e Morn.
1735/6
Charles Washington was Borne y.e 2.d Day of May about 3 in y.e Morn.e
1738
Mildred Washington was Born y.e 21.st of June 1739 about 9 at Night

Mildred Washington Departed this Life Oct.r y.e 23.d 1740 being Thursday
about 12 a Clock at Noon Aged 1 Year & 4 Months

Augustine Washington Departed this Life y.e 12.th Day of April 174.
Aged 49 Years

Facsimile of a record of births and deaths of children of Augustine and Mary Washington, found in her Bible. The entries were made on a detached sheet of paper that was affixed to a page of the Bible. It has been asserted that the handwriting is that of young George Washington but there is no authority for the statement. The identity of the scribe and the date of writing are not established.

The entering of GW's birthdate as "11th of February, 1731/32" is of course a reference to the "old style" calendar. By the "new style" Gregorian calendar adopted in 1752 it was February 22, 1732.

The original of this sheet is preserved at Mount Vernon with the family Bible and is on display with other Washington association items.

Creek was either repaired or replaced. Wakefield, as the property became known, was a residence for Augustine's son, "Austin," after the father's death. Whatever house stood there was burned at some undetermined date just before or during the Revolution. A massive chimney that stood on Pope's Creek some years later was assumed to be a part of the Washington residence, but actually may have been part of a farm building. The birthplace might have stood some distance away.

Augustine kept his family, which increased by one practically every year, at the Hunting Creek plantation until 1739, or until George was seven. Then the family moved again, to a property Augustine, Sr. acquired on the Rappahannock, opposite Fredericksburg. One reason for this new acquisition was that there were ore diggings to be developed.

William Byrd, in describing a trip up the Rappahannock in his famous diary, said of the village of Fredericksburg: "The inhabitants are few. Besides Col. Willis who is top man at the place, there are only one merchant, a tailor, a smith and an ordinary [tavern] keeper. . . . On the other side of the river . . . are England's iron mines, called so from the chief manager of them, though the land belongs to Mr. Washington. These mines are two miles from the furnace and Mr. Washington raises the ore and carts it thither for the 20 shillings the ton of iron the ore yields. The furnace is built on a run that discharges its waters into the Potomac. At Principia, at the head of the bay, they have also erected a forge and make a very good bar iron."

Fredericksburg was the largest town George saw until he was in his teens. At Hunting Creek, at Augustine's new plantation, which was called Ferry Farm, or in Fredericksburg, George had his first tutoring. Various names are given his tutors – William Grove, Hobby, the Reverend James Marye, Williams. Either Grove or Hobby was said to have been a convict servant obtained from England by Augustine to be a teacher. George was assumed to have attended the school opened in Fredericksburg in 1740 by Marye. There are no authentic records of George's instructions, but it is fair to assume that Augustine did not neglect to provide one or more instructors for the youth.

As noted above, he had sent his older sons, Lawrence and Augustine, Jr. to Appleby Charter School; and George probably would have gone to Appleby, too, at a suitable age, if Augustine had lived, and if his wife had consented to George's leaving her side.

There also is reason to assume from the subsequent course of George's interests that what he saw of the iron-mining, water-mill operation and other activities of his father was an influential part of the youth's education. It may be significant that he later said he resembled his father in appearance and character.

Augustine died at his Rappahannock Ferry Farm on April 12, 1743, aged forty-nine. Riding over his plantation, he was caught in a rain storm; he took cold and, after a brief illness, expired of what was described as rheumatic gout.

Augustine had begotten six children by Mary Ball. After George, they were Betty (1733), Samuel (1734), John Augustine (1736), Charles (1738), Mildred (1739). One clause of his will expressed his "desire that my said four sons' estates may be kept in my wife's hands until they respectively attain the age of twenty-one years, in case my said wife continues so long unmarried." He designated landed estates for Mary Ball's sons, cash for Betty. He had already given the Hunting Creek property to Jane Ball's son, Lawrence, and provided for the erection of a new house there. To it Lawrence soon carried a bride, Anne Fairfax. The will gave the Pope's Creek plantation to his second son, who soon gave it a new mistress

Design of monogram seal of Augustine Washington, George's father. He habitually abbreviated his signature as August: Washington. Note in later pages how George also abbreviated his.

Tilt-top table, only existing item of furniture known to have been owned by Augustine Washington and used at George's birthplace.

by marrying an Aydlett heiress. George was made heir to Ferry Farm.

Thereafter, George spent more time at the homes of his two elder half brothers than in his mother's household. It can be concluded that George did not get along well with his quick-tempered, strong-willed, possessive mother. She may have been all that adoring biographers have said of her, but these facts remain: of the three sons who remained closest to her and under her strongest influence, Charles died a drunkard; Samuel was a profligate who effected five marriages and ruinous debts ("In God's name how did my brother Samuel get so enormously in debt?" George wrote to another brother in 1781); and John Augustine achieved no distinction whatsoever.

Whatever the reasons for George's leaving his mother's side in his teens, the influence of his two older brothers must be accounted all to the

The burial plot at Bridge's Creek as re-established in 1930 by the Wakefield National Memorial Association. Here lie remains of the father (with his first wife, Jane Butler), paternal grandfather and great-grandfather of George Washington, together with twenty-nine other early members of the family. Two of the gravestones are the original ones; the others are replacements. A burial vault contains brick from the original family vault in which twelve members of the family were interred. (Photo from the National Park Service)

good, judged in the light of his subsequent career.

"Austin," having married wealth, lived in what was an advantageous environment for young George. Austin had a large library, a regular procession of visitors whose conversation was instructive and a stable of fine horses. Outdoor sports were engaged in vigorously as part of everyday life. There was a school at Bridge's Creek for the youths of the prosperous plantation families.

Lawrence Washington had entered the Virginia militia and served in the Cartagena expedition under Admiral Vernon, for whom he renamed the plantation at Hunting Creek. He regarded the royal service as a good place for his young half brother and, when George was fourteen, Lawrence obtained the issuance of a commission as midshipman for him. George's belongings were already aboard one of His Majesty's frigates in the Potomac when Mary Ball Washington's protests prevailed. She had been prompted in her decision by her half brother, Joseph, to whom she wrote in England for counsel. When a naval career was proposed for George, Joseph Ball replied: "I think he had better be put a prentice to a tinker," and more to that effect. Mary Washington objected to every step George subsequently made toward his military career.

At his mother's insistence, George returned to Fredericksburg for a time and attended school there. During this period he copied into a notebook the "100 Rules of Civility and Decent Behaviour" that have been identified with his name.

- Every Action done in company ought to be done with some sign of Respect to those that are Present.

- Sleep not when others Speak, Sit not when others stand, Speak not when you should hold your peace, walk not when others Stop.

- When in Company put not your hands to any part of the body not usually Discovered.

- If you cough, sneeze, sigh or yawn, do it not loud, but Privately, and speak not in your yawning, but put your handkerchief or hand before your Face and turn aside.

- Strive not with your Superiors in argument, but always submit your judgment to others with Modesty.

- When a man does all he can though it Succeeds not well blame him not that he did it.

- Associate yourself with Men of good Quality if you Esteem your Reputation; for 'tis better to be alone than in bad Company.

Those and one hundred and three other Rules of Civility that survive in Washington's youthful handwriting were declared by careless biographers to have been of his own composition. He copied them when thirteen or fourteen from a work published in London, *Young Man's Companion*, written "in a plain and easy stile," the title-page affirmed, "that a young man may attain the same, without a Tutor." It is evident that Washington put the rules into a copybook both as a means of committing them to memory and improving his handwriting. For the volume was

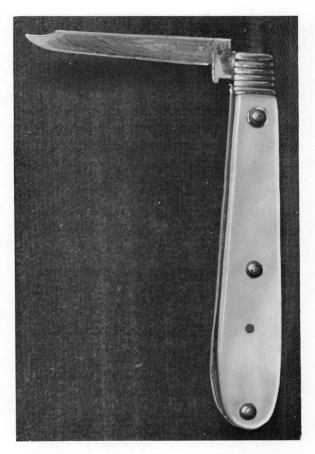

Right: Knife from England given by Mother Washington to George in his boyhood. He carried it the rest of his life. The knife is preserved at Mount Vernon.

a *vade-mecum*, or handbook intended to be carried about, with lessons in penmanship, letter composition, drafting of legal forms, making of ink and cutting of quills, figuring of interest, and oddments of instruction in care of the sick, navigation, hardening of cider as a potable, planting and grafting.

The *Young Man's Companion* enjoyed a popularity, or wide usage, contemporareously with *Joe Miller's Jests, or the Wits' Vade-mecum*, and it is logical to assume this was also among Washington's early reading, and also stamped upon his memory such anecdotes as:

"A Prince laughing at one of his Courtiers whom he had employed in several Embassies, told him he looked like an owl. I know not, answered

Model capital letters and script provided in *The Young Man's Companion* (including quotations from *Rules of Civility and Decent Behaviour*), reproduced above, are assumed to have formed, through studious copying and practice, Washington's penmanship. It is conjectured that such reading or copying he did away from tutors when he was young was done by the light of a fireplace designed like this, for he spent most of the daylight hours outdoors, vigorously. The artist who did this illustration for an old book on Washington has the flames too high. Generally a fire was kept low, for comfortable radiance of heat. Seasoned wood – chips or kindling – brought it up quickly for cooking. *Opposite page:* Specimens of Washington's handwriting at various ages. *Top to bottom:* When thirteen, nineteen, thirty-six, forty-four, and four days before his death. Additional specimens which appear in other pages of this work constitute an interesting comparative study for a hobbyist graphologist. An eminent New York City expert in autographs, Charles Hamilton, substantiates the statement in an earlier page that GW never signed as anything except G°Washington after youth.

Survey'd For Barnaby McHendry Four Hundred acres of Watered
Ungranted Land Situate Lying and being in the county of Frederick and in the Los River
or Cacaphon and Bounded as followeth Beginning at a Lyon Maple and mountain Burch on the East Side the River on a Mountain Side Lake Cottons and Run
thence No. 55. W Two hundred and Fofty three Poles to two white oaks and a Stick
amongst the Short Hills thence No. 35. Et Two hundred and Fifty three Poles to two
Chesnut Oak & and a white Oak thence S. 55 Et Two hundred and Fifty three Poles to
two mountain Burches and a white Oak on the Mountain Side thence S. 35 W
Two hundred and Fifty three Poles to the Beginning this Ninth Day of November
1749   by
  John Lomm }
  Edward Corder } Cha Men
  William Baker Marker

Washington

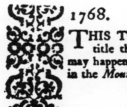

1768.
THIS TICKET [No. 258] ſhall entitle the Poſſeſſor to whatever PRIZE
may happen to be drawn againſt it's Number
in the *Mountain Road* LOTTERY.
G: Waſhington

Yr. most affect. Brother,

G: Washington

New York 29th of April 1776

Mount Vernon G: Washington
December 10th
1799

the Courtier, what I look like; but this I know, that I have had the Honour several Times to represent your Majesty's Person."

"A Lieutenant-Colonel to one of the Irish Regiments, in the French Service, being dispatched by the Duke of Berwick to the King of France, with a complaint, relating to some Irregularities that had happened in the Regiment, his Majesty, with some Emotion of Mind, told him, That the Irish Troops gave him more Uneasiness than all his Forces besides. Sir (said the Officer) all your Majesty's Enemies make the same Complaint."

That Washington had gifts as wit is documented in a subsequent chapter (page 239 *et seq*), but there is no evidence it was derivative of the collectors who put Joe Miller's name on their mélange. There is evidence of the influence of the *Young Man's Companion* in his career. Certainly his handwriting remained modeled after the copy-sheet in the volume.

To sum up, the boy Washington had some schooling between six and perhaps fourteen, in classes conducted at or near the family residence on the Rappahannock near Fredericksburg. Certainly he learned to read, to cipher. He appears to have been taught the first elements of Latin, perhaps by the Reverend James Marye, in Fredericksburg, for the fly-leaf of a Latin translation of Homer, printed in 1742, has an inscription signed *Est mihi nomen, Georgio Washington*.

During this period George found and took possession of the manuals on surveying and the surveying instruments his father had used in the mining operations. They were to give a decisive turn to Washington's career as soon as he left his mother's household again, never to return except as a visitor. He went to live for good with Lawrence at Mount Vernon and, fortuitously, was received as an intimate of the Fairfax family, Lawrence's neighbors and relatives by marriage.

Thomas, Lord Fairfax, had inherited vast estates in the northern neck of Virginia and in the Shenandoah Valley through his mother, the daughter and heiress of Lord Culpeper, royal grantee. His domain comprised over 5,000,000 acres of land, nearly one quarter of the common-wealth of Virginia. Lord Fairfax, who did not settle in Virginia until 1747, lived for several years at Belvoir, the home of Sir William Fairfax, to whom he had entrusted some of the management of his estates. Sir William was the father-in-law of Lawrence Washington.

Lord Fairfax remained a bachelor (in consequence, it was said, of having been jilted by the lady he loved) and, lacking sons, took an interest in his cousin's son, George William Fairfax, and in Lawrence Washington's young half brother, George. Washington Irving concluded, "An intimacy with a family like this, in which the frankness and simplicity of rural and colonial life were united with European refinement, could not but have a beneficial effect."

"Associate yourself with Men of good Quality if you Esteem your Reputation; for 'tis better to be alone than in bad Company," the *Young Man's Companion* had advised in its *Rules of Civility*, adopted in translation from a French credo.

Young George was at sixteen tall, well-formed, muscular, athletically inclined and skillful in the competitive sports which won attention among gentlemen — fox hunting, marksmanship, fishing and such. He had learned at his father's farm the management of small boats. He had his father's resourcefulness, also Augustine's combativeness. George had a temper and used his fists.

Lord Fairfax wrote to Mary Washington when George was still a youth: "I wish I could say that he governs his temper. He is subject to attacks of anger on provocation, sometimes without just cause." (Instances of his violent temper in later life will be mentioned in succeeding pages.)

OPPOSITE PAGE: George William Fairfax, a portrait by an unidentified artist in England after 1773, of George Washington's benefactor in his teens and long-time friend. Fairfax, born in the Bahamas in 1724, was therefore eight years older. When they met, George was sixteen and Fairfax was Burgess for Frederick County. He is referred to in Washington's earliest diary as "George Fairfax, Esq." A few months after this entry, Fairfax was to marry Sarah "Sally" Cary; the lady became a legendary figure in Washington's life, somewhat unjustifiably as Ann Rutledge was to be in Lincoln's.

Existing letters indicate that the Fairfaxes sympathized with their admirable young friend in his distaste for being a mama's boy at Fredericksburg. Sir William Fairfax abetted Lawrence's effort to get George into the navy as a midshipman. The Fairfaxes succeeded in effecting a decisive change in George's life in 1748, when he was sixteen. Lord Fairfax wanted to know more about his lands on the remote south branch of the Potomac. Young Washington's discovery of his father's surveying instruments and books had stimulated his interest in technology, and this was known to the Fairfaxes. When Lord Fairfax organized a surveying expedition to his western lands, George was invited to go along for the experience in surveying it would give him under a good instructor, and to provide companionship for George William Fairfax. James Genn, who held a commonwealth commission as surveyor, had been hired to direct the expedition. Fortunately, the Widow Washington did not object to George's making the journey into the wilds. It was to demonstrate his mettle, make him a sur-

veyor and frontiersman, and lead directly to his military career. We have a first-hand account of his experiences, for they are noted in the earliest existing Washington diary.

"Fryday March 11th 1747/8. Began my Journey in Company with George Fairfax, Esqr., we travell'd this day 40 miles . . ."

There were brief notations for March 12th, 13th and 14th, then:

"Tuesday 15th We set out early with Intent to Run round ye sd. Land but being taken in a Rain and it Increasing very fast obliged us to return it clearing about one oClock and our time being too Precious to Loose we a second time ventur'd out and Worked hard till Night and then return'd to Penningtons we got our supper and was lighted into a Room and I not being so good a Woodsman as ye rest of my Company striped myself very orderly and went to ye Bed as they called it when to my Surprise I found it to be nothing but a Little Straw-Matted together without Sheets or any thing else but only one thread Bear blanket with double its Weight of

Right: Lawrence, George's favorite half brother, as drawn and engraved in the 1850's by Benson J. Lossing for his *Mount Vernon and Its Associations*, after a life-portrait now owned by the Mount Vernon Ladies' Association of the Union. Attributed to John Wollaston, who painted other Washingtons.

Mary Washington, writing to her brother in 1759, expressed relief that her son George had given up his military career. (Original preserved by Historical Society of Pennsylvania.)

Vermin such as Lice Fleas &c I was glad to get up (as soon as ye Light was carried from us) I put on my Cloths and Lay as my Companions. Had we not been very tired I am sure we should not have slep'd much that night I made a Promise not to Sleep so from that time forward chusing rather to sleep in ye open Air before a fire as will appear hereafter."

A meeting with Indians prompted one of the longest entries in this first of Washington's diaries:

"Wednesday 23d Rain'd till about two oClock and Clear'd when we were agreeably surpris'd at y. sight of thirty odd Indians coming from War with only one Scalp. We had some Liquor with us of which we gave them Part it elevating there Spirits put them in y. Humour of Dauncing of whom we had a War Daunce there manner of Dauncing is as follows Viz They clear a Large Circle and make a Great Fire in y. middle then seats themselves around it y. Speaker makes a grand speech telling them in what Manner they are to Daunce after he has finished y. best Dauncer jumps up as one awakened out of a Sleep and runs and Jumps about y. Ring in a most comical manner he is followed by y. Rest then begins there Musicians to Play y. Musick is a Pot half [full] of Water with a Deerskin Stretched over it as tight as it can and a goard with some Shott in it to Rattle and a Piece of an horses Tail

The old home of Mary Ball Washington at 1200 Charles Street, Fredericksburg, Va., as it looked before restoration was completed. This is the only one of the dwellings of Mrs. Washington now standing (she never lived at Mount Vernon). It was purchased in 1890 by the Association for the Preservation of Virginia Antiquities, to which in 1929 George A. Ball of Muncie, Indiana, gave funds for extensive restoration work.

It was here that Washington came as President-elect on March 12, 1789, to pay his respects to his mother. She died less than six months later.

Visitors to Fredericksburg can also see Kenmore, the home of Fielding Lewis and his wife, Betty Washington; and George's boyhood Ferry Farm.

Contemporary silhouette of Mary Ball Washington.

There are questions about the authenticity of various portraits of Mary Ball Washington. These (*top left above*) are two of them. Probably the best is the one discovered in the possession of a member of the Ball family in Fredericksburg in 1850 by Dr. Shearasjahub Spooner, and acquired by W. Lanier Washington. It is attributed to Robert Edge Pine. She is identified as the subject of a painting by John Wollaston, discovered in Fredericksburg by another researcher and also acquired by W. Lanier Washington. It shows a younger woman than the Pine portrait does, and is assumed to have been painted in the 1750s.

Wallaston, who had a vogue as a portraitist in New York and Philadelphia in the middle of the eighteenth century, is also claimed to have painted the earliest portrait of George Washington.

Opposite: Portrait of Mary Ball Washington credited to Robert Edge Pine. Reproduced here from a print in New-York Historical Society.

tied to it to make it look fine y. one keeps Rattling and y. other Drumming all y. while y. others is Dauncing"

There was trouble with squatters who refused to acknowledge the Fairfax title to the land. There were Indians lurking about. Daily, the party blazed trails or swam icy flooded rivers, and surveyed 400-acre plots. Nights, they lay down exhausted, beset by vermin, vulnerable to fire or rain, surrounded by other dangers.

There was pay for Washington also.

"A Doubleoon a day is my constant gain every day that the weather will permit my going out and some times six pistoles. . . . I have never had my Cloaths off but lay in sleep in them," he noted in his journal. Six pistoles was high pay — some seven dollars in later-day equivalent — for a lad of sixteen, engaged in platting of 400-acre farms the Fairfax land-agent would sell to settlers coming from the British Isles and the Continent.

It was a time of maturity in more than one way. Washington mingled with Indians and stored knowledge of their crafts, got acquainted with wildcat distillates at settler houses that functioned as ordinaries, or travelers' makeshift stopping places, where meals of sorts were served. He engaged in rough sports that were spontaneous at such places on occasion, wrestling, leaping, tossing logs, running, throwing tomahawks or knives at targets.

One night his straw pallet caught fire, and was "Luckily Preserv'd by one of our Men awaking when it was ablaze." A rattlesnake made itself evident, their provisions ran out and they knew hunger, but Wednesday, April 13, 1748, after a month of trial, "Mr. Fairfax got safe home and I myself to my Brother's."

Obviously, he liked the experience that was so challenging to one of vigor and fortitude. And opportunity as surveyor — a position of importance among Men of good Quality — was at hand.

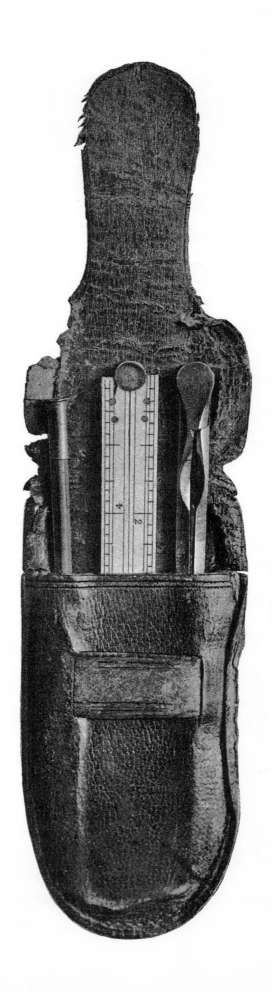

Washington went alone later in 1748 to William and Mary College at Williamsburg to qualify himself for a license as surveyor. Culpepper County was being formed and in need of one. Barely seventeen, but with the recommendation of Lord Thomas Fairfax, George Washington was appointed to the position. That summer, he went into the wilderness on his own. His friend, George William Fairfax, several years older, was preoccupied elsewhere. He had gone down the James to marry and bring into George's life Sally Cary.

In 1751 George had to take leave of his surveying duties. Lawrence Washington's ailment — "consumption" — had reached a virulent stage.

Right: Facsimile of title-page of book in which Washington preserved copies of early surveys. *Below*: Portion of a survey he made in 1750 for Lord Fairfax. Checkups made by modern surveyors of existing plats have confirmed Washington's skill. *On opposite page*: Red morocco pocket case, containing ivory scale, dividers and lead pencil, used by Washington in surveys. Loaned by Edmund Law Rogers, Baltimore, Md., to the Washington Inauguration Centennial Exhibition of relics, in 1889.

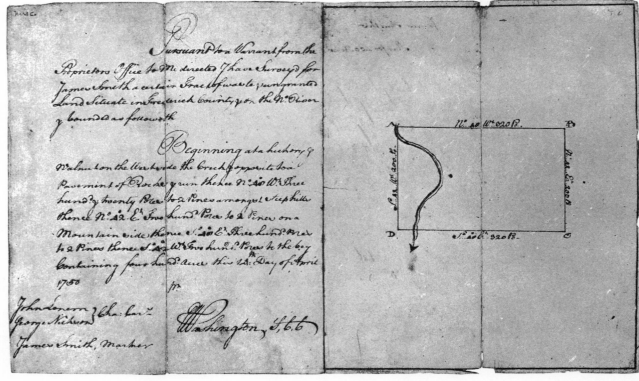

He was induced to go to Barbadoes in the belief that such a journey would enable him to overcome the ravages of the disease now known as tuberculosis. Lawrence's wife would remain in Virginia with the children while George served as Lawrence's companion on the voyage — the only time that Washington ever was to go outside the boundaries of what would be the United States of America.

The brothers sailed from the Potomac September 28, 1751, and landed at Bridgetown November 3. George kept a meticulous diary during the voyage: "We were greatly alarm'd with the cry of Land at 4 a.m.: we quitted our beds and found ye land appearing at bout 3 leagues distance when by our reckoning we should have been near 150 Leagues to the Windward."

On the fourth "came Dr. [William] Hillary, an imminent physician recommended by Major [Gedney] Clarke, to pass an opinion on my brother's disorder, which he did in a favorable light, giving great assurance, that it was not so fixed but that a cure might be effectually made. . . ."

Major Clarke, the brother of the third wife of William Fairfax, who was Lawrence's father-in-law, had been informed by Fairfax of the brothers' voyage and its purpose. He invited them to breakfast and dinner. They went, George "with some reluctance, as the smallpox was in his [Clarke's] family." Nevertheless, he was persuaded — or persuaded himself — to make successive visits to the Clarke household, which included a comely Miss Roberts, a niece of Mrs. Clarke. As a result he finally contracted the disease, which left permanent blemishes on GW's otherwise handsome countenance — blemishes that the portrait artists did not show.

Introduced to the theater in Barbadoes, George seemed unsure of the quality of the performance; he saw "the Tragedy of George Barnwell acted: the character of Barnwell was said to be well perform'd. There was music adapted and

George Washington and his friend, George William Fairfax, enjoying a hunt — an engraving from Irving's *Life of Washington*. The Fairfaxes were among the leading devotees of fox-hunting in Virginia. Washington's diary for November 22, 1768, has an entry typical of many: "Went a fox huntg. with Lord Fairfax and Colo. Fairfax & my Br. Catchd 2 Foxes." For two weeks thereafter they hunted foxes almost every day.

regularly conducted." This was an allusion to *The London Merchant*, a prose play by George Lillo that was based on a seventeenth-century ballad. Barnwell was a London apprentice seduced by a much older woman, Sarah Millwood, to whom the youth gave £200 of his master's money. To meet her demands, Barnwell robbed and murdered his uncle; and when Sarah had spent the money she turned Barnwell out. Each of them informed against the other when suspicion centered on him, and both were hanged.

From that time on George was a devoted patron of theatricals. At least once he expressed a wish to take part in an amateur production of *Cato*, a dramatization of scenes in the career of the great Roman patriot.

Fanciful representation of Washington as an official surveyor before he was thrust into the military limelight — an illustration by Felix O. C. Darley, engraved by G. R. Hall, for Irving's *Life of Washington*.

GW having recovered sufficiently from smallpox to venture on the voyage (and to be allowed aboard) he embarked in the ship *Industry* December 22, and in January 1752 he was back in Virginia with letters and messages for Lawrence's wife and associates. He had left his brother in the Barbadoes in an apparent state of convalescence. This was soon to prove an illusion. Lawrence returned to Virginia in July to die.

He had given thought to his half-brother's future. In resigning the duties and prerogatives of adjutant-general for one of Virginia's four military districts, Lawrence had requested the appointment of GW to the post. To insure that George's prospects of advancement in the affairs of the Colony would not suffer from practical knowledge of soldier craft, Lawrence arranged with a respected former comrade-in-arms, Jacob Van Braam, a Dutch mercenary in English wars, to tutor GW in basic military science at times George wasn't surveying. (Van Braam was to continue the tutelage after Washington became a militia officer, and would be with him, bolstering morale, after Washington's first defeat in action.)

Lawrence Washington died July 26, 1752. He had made GW his executor and contingent heir. His will specified that in the event of the death of his daughter, Sarah, George should receive Mount Vernon and attendant property and provide Lawrence's widow with an annuity. The frail Sarah died within two months, whereupon GW was master of Mount Vernon's 2500 acres, manor house and appurtenances, in addition to the properties he had accumulated for himself:

The "Bullskin Plantation," so-called from its adjacency to Bullskin Creek in Frederick County. He obtained the tract of wild land — five hundred-odd acres — as a surveyor's fee, in 1748 (when only sixteen).

A cultivated farm of about 450 acres, acquired in 1750 for £112, cash, accumulated from surveyor's fees.

Another undeveloped 550 acres bought in 1752 for cash.

These holdings, and his subsequent management of lands, leave little doubt that GW would have become well-to-do even if he had not inherited Lawrence's property and married a wealthy widow.

Anyway, GW before his twenty-first birthday was the virtual owner of more than 3500 acres of Virginia lands.

He was an accomplished surveyor.

He was Adjutant-General of the Southern District of Virginia, with the rank of Major and supervision over all militia in the district. The pay was £150 annually, a goodly sum in Virginia then. (He was soon transferred to the preferable Northern Neck and Eastern Shore District.)

He was on his way to greatness.

Two years before Washington became official surveyor for Culpepper County, The Ohio Company of Virginia was formed by gentlemen investors — Virginians, Marylanders and a London merchant — to trade with Indians in lands claimed by Virginia under the royal charter, to obtain grants of lands for settlement and to secure buyers of tracts from the Company at a profit. In 1749, the Governor of Virginia was directed by his superiors in London to accede to the petition to the extent of 200,000 acres, with the stipulation that 200 families be settled permanently in the area within seven years. Lord Thomas Fairfax was one of the investors in the Company, as were Lawrence and Augustine Washington.*

The Company had a storehouse for trade goods set up on the Potomac headwaters, opposite Wills Creek, and employed Christopher Gist to explore the grant and establish relationships with the Indians.

Gist** was outstanding among pioneers of the new West. He, not Daniel Boone, might well have been the prototype of the frontiersman that

---

* It should be made clear that far from being an enterprise in which Fairfax and the Washingtons could have dictated the subsequent role of young George in its affairs, the incorporators included Arthur Dobbs, Samuel Smith, James Wardrop, John Hanbury (of London), John Taylor, Presley Thornton, Nathaniel Chapman, Thomas Cresap, John Mercer, James Scott, Robert Carter, Richard Lee, Thomas Lee (President of the Council of Virginia) and the Governor himself, Robert Dinwiddie.

** In England, the family name had been spelled Guest.

John Filson and James Fenimore Cooper introduced into literature. Born in western Maryland in 1706, and a contemporary of Boone's in North Carolina, he penetrated the Ohio valley via the river as Indian trader and saw Kentucky long before Boone went through Cumberland Gap into that region. He established a cordial relationship with Indians, who gave him the name *Assosanah*, which he conscientiously preserved, and never suffered the humiliations at Indian hands that Boone brought upon himself.

Gist's father, Richard, was an educated man who practiced surveying (and was one of the commissioners who laid out the town of Baltimore). Evidence that Christopher himself had a good education and experience as a surveyor is in the *Journal* of his expedition in 1750 for The Ohio Company, that ensued after he was sought

out in retirement on the Yadkin, in North Carolina, to undertake the mission.

Gist's instructions from the Committee of The Ohio Company, September 11, 1750, began: "You are to go out as soon as possible to the Westward of the great Mountains, and carry with you a Number of Men as You think necessary, in Order to Search out and discover the Lands upon the river Ohio, & other adjoining Branches of the Mississippi down as low as the great Falls thereof."

Gist went down the Ohio as far as the great Falls, at the future site of Louisville, then returned to Virginia by following rivers upstream to the mountains and through them into North Carolina, thence to Williamsburg. His second trip into the Ohio country for the Company in 1751-2 was via different routes. Thus, with all his earlier

Washington and Christopher Gist crossing the Alleghany River in their mission to Fort Le Beouf with four companions. From an engraving by Alonzo Chappel in the author's collection.

explorations and two journeys for the Ohio Company, he was an ideal guide and tutor for George Washington when the youth was chosen in 1753 by Governor Dinwiddie to go to the French with warnings against their interference with the Ohio Company's advances in the Valley.

It is clear that Washington, now twenty-one and Adjutant of the Southern District of Virginia, volunteered for the assignment that was to prove so consequential in his life.

An earlier choice of Government Dinwiddie, Captain William Trent, had failed in his mission as intelligence officer. He had been sent to reconnoiter new outposts the French had thrust into territory west of the Alleghanies claimed by England. Following French traders who had won Indians as customers, troops had come down Lake Erie, set up a fort at Presque Isle, cut roads, and fortified themselves also at Le Beouf, on a tributary of the Alleghany. Dinwiddie realized the threat not only to the frontier, but to the designs of The Ohio Company. "They will take possession of the river Ohio, oppress our trade and take our traders prisoner. . . ."

Trent was to have found out the strength of the French forces after a summer in which, it was known from Indians, disease had taken toll in the garrisons, and to propose some plan for blocking further advances. Trent had not approached Le Beouf any closer than Logstown, near the Monongahela, chief village of the Lenni-Lenape. He had no such degree of adaptation as Washington had acquired to the rigors of wilderness travel and existence. Such information as he had obtained from Indians newly committed to the French was unreliable.

Washington learned from items in the *Virginia Gazette* and from stories of hunters and traders of the French activities. Perhaps the ineffectualness of Trent passed as gossip from Williamsburg among militia officers. The seriousness of the situation was emphasized by the special session of the General Assembly called by the Governor for November 1. Burgesses were arriving for it when Washington rode in about

October 24 or 25 to call on the governor. By chance, a newly arrived ship had brought a response from London to Dinwiddie's account of French encroachments and proposal that counter fortifications be established.

George II, mindful of his treaty with the French sovereign, directed that before hostile acts be committed, the French should be warned of their invasion of His Majesty's domain and be told to abandon it. Washington's well-timed offer of his services as emissary was accepted without hesitation. The role of King's messenger to Le Beouf presented ample opportunity for acquisition of data on military forces, defenses, armaments and, perhaps, plans. Besides a formal letter to the French commander, he carried a request to Christopher Gist, at Will's Creek, on the Potomac, to be Washington's guide, and Washington had verbal orders in some detail. One was to secure an interpreter capable of conversing and translating in French. Washington found Jacob Von Braam, who knew the language from military experience on the continent, at Fredericksburg, and Van Braam was with him when the letter to Gist was delivered.

Gist assented, and four others with experience on the frontier were chosen to join the party as attendants. When equipment had been put into shape or acquired — arms, ammunition, gifts for the expected Indian hosts and informants, food for themselves, corn for the horses — the expedition struck out November 15, to cross ridges of the Alleghanies in the direction of the Monongahela. Eight miles were made the first day, then progress was slower.

"The excessive Rains and Quantity of Snow which had fallen, prevented our reaching Mr. Frazier's, an Indian Trader, at the mouth of Turtle Creek, on the Monongahela, till Thursday the 22nd.," Washington was to write in his report to Governor Dinwiddie. "The Waters were quite impassible without swimming our Horses; which obliged us to get the Loan of a Canoe from Frazier, and to send Barnaby Currin and Henry Steward down the Monongahela, with our Baggage, to meet us at the Forks of Ohio, about ten miles, there to cross the Alighany.

"As I got down [arrived at the Forks] before the Canoe I spent some time in viewing the Rivers, and the Land in the Fork; which I think extremely well situated for a Fort, as it has the absolute command of both Rivers."

In consequence of his subsequent recommendation to Governor Dinwiddie, erection of a fortification at the Forks was to be the chief outcome of the expedition. In the following century the great city of Pittsburgh was to rise there.

A purported drawing of Fort Le Beouf from an unidentified source. *Right:* Title-page of the original printing of Washington's Journal of his mission to the French and a text page from it. Only two copies of the first edition were known to exist when this biography of Washington was being prepared, but facsimile copies are numerous. Gist's journal of his earlier travels in the region, 1751, were put into print by the Filson Club, Louisville, Kentucky, for its members, in 1908.

A nineteenth-century artist's illustration of Washington and Gist with the French commander.

THE
JOURNAL
OF
Major *George Washington,*
SENT BY THE
Hon. *ROBERT DINWIDDIE,* Esq;
His Majesty's Lieutenant-Governor, and
Commander in Chief of *VIRGINIA,*
TO THE
COMMANDANT
OF THE
FRENCH FORCES
ON
OHIO.
TO WHICH ARE ADDED, THE
GOVERNOR's LETTER,
AND A TRANSLATION OF THE
FRENCH OFFICER's ANSWER.

WILLIAMSBURG:
Printed by WILLIAM HUNTER. 1754.

(3)

THE
JOURNAL, &c.

Wednesday, October 31st, 1753,

I WAS commissioned and appointed by the Honourable *Robert Dinwiddie,* Esq; Governor, &c. of *Virginia,* to visit and deliver a Letter to the Commandant of the *French* Forces on the *Ohio,* and set out on the intended Journey the same Day ; the next, I arrived at *Fredericksburg,* and engaged Mr. *Jacob Vanbraam,* to be my *French* Interpreter ; and proceeded with him to *Alexandria,* where we provided Necessaries ; from thence we went to *Winchester,* and got Baggage, Horses, &c. and from thence we pursued the new Road to *Wills*-Creek, where we arrived the 14th of *November.*

Here I engaged Mr. *Gist* to pilot us out, and also hired four others as Servitors, *Barnaby Currin,* and *John Mac-Quire,* Indian Traders, *Henry Steward,* and *William Jenkins,* and in Company with those Persons, left the Inhabitants the Day following.

The excessive Rains and vast Quantity of Snow that had fallen, prevented our reaching Mr. *Frazier*'s an Indian Trader, at the Mouth of *Turtle*-Creek, on *Monongahela,* till *Thursday* the 22d. We were informed here, that Expresses were sent a few Days ago to the Traders down the River, to acquaint them with the *French* General's Death, and the Return

A 2

Not surprisingly, the demand presented by GW in behalf of Governor Dinwiddie, for French withdrawal from the Ohio country, was disregarded in spite of the personal impression the young major made upon its recipients. Dinwiddie sought an appropriation from the House of Burgesses for militant measures against the intruders. The request was rejected; to a majority of the burgesses, this was an objective solely for the benefit of a select group of land speculators. Dinwiddie turned then to stockholders in The Ohio Company: he stressed how valueless their shares would be made by French possession of the disputed region. The appeal to their purses rather than their patriotism induced the managers to send out, at the Company's expense, the aforementioned Captain William Trent with thirty-three men. The mission was to preempt the commanding position at the Forks of the Ohio — the junction of the Monongahela and Alleghany Rivers — for a fort.

It would have been natural for the burgesses to be cynical of the effectiveness of colonial militia against the French professionals. They knew how much was to be expected of colonial militia not fighting for their own homes and immediate security. Expeditions of colonial pick-up forces against French regulars in Canada in 1711 and again in 1745 had been far from conclusive in a military sense. British regulars were quite contemptuous of the *Yankey* irregulars, as was made evident in a song that originated in ridicule of them, *Yankey* [later Yankee] *Doodle*. The militiamen were generally poorly equipped, ill-trained, undisciplined, unreliable as a group unless under a stirring, dedicated leader of the caliber of the exceptional Robert Rogers. GW was not yet such a leader.

Dinwiddie realized Trent's venture with thirty-three assorted men, whatever their qualities, was a hazardous stopgap. The Virginia governor appealed to the colonial governments in Pennsylvania, New York, Maryland, for support in the common interest against the French menace. He received no encouragement. The Pennsylvania Assembly (of which Benjamin Franklin was a member then) responded that in its members' collective opinion, any British claim to the Ohio country had doubtful basis.

Opportunistically, Dinwiddie juggled funds at his official disposal. Some five hundred men were induced to join, at six pence per day, a regiment that was to be ordered to the Forks of the Ohio, to help Trent complete the fort, and then be its garrison. Joshua Fry, Oxford-educated professor of mathematics at William and Mary College, member of the governor's council, and, at that stage, GW's superior in more than one sense, was designated as colonel. The twenty-two-year-old GW was placed second in command.

Washington was at the mouth of Will's Creek, headwater of the Potomac [now Cumberland, Maryland], with an advance detachment of some hundred and fifty men, when news was brought by Indian scouts of a French march to the Forks of the Ohio. Word was passed on back to Fry, who remained in Virginia, hopefully recruiting, drilling and maneuvering additional strength for the regiment. Fry could not act on the news: He was killed in a fall from a balky horse. Washington was now in command and dependent on his own judgment in dealing with some five hundred French, having nine pieces of artillery, who were within striking distance.

For days Washington obviously was undecided on conclusive moves. He was reinforced until the total was over three hundred and fifty, including a company of regulars. Typically, and

"Training Days in the Olden Time" is the title of a popular early nineteenth-century print of a scene in previous century, when regular annual "training days" were provided by colonial law for able-bodied males, as preparation for militia service. The settlers were averse to spit-and-polish drilling and made a poor appearance in military turnouts.

indicative of the attitude of one holding the King's commission, the captain of the company of regulars, one Mackaye, refused to take orders from any Provincial officer, and hence sat apart in councils.

GW received information, again via Indians, that a detachment of French was encamped near the uncompleted English fort. Impetuously, without having provided for a strong position to which to retire, if necessary, GW led his column, with Indian guides, to the bivouac.

All the thirty enemy were asleep at dawn or under cover because of driving rain, May 28, when Washington surprised them.

Possibly as a face-saver, French spokesmen represented that the detachment was under a flag of truce it assumed would be respected.

Ten French were killed, including the detachment's commander, Jumonville; a wounded man and more than a dozen were captured.

Reports carried to the main force by some who escaped the attackers brought about seven hundred French with their Indian allies swarming after Washington and his troops. Meanwhile, the small company at the Forks had been overwhelmed in Trent's absence. French military engineers — then the world's best — took over completion of the works renamed Fort Duquesne. Trent, advised of the approach of a substantial force of Virginians, had gone off to urge their commander to hurry up.

A month after the Jumonville engagement or massacre, Washington's force was cornered, entrapped, at a hastily improvised "Fort Necessity" misplaced at a low point beside a creek in what were described correctly as the Great Meadows. The meadows were made lush by overflows of the creek during rainy seasons. Downpours fell one after another that June of 1754, and on July third French besiegers strung out along the slopes could look down upon, and shoot at, Virginians struggling for footing in the water and mud that lay within the "fort."

It is a critical question why anyone trained as a surveyor had made this strange choice of ground for a defensive position. Here one must consider that the young commander's education for military leadership had been limited; that most of what he knew of foreign affairs at this stage of his career had come from newspapers (of which he was ever an intent reader) and conversation; that dutiful study of military manuals was prompted by what happened.

After hours of attack on July 3 Washington raised a white flag for a surrender parley. Either because he was not given a realistic understanding of the French in which the terms were written (his interpreter and translator was his erstwhile tutor, Jacob Van Braam), or disbelieved he had a choice, GW signed a paper attesting responsibility for *l'assassinat* of Jumonville. He gave his word that Virginia would not attempt to build another fort along the Ohio for at least a year. In exchange he was allowed to march his men back to Virginia, without weapons.

GW was treated as a hero in Virginia, though voices were raised critically among burgesses who understood French over the commander's having impolitically admitted "assassination." His men were voted small bonuses. In contrast, poor Trent had been treated with disdain on *his* return from a humiliating surrender.

In a letter to his brother John Augustine after this campaign, GW noted with a youthful verve, "I have heard the bullets whistle; and, believe me, there is something charming in the sound." Somehow a copy of the letter reached London, was printed, and for the first time the Virginia colonel came to the attention of a royal sovereign. George II was quoted as remarking, "He has not heard many, or he would not think them very charming."

His first experience in command had been a failure, but it made him a man of mark nevertheless, and GW proved that he had learned something from it. This was not evident immediately, though he could not be blamed fairly for the disastrous outcome of the expedition in 1755 of General Edward Braddock.

In brief, Braddock, who had fought with some success European armies that adhered to classical European tactics, made no allowances for what the French in America might have learned by hard experience from Indian foes and allies. Sent to America as new British C-in-C in 1755, and faced with the necessity of waging the war that ensued after Washington's attack on Jumonville, Braddock obviously assumed the

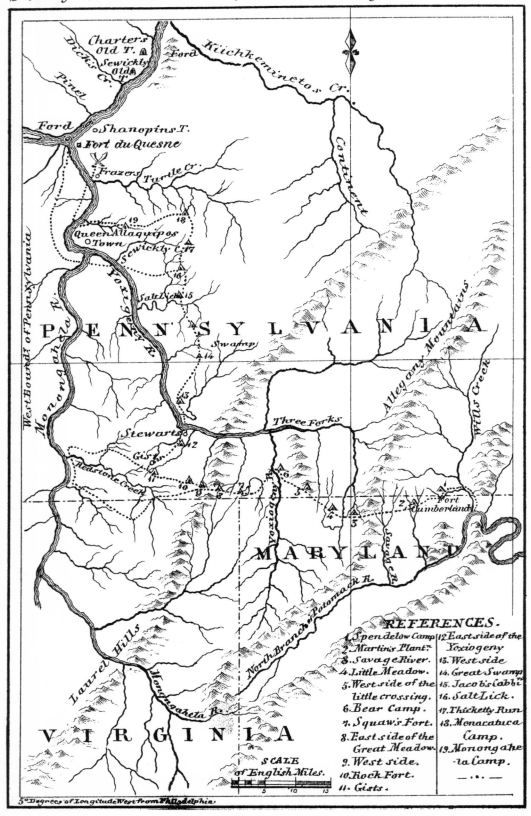

A MAP OF THE COUNTRY

BETWEEN WILLS' CREEK & MONONGAHELA RIVER,

Shewing the route and Encampments of the English Army in 1755.

REFERENCES.

1. Spendelow Camp
2. Martin's Plant.
3. Savage River.
4. Little Meadow.
5. West side of the little crossing.
6. Bear Camp.
7. Squaw's Fort.
8. East side of the Great Meadow.
9. West side.
10. Rock Fort.
11. Gists.
12. East side of the Yoxiogeny
13. West side
14. Great Swamp
15. Jacob's Cabbi
16. Salt Lick.
17. Thicketty Run
18. Monacatuca Camp.
19. Monongahe-la Camp.

SCALE of English Miles.

5   10   15

5° Degrees of Longitude West from Philadelphia.

French in America would fight in accordance with European established principles, and was not responsive to contrary advice. Progress of his strike at Fort Duquesne was heralded by the hacking of a road through the Alleghanies. Consequently, he was a victim with his men of an ambuscade at a place — some twenty miles from the fort — and time chosen by foes fighting in Indian guerrilla fashion. Probably only the Indians' habit of collecting scalps from fallen antagonists and the knowledge of Indian fighting impressed on the Virginians under Washington saved Washington and most of his regiment from swelling the casualties Braddock's column suffered. Most of the Virginians' number escaped safely to the base camp at Fort Cumberland.

A subsequent letter of Washington's describing bullets' whistle as "charming" was not revealed in my research.

After "Fort Necessity" GW was never wholly responsible for the outcome of any engagement or battle. Many, if not all, of them are contentious subjects that cannot be fairly or objectively reported or discussed in limited space. Entire volumes are devoted to some of them by individual commentators. For purposes of this book, Washington's military operations 1775-81 will be simply outlined. For comprehensive details, the reader is referred to authoritative accounts listed in a bibliographical appendix, pages 255-256.

"Dear Sir:
"After thanking Heaven for your safe return, I must accuse you of great unkindness in refusing us the pleasure of seeing you this night . . .
"If you will not come to us to-morrow morning very early, we shall be at Mount Vernon.
"S[ally] Fairfax
"Ann Spearing
"Eliz'th Dent."

On the opposite page: Map of the country between Williamsburg and Forks of the Ohio, through which Washington traveled as emissary to the French, and where General Braddock's campaign had to be conducted. Though forewarned of the roughness of the terrain and of water that had to be crossed, Braddock rode in a carriage and greatly impeded the advance.

Braddock had told Franklin, "These savages may, indeed, be a formidable enemy to your raw American militia; but upon the King's regular and disciplined troops, Sir, it is impossible that they should make any impression." The Regulars' resplendent uniforms (*left*) made them easy marks.

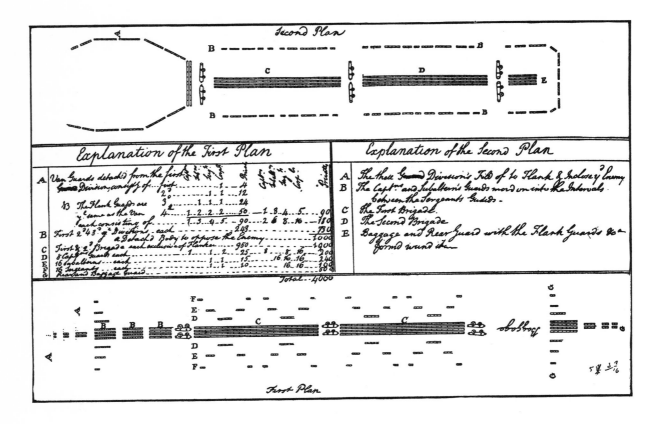

Note this letter dated July 26, 1755, when Washington was back from the Braddock campaign, and signed with three names, had the pronoun 'I,' indicating that the writer was Sally Fairfax, and suggestive that there was a closeness between the addressee and that writer. There was indeed a kind of flirtatious correspondence between the young Colonel and the wife of his long-time friend, but it is significant that when Sally teased him about another woman, Washington wrote to her:

" 'Tis true I confess myself a votary of love. I acknowledge that a lady is in the case, and further confess that the lady is known to you. Yes, Madame, as well as she is to one who is too sensible of her charms to deny the Power whose influence he feels and must ever submit to...."

She was not the woman he married.

Above: The young Colonel Washington's plan for a line of march in the forest country, submitted to General Forbes in October 1758 in response to a request for a tactical plan — the first advice sought by the British Regulars of an American militia officer for the conduct of a campaign. "Here was a milestone that marked the progress of the military education of George Washington," Thomas G. Frothingham observed. "A British general was asking a young Virginia colonel of twenty-six, not merely for a suggestion as to some detail of tactics, but for a tactical scheme for the conduct of an expeditionary force of four thousand men." The young Virginia officer was fully prepared to offer the solution of a problem new to British officers who had never coped successfully with savages in a wilderness, with flexible tactics that would change quickly the line of march into a line of battle, in case of an attack. The advantages of this scheme, as elucidated by Washington in his covering letter, were apparent to Forbes and his staff. The plan was adopted.

In 1756, the Virginia colonel had occasion to journey to Boston for militia business with Gov. Shirley, British C-in-C in North America. He stopped in New York on the northward journey for a visit with a Virginia acquaintance, Beverly Robinson. Robinson was the son-in-law of Frederick Philipse II, inheritor of a large fortune accumulated by a one-time Dutch carpenter, in land speculation and as sponsor of privateering against Moslem shipping in the Red Sea and Indian Ocean. Susannah Philipse Robinson had an unmarried sister, Mary, then twenty-five (a year older than Washington). The opportunity to meet again this attractive heiress obviously prompted Washington's stopping in New York for a week on his southward journey. His account books document spending of pounds "for treating the ladies" and extensive tailors' bills.

There is evidence that Washington proposed to Miss Philipse, but none that her rejection (if there was one) affected his heart or subsequent happiness. Mary Philipse remained a spinster till twenty-seven, when her bridegroom was Lieutenant-Colonel Roger Morris, an associate of

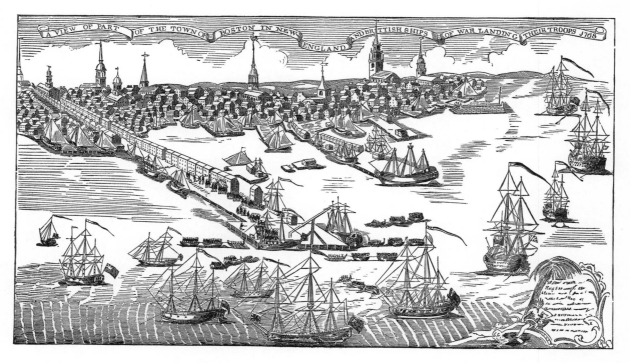

Boston as it looked about the time Washington paid his first visit to New England, to state his grievances to Governor Shirley. From an engraving published in London in 1768. Shirley was typical of British factotums whose actions were to be such rousing influences against British rule in the Colonies. Educated as a lawyer, he wangled politically an appointment as judge of admiralty court at Boston in 1733, and pushed himself into the position of royal governor. He had proved his lack of qualifications as a general, and military incompetence, during an expedition to French Fort Niagara, of which he assumed command. Nevertheless, he became Braddock's successor as British commander-in-chief in the Colonies after the Braddock fatality. (Shirley's son was killed in action with Braddock). Washington's mission to the town where he was to take command nine years later was to acquaint Shirley with the plans of Virginia's Governor Dinwiddie for undoing the defeat of Braddock, and also to plead for an equality in authority of officers of the colonial militia with British regular officers of the same rank. He had learned by experience of the contempt of British officers, trained in European military traditions, for the advice of men who knew how different strategy and tactics of wilderness warfare had to be. The seventy-two-year-old Shirley was no man to recognize the wisdom of a twenty-four-year-old.

Washington's in the Braddock campaign.

How fortunate it was for the nation, perhaps, that Washington didn't marry into the Philipse family was indicated in 1775. The Philipses remained staunch Tories and, doubtless under Mary's influence, Roger Morris turned against the patriot cause in which other New York Morrises were important figures. The splendid mansion Roger Morris was enabled to build with Philipse money was confiscated in 1776 by the patriot government, and the two were fugitives when its situation made it headquarters for Washington* during the battles preceding his movement into New Jersey.

In a later-day conversation with one of the Philipses, a gentleman remarked how different Mary Philipse's life would have been had she married Washington. "You mistake, Sir," was the quoted response. "She had immense influence over everybody, and had she become the wife of Washington he would not have become leader of the rebellion; she would have prevented it."

It is especially interesting to consider this remark in the light of an exclamation attributed to John Adams, in one of his recurrent moods of bitterness and jealousy toward Washington while the first sufferer from the obscurity and ineffectualness of being Vice President: "Would Washington have been the commander of the

* Washington was to visit it again in 1790, while President at New York. A new owner let the hilltop premises be used for picknicking by ladies and gentlemen seeking relief from the town's summer dismalness. Washington noted in his journal, "Dined on a dinner provided by Mr. Marriner at the House lately Colo. Roger Morris', but confiscated and in the occupation of a common Farmer." Among subsequent owners was Stephen Jumel, who made a splendid place of it again, in French style, and entertained numerous personages before his mysterious death. Mrs. Jumel, half her late husband's age, then married aging Aaron Burr, but it remained known as Jumel Mansion. Fortunately, the residence was restored to its Revolutionary War aspect, with original and contemporary furnishings, by the Washington Headquarters Association and Daughters of the American Revolution, and is maintained as a museum. Perhaps next to Mount Vernon and his dwelling at Valley Forge, it is the most visited of places associated with Washington's life.

"Washington Raising the British Flag at Fort Du Quesne," a popular engraving in the Eighteen-Fifties, published by Virtus Emmons & Co., New York City. J. R. Chapin and T. B. Smith were credited as artist and engraver, respectively. [Author's collection.]

Revolutionary Army or President of the United States if he had not married the rich widow of Mr. Custis?"

Martha Dandridge Custis, like Mary Philipse, was about a year older than Washington. They met in March 1758 (within a short time of Mary Philipse's taking Roger Morris as husband). Malarial fever and dysentery plagued Washington after the Braddock expedition and induced him to take leave of the Virginia Regiment and seek relief at Mount Vernon. Weeks later he wrote, "I have never been able to return to my command . . . my disorder at times being obstinately upon me, in spite of all the efforts of the sons of Æscukapius, whom I have hitherto consulted. . . . I am now under a strict regimen, and shall set out tomorrow for Williamsburg to receive the advice of the best physician there."

The Philipse Manor House on the Hudson, near Yonkers, where Washington paid court to Mary Philipse. The engraving of her above is from a life portrait by John Wollaston, in 1756, the year she became briefly the object of Washington's attentions.

Martha Dandridge portrayed as a young woman — an engraving after a painting by Alonzo Chappel. John Wollaston painted her while she was John Custis' wife. The portrait, which hung at Mount Vernon during her life there, is owned now by Washington and Lee University.

It appears that during this visit to the Capital he met Martha Dandridge Custis, "the prettiest and richest widow in Virginia." He was soon a well man, and back in service. General John Forbes had been sent to accomplish the task in which Braddock had failed, and Washington's aid was welcomed. However, almost coincidental with Washington's taking possession of Fort Duquesne (which Forbes renamed Fort Pitt), news came that the French were withdrawing from America. Washington resigned his commission to retire to Mount Vernon with, he expected, a wife.

On the way to Martha Custis' side, he wrote a curious letter to Sally Fairfax that could be interpreted as an affirmation of continuing affection for her. Nevertheless on Saturday, January 6, 1759, he and Mrs. Custis were married at the bride's residence, "White House," New Kent County, Virginia, by the rector of her parish church. The time was high noon. The bridal gown was heavy brocaded silk interwoven with silver threads; there was at least one satin petticoat. Her shoes were high-heeled, satin uppers with buckles inset with brilliants. Besides a pearl necklace, she had earrings and bracelets. On this occasion some attention was also paid to the bridegroom, an imposing figure, standing several inches higher than the bride. Though a sword hung at his side, he was clad in citizen's dress of blue broadcloth, the coat lined in red silk and ornamented with silver trimmings; the waistcoat of embroidered white satin. Buckles of gold were upon his shoes and at his knee. His hair was, of course, an arrangement by an expert at male coiffure, and powdered white.

The honeymoon was spent at White House, from which Washington wrote to his overseer at Mount Vernon, "You must have the House very well cleaned, and were you to make Fires in the Rooms below it w'd air them. You must get two of the best Bedsteads put up. Enquire abt. in the neighborhood, and get some Eggs and Chickens, and prepare in the best manner you can . . ."

The mansion at Mount Vernon as a visitor afoot sees it, walking upon the lawn that stretches down to the Potomac River. Washington watched boats sail up from Chesapeake Bay.

II

COUNTRY GENTLEMAN

"The life of the Husbandman, of all others, is the most delightful. It is honorable, it is amusing, and, with judicious management, it is profitable."

— GEORGE WASHINGTON, 1788

As a teen-ager, Washington had transcribed into a copy-book, along with Rules of Civity from *Young Man's Companion,* verses entitled *True Happiness:*

There are things, which once possess'd
Will make a life that's truly bless'd
A good Estate on healthy Soil,
Not Got by Vice nor yet by toil;
Round a warm fire, a pleasant Joke,
With Chimney ever free from Smoke:
A strength entire, a Sparkling Bowl,
A quiet Wife, a quiet Soul,
A Mind, as well as body, whole;
Prudent Simplicity, constant Friend,
A Diet which no art Commands;
A Merry Night without much Drinking,
A Happy Thought without much Thinking;
Each Night by Quiet Sleep made Short
A Will to be but what thou art:
Possessed of these, all else defy
And neither wish nor fear to Die
　　These are things, which once Possess'd
　　Will make a life that's truly bless'd.

George Washington, at twenty-seven, the

Squire of Mount Vernon and extensive other lands; a person who had earned distinction in Virginia's far-reaching military affairs, and a respected member of its political councils; the husband of Martha Custis Washington and thus, under the law, administrative master of her inherited fortune* — had he not realized true happiness as specified in the verses?

The 2500 acres of Mount Vernon was not yet his completely; for Lawrence's widow, Anne Fairfax Washington (who soon married George

---

* It consisted of money on bond and stock in the Bank of England, the Custis plantation in New Kent County, many slaves, various chattels. Immediately, Washington sent marriage papers to the necessary authorities in London and asserted his legal authority over the Custis Estate. Thereafter, as his journals show, when Martha wanted to spend anything, she had to ask George. "By cash to Mrs. Washington for Pocket Money £4" was a typical entry after the honeymoon at White House was over and the couple moved to Mount Vernon with Mrs. Washington's children, Martha and John. Washington also now had the management of the property of these two surviving children for whom Daniel Parke Custis made individual provision in his will.

Lee) had been bequeathed a life interest. George Washington was obligated to pay her annually 15,000 pounds of tobacco, or its equivalent in current money, until her death in 1761. The holdings he acquired by his own efforts before 1759 were only promising: 550 acres of wild land in Frederick County, "my Bullskin Plantation"; 500 acres on Dogue Run; plus claims in the unsettled west amounting to some 12,000 acres that needed settlers, cultivation, roads and peace to be productive of income.

Settling down at Mount Vernon in 1759 as gentleman farmer was as formidable a challenge to Washington's capabilities as any he had faced previously. These home acres were not "a good Estate on healthy soil," prescribed in that formula for true happiness. Little more than half of the 2500 acres was tillable, and these were of generally mediocre quality. Around, aside from the Fairfaxes, were plantation owners in debt because of conditions with which Washington was going to have to cope. His lands apart from Mount Vernon could not be looked after in person properly; they had to be entrusted to managers, rented, or left idle. Mount Vernon had no substantial market close by, and the cost of transportation was so great, it had to produce for sale articles of relatively little bulk compared to value. Production was afflicted with the most inefficient labor system man ever devised: slavery. Washington's problem with it was compounded by the increasing number of slaves for whom food, clothing, housing, fuel, had to be provided due to his humanitarian refusal to send away the aged, nonproductive, or unfit, or break up families.

He saw the unwisdom of dependence year after year upon the money crop that was the basis of plantation economics in Virginia and Maryland — tobacco — even while his methods were increasing productivity. In 1759 there were 34,000 pounds of tobacco to send to market. Within four years the yield was increased to 89,000 pounds. He also produced pork, corn and wheat; he had a herring fishery in the Potomac; he operated a public ferry; and he had his own mill to grind his grain. The flour was divided into superfine, fine and middlings grades, and put

A Washington table, with silver-plate, drinking glass, candlestick and, right, a stand for a toureen with pit in center for candle to keep contents warm.

Daniel Parke Custis, the first husband of Martha Dandridge, from a drawing in B. J. Lossing's *Mount Vernon and Its Associations*. Martha bore him four children, including two sons who died before Custis left her a widow, aged twenty-six, in 1757.

Mantelpiece at Mount Vernon, with decorative tiles, jars, and oil lamps.

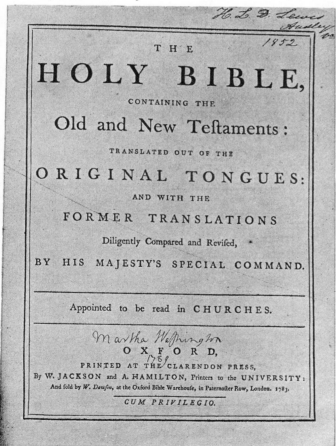

into barrels made by his own coopers, for export to the West Indies. He experimented with fertilizers, crop rotations, animal breeding, plows, seeders; he methodically secured reports on English agricultural advances and exchanged information with their writers. He earned the title of "America's first scientific farmer," before the Revolution and he continued acquisition of information on farming all his life. In his surviving papers are lengthy notes taken from Jethro Tull's *Horse-Hoeing Husbandry*, Duhamel's *Practical Treatise on Husbandry*, Home's *The Gentleman Farmer* and, particularly, Young's *Annals*, a periodical to which George II contributed under the name of "Ralph Robinson." (Possibly inspired by the "Farmer King," his Prime Minister, William Pitt, penned the article for Young's *Annals* on storing turnips for winter of which Washington took note.)

While turning Mount Vernon's soil, and Dogue Run's and Bullskin Plantation's, to profit, Washington added to his holdings optimistically — undoubtedly with the aid of Mrs. Washington's money — and in 1771 he was paying quit-rents on 5500 acres in Fairfax County, 2500 in Frederick County, 1200 in King George County, 240 in Hampshire, 275 in Londoun. In addition there were the tracts beyond the mountains that were just lying there.

The sixty miles a day he often rode in over-

Martha Washington's snuff-box, and a drawing of the watch given to her in 1759 as a bridal gift.

•

Left: Title-page of Martha Washington's Bible. It is preserved at Mount Vernon.

seeing personally what was being done on his lands closest to Mount Vernon could not be reckoned as pleasure. But he was often in the saddle for pleasure, fox-hunting, with the baying of his hounds music in his ears. He raised Thoroughbreds and put them in meets in Virginia and Maryland. He was a devotee of fishing; he often had his early morning catch in the Potomac or a creek for breakfast. His diaries have scores of entries relating to his enjoyment of gaming with cards. He loved dancing. He had abundant friends. They included Sally Fairfax and her husband, who were neighborly dining, card-playing, fox-hunting, dancing intimates of George and Martha for fourteen years before George William Fairfax moved to England for business reasons and took Sally with him. (When *Belvoir*'s effects were put up at auction after the Fairfaxes' departure, Washington attended the sale and bought many pieces of the furniture.)

Colonel Washington, his wife, young Martha and Jack Custis, with a servant at Mount Vernon — from an engraving by Phillabrown of an illustration painted by Alonzo Chappel. The servant and the horse here depicted were given to Washington by the dying Braddock on the fatal field of the Monongahela. The setting was a porch formerly attached to the south end of the mansion, off the library.

In Washington's diaries are hundreds of entries about his mills on Dogue Run and Four Mile Run, one of which is shown below. Washington also owned a grist mill on a small stream emptying into the Youghiogheny River — one of the first mills erected west of the Alleghenies — and in 1774 he sent a group of settlers, including a miller, there to break to the plow and cultivate one of the tracts of land he started acquiring as a teenage surveyor. *Left:* His desk in his library, as sketched by Benson J. Lossing.

20ᵗʰ Began to manufacture my Wheat with the water of Piney Branch, which being insufficient to keep the Mill constantly at work, & Country Custom coming in, no great progress coud be made—

General and Mrs. Washington, painted in oils, at
Mount Vernon in 1790. With them are her grandchildren, George Washington Parke Custis and Eleanor Parke Custis, who were adopted by the General.
In the background is the Potomac River; at right, the
servant, Billy Lee. The artist was Edward Savage and
the original is in the Mellon Collection at the National Gallery of Art in Washington. Savage made
mezzotints of this group portrait, and some of the
prints remain to be found by lucky collectors. (For
earlier portraits from life of General and Mrs. Washington, see pages 132-155.)

What of Washington's religion? The clergyman in the parish in which the boy George spent his first years of comprehension reported to superiors that he, the rector, catechised all youth "in Lent and a great part of the summer." Of course, George, the son of one of the vestrymen, received this drilling.

The extent of his religious devotion before he kept his diaries can only be conjectured. The first diary reference to church, November 11, 1751, when he was nineteen, says: "Dressed in order for Church, but got to town two Late dined at Majr. Clarkes with ye S:G: went to Evening service and return'd to our lodgings." That was while he was in the Barbadoes with the tubercular-stricken Lawrence. ("Ye S:G:" was the Surveyor-General.)

During the next eight years, Washington's activity as surveyor and soldier would necessarily have limited his church-going, but after his marriage and settling down at Mount Vernon, he was not a regular attendant, either. His daily itemization of "where and how my time is spent" in his diaries attests his being at church only sixteen times in 1760. However, in 1762 he was chosen vestryman of Truro Parish, Fairfax County; the next year he was elected warden of Pohick Church of Truro Parish.

The Reverend Lee Massey, rector at Pohick before the Revolution, was quoted as effusing, "I never knew so constant attendent in church as Washington. . . ." If that was so, he had a parish full of irregular attendants, indeed, for Washington's diary for 1768 records his church attendance only fourteen times in that year. Truro could not count Washington as one of its communicants

General Washington's bedroom at Mount Vernon, looking in through the doorway to the hall. One stairway from this hall enabled him to go up to Mrs. Washington's room on the third floor.

On opposite page, as indicated, are floor plans of the Mount Vernon residence embodying changes Washington made in the arrangements during his forty years of ownership.

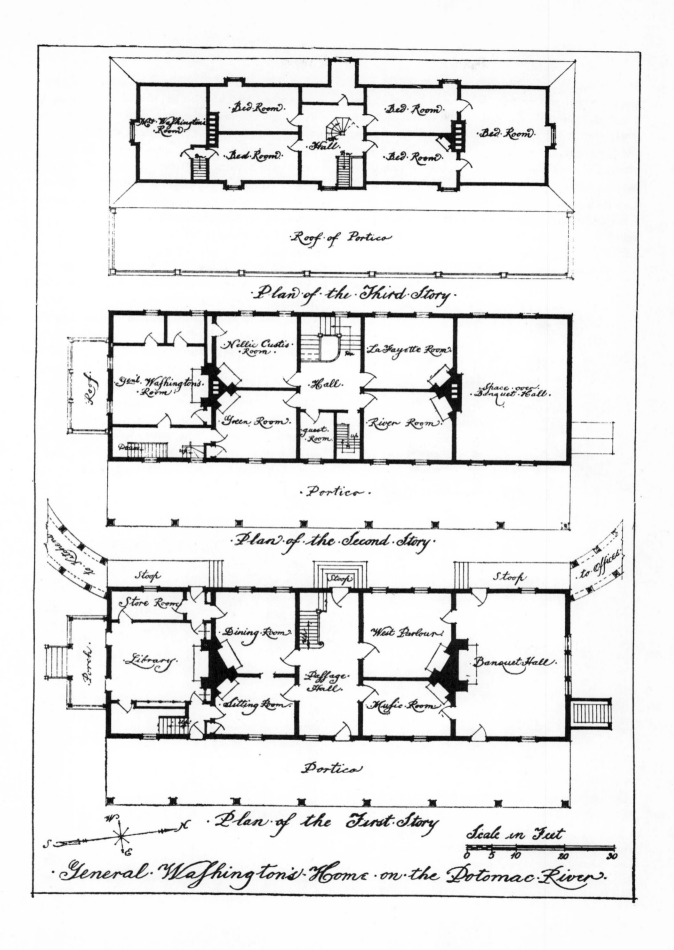

Roof of Portico.

Plan of the Third Story.

Portico.

Plan of the Second Story.

Portico

Plan of the First Story

Scale in Feet

0 5 10   20   30

General Washington's Home on the Potomac River.

after 1773. When building of a new church was proposed in the parish, Washington drew the plans and subscribed a sum to the building fund, with the expectancy of having a family pew. Subsequently, it was decided by vote of the vestry that there would be no private pews. Washington was incensed by what he deemed a breach of contract, and in 1773 transferred to the new Christ Church in Alexandria. He bought a pew there for £36/10 per annum, the highest price paid by any parishioner.

The inventive Jared Sparks quoted Madison as saying that when Washington belonged "to the vestry of a church in his neighborhood [presumably Pohick], he sometimes spoke with great force, animation, and eloquence on the topics that came before them." This was contrary to Washington's usual conduct in meeting places. He was animated, stimulating and persuasive in small conversational groups or military conferences, but never a speechmaker.

He faltered in addressing the Virginia House of Burgesses. He was "prominent, but silent" in the Continental Congress." At his inauguration as President, Maclay noted, "this great man was agitated and embarrassed more than he ever was by the leveled cannon or pointed musket." It is difficult to imagine his haranguing a congregation in church, as Sparks suggests.

During the Presidency, when the public eye came upon his every move, he attended church regularly, doubtlessly from a sense of duty. Back at Mount Vernon, he attended one or two times a month. On Sundays he wrote letters and kept his accounts, made land purchases, sold wheat, went fox-hunting and entertained visitors. In 1799, a diary entry notes his inattendance at church for two Sundays because of visits from

Above: Early drawing of Christ Church, Alexandria, as it appeared in Washington's time.

Center: Pulpit in Pohick Church from which the rector preached sermons Washington heard. *At right:* One sheet of plans Washington drew for a new church in Truro Parish. He transferred away from the parish as a result of a disagreement over the new church.

"Strangers, with whom I could not use the freedom to leave alone, or recommend to the care of each other, for their amusement."

Unquestionably, he was tolerant and considerate of the religious beliefs and practices of others. In a letter he wrote, "Of all the animosities which have existed among mankind, those which are caused by difference of sentiments in religion appear to be the most inveterate and distressing, and ought most to be deprecated." His friends included Jews, Roman Catholics, Quakers, agnostics and atheists.

A marked trait of Washington's character, his peculiarity about his clothes, was noted by Paul Leicester Ford and others. "There can be little question that he was early in life a good deal of a dandy and this liking for fine feathers never quite left him," Ford commented. When George was about sixteen years old he noted in his journal:

"Memorandum to have my Coat made by the following Directions: to be made a Frock with Lapel Breast the Lapel to Contain on each side six Button Holes and to be about 5 or 6 Inches wide all the way equal and to turn as the Breast on the Coat does; to have it very long Waisted and in Length to come down to or below the bent of the knee. The Waist from the armpit to the Fold to be exactly as long or Longer than from thence to the Bottom. Not to have more than one fold in the Skirt and the top to be made just to turn in, and three Button Holes the Lapel at the top to turn as the Cape of the Coat and Bottom to Come Parallel with the Button Holes, the Last Button Hole in the Breast to be right opposite to the Button on the Hip."*

---

* Punctuation was inserted in this passage for clarity; GW didn't use it.

Above: The kitchen, as restored by the Mount Vernon Ladies Association of the Union. It is reached from the dining room through a storeroom and a gallery.

Such meticulousness in dress at that age could be attributed to the influence of the example set by young Fairfax, with fashion bents of the "Macaroni," fops who looked beyond London to Italy for manners in dress and conduct. They went to such extremes as eating with fork as well as knife and spoon. To insure having all three at hand, they carried a set in a silver case in their goings about.

Washington did not go to extremes in dress; he suited clothes to occasions. In that first venturesome trip to the Ohio for Governor Dinwiddie, he left gentlemanly habiliments at Williamsburg and started in garb for roughing it. This, too, was discarded. "I put myself in an Indian walking Dress," he wrote in his journal; and "tied myself up in a Match Coat," the latter meaning a blanket.

As husband and holder of the purse-strings, he exerted an influence on Mrs. Washington's attire, and ordered some of the gowns as well as accessories she wore. In their travels each had one or more trunks filled with clothing for formal and informal appearances at Alexandria, Williamsburg, Annapolis, Philadelphia or wherever.

Martha had to accept constant streams of visitors to Mount Vernon, and repeated absences

Here: One of Washington's trunks used in his travels during the War of Independence. *Above it:* Types of luggage designed to accompany the traveler by fast coach, in which space was at a premium. The Washington trunk, of leather, is preserved at Mount Vernon.

Opposite page: Procession of dress in England and the Colonies during the lifetimes of Mr. and Mrs. Washington, as assembled from prints published in London. Until the War of Independence, both obtained clothes, or fine materials for them, from London. "Whatever goods you may send me," Washington wrote to his agent in London, "let them be fashionable."

1727   1730   1737   1744   1750

1750   1760   1770   1772   1775   1780

1790   1790   1793   1796   CLERGYMAN   WORKMAN AND WIFE

HEAD-DRESSES OF THE PERIOD   HATS OF THE PERIOD.   HEAD-DRESSES OF THE PERIOD

of her husband for days or weeks at a time. His brother Sam, Sam's wife and their children, his brother Charles, his sister and her husband came often. He was sought as referee in court matters. Officers, who had entrusted him with securing their claims to a share of 200,000 acres of land proclaimed as a grant to officers in the Virginia Regiment against the French, called or came to confer. His diaries for September 1770 had such typical entries as "Major Wagener dind here and went away in the afternoon"; "Miss Massey still here, and Mr. Semple came in just after we had dind and went away after dinner was got for him"; "Miss Massey went away and in the Evening, Mr. Boucher, Majr. Taylor and Jackey Custis

came here"; "Colo. Fairfax and Lady and Mrs. Ambler dind here with the gentleman that came yesterday — and went away after"; "Captn. Ingles, and his Master, Mr. Bruce, and Mr. John West dind here — all of whom returned afterwards"; "John Savage, formerly Lieutt. in the Virga. Service, and one William Carnes came here to enter their claim to a share in the 200,000 acres of land...."

Three days after that entry, October 5, 1770, Washington noted, "Set out in company with Doctr. Craik for the Settlement on the Redstone, etca. Dind at Mr. Byron Fairfax's and lodged at Leesburg." Systematically, he entered an expense: Mass' Ordinary, 3s., 6 d.

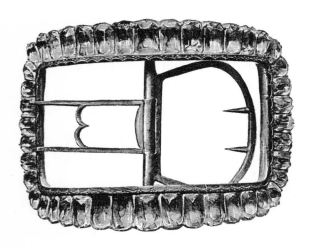

One pair of the silver knee buckles worn by GW with his breeches on occasion. They are exhibited at Mount Vernon. Washington shared the liking of gentlemen dandies for gold and silver ornamentation. In 1754, his accounts show, he bought "a superfine blue broad cloth coat with silver trimmings" and "silver lace for a hat." Clothes he ordered from London in the 1750's included three "gold and scarlet swordknots, 1 fashionable goldlaced hat," and a "riding waistcoat of superfine scarlet cloth and gold lace."

(→) GW depicted at Lake Drummond, Dismal Swamp, in an engraving in Irving's biography. It is unlikely the Colonel, who suited dress to the occasion or work, wore such gentlemanly attire for sloshing around, surveying, and mapping in a mosquito-infested morass.

Redstone Creek emptied into the Monongahela River about thirty-seven miles above the Forks of the Ohio, which Washington had envisioned earlier as the future site of a great city (and Pittsburgh was to rise there). From the Monongahela, Washington and Craik went as far down the Ohio as the Great Kanawha, before turning back.

Craik was the man whom Washington was to describe nearly three decades later as "My compatriot in arms, my old and intimate friend" — a unique compliment from Washington. A year younger than Washington, Craik was a Scot educated at Edinburgh to be a surgeon in the British army. However, he migrated to Virginia before the hostilities on the frontier brought him in service with Braddock in the disastrous campaign of 1755 and intimacy with Washington. Craik attended the wounded Braddock, and lacked skill to save him.

The doctor obtained and recorded the account of Washington's remarkable escape from being a casualty with Braddock. While exploring in western Virginia a few years after the battle on the Monongahela, Craik met an aged Indian chieftain who told him, through an interpreter, how the Indians had staged the surprise. One of the details was that he had fired at least fifteen

musket shots at the tall colonel who was rallying the Virginia troops and had ordered his men to make Washington a target, without effect.

Though the journey to the Ohio for which Washington absented himself from Mount Vernon nine weeks after the harvest supervision was taken in the interest of locating and patenting the 200,000-acre tract in behalf of the officers, "his weakness for acquiring good land was, undoubtedly, a large factor in the matter," John C. Fitzpatrick remarked, and the use of "weakness" to describe the impulse is odd. Washington noted later, "After the Patents were granted and the Land thereby secured, I concerned myself no further with any part thereof excepting my own." The reason for his going some 300 miles out of the way from Redstone Creek was made apparent by an advertisement the first major real-estate promoter in the West placed in the Maryland Advocate & Commercial Advertiser in 1773:

"The subscriber having obtained patents for upwards of TWENTY THOUSAND acres of Land in the Ohio and Grand Kanawha . . . proposes to divide the same into any sized tenements that may be desired, and lease them on moderate terms, allowing a reasonable number of years rent free, provided that within the space of two years from next October three acres for every fifty contained in each lot . . . shall be cleared, fenced, and tilled; and that by or before the time limited by the commencement of the first rent, five acres for every hundred . . . shall be enclosed and laid down in good grass for meadow; and moreover that at least fifty good fruit trees for every like quantity of land shall be planted on the premises. . . .

"As these lands are among the first which have been surveyed in the part of the country they lie in, it is almost needless to premise that none can exceed them in luxuriance of soil or convenience of situation, all of them lying upon the banks of either the Ohio or Kanawha and abounding with fine fish and wild fowl. . . .

"From every part of these lands water carriage is now had to Fort Pitt, up the Monongahela to Redstone, vessels of convenient burden may and do pass continually. . . ."

When Washington got patents for many square miles of land in the vicinity of what he confidently expected to be the first center of the development of the Ohio country, he was substantially involved in a company designated, "Adventurers for Draining the Dismal Swamp." The marshy region overlapping the Virginia-North Carolina boundary promised to be very fertile and profitable land if drained, and a drainage canal could be a natural course for water transport of tobacco and other products from Albemarle Sound into Nansemond and Elizabeth rivers, Virginia. Washington made a half dozen trips to the Swamp between 1763 and 1770, at which time shingles were the principal product of the 40,000 acres of the area the company had acquired. Washington resumed close attention to the project after the Revolution and in 1793 appraised his Swamp holdings at £5000.

The 1760s had brought an awakening of interest in canal projects. With highways few and generally poor, railways in the future and shippers or buyers as well as passengers at the mercy of rains, floods, snows or whatnot, inland water transport was essential. Philip Schuyler, who was in England when James Brindley completed the Duke of Bridgewater's canal to carry coal from mines to Manchester, came back to urge upon his fellow countrymen the importance of such interconnections of the inland reaches. Washington's mind was stimulated by the Dismal Swamp reclamation and his possession of lands along the Potomac, in western Virginia, and beyond in the Ohio Valley to envision a number of canals. In 1772, he secured from the Virginia Assembly an act incorporating a company for promotion of improvement of the Potomac. He foresaw a canal connecting the Potomac with a tributary of the Ohio. This was one of the matters from which he was made to turn by the crises that festered after the Stamp Acts of the British Parliament, the forming of resistance in the Colonies and the punitive counter-measure of the king's ministers, the Boston Port Bill.

After the Revolution, Washington's resumption of his Potomac River projects and the attendant difficulties in obtaining cooperation of the States concerned was to make him a prime mover for altering the loose Confederation of assertedly self-sufficient States into a National Union.

III

MAKING OF A REVOLUTION

"Unhappy it is, to reflect, that a brother's sword has been sheathed in a brother's breast, and that the once happy and peaceful plains of America are either to be drenched with blood, or inhabited by slaves. Sad alternative! But can a virtuous man hesitate in his choice?"

— GEORGE WASHINGTON, 1775

M AY, 1774, when a courier in the service of the Committee of Correspondence brought to Williamsburg news of the punitive Boston Port Bill enacted by Parliament, the Burgesses appointed a day of fasting. The royal governor, Dunmore, reacted the next day by ordering the Assembly dissolved; the doors of the Capitol were closed. Washington and fellow burgesses met instead at Raleigh Tavern, to effect renewal of non-importation agreements and to advance the calling of an intercolonial congress — a matter Washington had discussed with officials in other colonies in the course of a journey to New York a year earlier. A call went out for a Virginia convention, to meet August 1.

In the preliminary Fairfax County Convention in July, Washington was chosen to preside. When the Fairfax County Resolves had been adopted, he was sent as delegate to the First Virginia Provincial Convention at Williamsburg. Thus the forty-two-year-old planter was thrust into the making of epochal events.

In the meeting at Williamsburg, August 1-9, 1774, Washington was reported as voicing the first determination by any responsible man in the Colonies to resist British measures by force of arms: "I will raise one thousand men, subsist them at my own expense, and march to the relief of Boston." These words soon were to be quoted and requoted as stirringly as Patrick Henry's assertion, in 1765, of the legislative independence of Virginia, with its closing challenge, "If this be treason, make the most of it."

Elected one of the Virginia delegates to the intercolonial Congress summoned to meet in September, Washington noted in his diary on August 31: "After dinner in company with Patrick Henry and Mr. [Edmund] Pendleton started to attend the General Congress at Philadelphia." Benjamin Harrison, Richard Bland, Richard Henry Lee and Peyton Randolph were the other Virginia delegates. Peyton Randolph was chosen the President of the Philadelphia assemblage, which was designated the Continental Congress to distinguish it from congresses in individual colonies.

In summing up ability in that Congress, whose fifty-four delegates also included John and Samuel Adams, John Dickinson, John Jay, Thomas McKean, John Rutledge and Philip Liv-

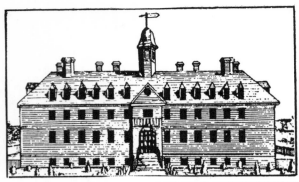

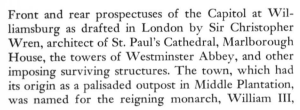

Front and rear prospectuses of the Capitol at Williamsburg as drafted in London by Sir Christopher Wren, architect of St. Paul's Cathedral, Marlborough House, the towers of Westminster Abbey, and other imposing surviving structures. The town, which had its origin as a palisaded outpost in Middle Plantation, was named for the reigning monarch, William III, when the seat of dominion government was moved from the first settlement, Jamestown. *Above:* Speaker's Chair in the Hall of Burgesses, to which Washington was elected as Member from Frederick County in July 1758, and a stove preserved from Capitol's early days. *Below:* General Court chamber as restored. Photo by Thomas L. Williams.

The reconstruction of the Capitol at Williamsburg, which had been completed in 1705 from plans drawn by Sir Christopher Wren. It was twice burned and underwent modifications. Here, in 1753, Governor Robert Dinwiddie appointed Washington emissary to the commandant of the French forces on the Ohio. Here Washington was commissioned as commander of the Virginia militia. Here he sat in the Hall of Burgesses from 1759 until the Revolution. There are references in his diary to his attendance at balls in the Capitol as well as at the Palace of the Governor. Nearby was a theater he attended — "Once even five times in a row to see a particular red-haired actress perform," it is stated by a Colonial Williamsburg historian. Incidentally, the estate left Mrs. Washington by her first husband included a large brick house in Williamsburg.

ingston, Patrick Henry was to say, "If you speak of eloquence, Mr. Rutledge of South Carolina is the greatest orator; but if you speak of solid information and sound judgment, Colonel Washington is by far the greatest man on the floor."*

In anticipation of subsequent events, it is pertinent to note that on the motion of Sam Adams of Massachusetts the first prayer of the Congress was offered by the eminent Church of England reverend, Jacob Duche. After reading the Thirty-fifth Psalm, Duche extemporized a fervent invocation of divine favor on the pro-

ceedings. (In a change of heart, the good man was to plead with Washington in 1776 to resign and "to represent to Congress the indispensable necessity of rescinding the hasty and ill-advised Declaration of Independence." George Washington transmitted the letter to Congress, quotations from it got into the press, and Reverend Duche found it expedient to go to England when the British, whose capture of Philadelphia had made him so despairing, gave up possession in mid-1778. His estate was confiscated and he was declared a traitor by the Pennsylvania government.)

* This observation may appear to refute the opinion of Washington as an orator given in the previous chapter. Note, however, that Patrick Henry gives John Rutledge the palm as orator. His reference is to Washington's influence in the discussions by small groups in which the actions of any political gathering are decided.

Opposite page: The Governor's Palace at Williamsburg, as it looked soon after the munificence of John D. Rockefeller, Jr. made it possible to see the Virginia colonial capital as portions of it looked during the years when Washington strode its streets as Burgess, Colonel of Virginia militia, Commander-in-Chief, President and retired gentleman. The young boxwood in the foreground has grown up now to form a maze duplicating one in the original garden.

The restored Raleigh Tavern, where Washington often danced and where (as his diary shows) he often engaged in games of chance. His journals record purchases of "one dozen packs playing cards," winnings and losings at whist and loo. He wagered on horse-races, and played billiards avidly. He "invested" repeatedly in lotteries. (→). See page 13.

Numb. 1768.
185

THIS TICKET [No. 185] fhalʳ. entitʳe the Poffeffor to whatever PRIZE may happen to be drawn againſt its Number in the *Mountain Road* LOTTERY.

G Waſhington

Samuel Adams was declared a traitor before this First Continental Congress began its session. Sam Adams was the man contemporaries regarded as "Father of the Revolution." Because of him, Boston certainly was the first dormant volcano of rebellion to erupt against George III's ministry. Others spoke fire, James Otis and John Hancock notably, but none more insistently and effectively than Sam Adams. Sam's younger cousin John's was more a voice of reason than of persuasive arousement. Otis, the most brilliant lawyer in Boston, acknowledged Sam as master: he promoted the latter's election to the House of Representatives and his choice for all the important committees; Otis carried drafts of his own articles for the press and speeches to Sam "to pour a little oil into them." As for Hancock, a dozen years his junior, Sam had won this merchant prince — richest man in Boston — over to support of the Whig cause, for a reason made plain privately to John Adams: "I have done a wise thing by making his fortune our own. He has great riches, and we can give him consequence to enjoy them."

Benj. Franklin

Boston's greater son, Benjamin Franklin, was absent from the Colonies when ferment over the provocative stamp taxes came to a head. George Grenville, as Chancellor of the Exchequer to George III, had given notice of the proposed stamp-taxes for defraying part of the expenses of the war with France in America. Franklin was sent to London a second time as agent for Pennsylvania (he had represented it there 1757-1762 and returned with honorary degrees from universities of Edinburgh and Oxford). He used his persuasive powers to the utmost, and won some sympathizers for the Colonies' grievances, yet when the obnoxious law was passed in 1765, Franklin counseled submission.

"In this case, however, the wisdom of Franklin proved inferior to the collective wisdom of his fellow-countrymen," it was remarked. By falling equally on all persons, stamp-taxes gave everyone a grievance. They united all the Colonies for the first time, in large part due to the opportunism of Sam Adams.

He wrote letters and newspaper articles furiously; he bestirred organization of "Sons of Liberty" — a phrase taken from a speech in Parliament by Colonel Isaac Barre.

To the PUBLIC.

THE FLYING MACHINE, kept by John Mercereau, at the New-Blazing-Star Ferry, near New-York, ſets off from Powles Hook every Monday, Wedneſday, and Friday Mornings, for Philadelphia, and performs the Journey in a Day and a Half, for the Summer Seaſon, till the 1ſt of November, from that Time to go twice a Week till the firſt of May, when they again perform it three Times a Week. When the Stages go only twice a Week, they ſet off Mondays and Thurſdays The Waggons in Philadelphia ſet out from the Sign of the George, in Second-ſtreet, the ſame Morning. The Paſſengers are deſired to croſs the Ferry the Evening before, as the Stages muſt ſet off early the next Morning. The Price for each Paſſenger is *Twenty Shillings*, Proc. and Goods as uſual. Paſſengers going Part of the Way to pay in Proportion.

As the Proprietor has made ſuch Improvements upon the Machines, one of which is in Imitation of a Coach, he hopes to merit the Favour of the Publick.

JOHN MERCEREAU

Reduction of the transit time between New York and Philadelphia to one day and a half made "flying machines" of the coaches of a line opened across the Jerseys in 1757. Competition soon provided "wagons" practically daily. Philadelphia-New York routes became great avenues of travel and communication north or south for persons not satisfied with vagaries and slowness of ships.

•

At left: Franklin, an engraving after a painting by Alonzo Chappel. Washington may have had his first meeting with Franklin when the latter came to Braddock's headquarters at Frederick back in 1755.

Samuel Adams, the fomenter of resistance and rebellion at Boston — a contemporary woodcut that reversed an original engraving, 1774, by Paul Revere.

The Stamp Act of 1765 imposed taxes on all the British Colonies in America (including newly acquired Canada and those in the West Indies). Stamps in specific denominations were required for all legal and commercial papers (such as wills, deeds, notes, bonds, mortgages), newspapers, pamphlets, ships' clearance papers, packs of playing cards, sets of dice. No such clamor arose in Jamaica, the Bahamas, et al., as swept from Massachusetts (which then included Maine) down through the Carolinas.

The imposts were impressed most numerously upon lawyers, who were generally experienced as rousing orators. The brilliant Patrick Henry communicated the feeling of Sam Adams and James Otis in Massachusetts to fellow Virginians in the House of Burgesses: "Caesar had his Brutus, Charles the first his Cromwell, and George the Third" [interrupted here by cries of *Treason! treason!*, Henry waited till he could be again heard] " — and George the Third may profit by their example!"

At the top of this page: Facsimiles of British tax stamps issued for the Colonies, and (*at far right*) a riposte of the Pennsylvania Journal in 1765. *Above, here,* an early woodcut of a disturbance in New York City arising from a Stamp Tax protest. A banner surmounted by a deaths-head and inscribed "The folly of England and the ruin of America" is followed by gallows with effigies hanging.

Opposite page: Tarring and feathering of a British tax official at Boston, perhaps at the hands of Sons of Liberty, as depicted in an old illustration.

Sons of Liberty arose in New York, Philadelphia, other cities and towns on news from Boston. Effigies of royal officials were hanged from elms and oaks on town commons, and these became rallying places: Liberty Trees. Boycotts of trade with England were begun. January 1, 1766, John Adams noted in his journal:

"This year brings ruin or salvation to the British colonies. The eyes of all America are affixed on British parliament. In short, Britain and America are staring at each other."

Britain was stared down. Manufacturers, merchants, shipowners made their voices heard in parliament. The Stamp Act was repealed in March 1766. A new Chancellor of Exchequer, Charles Townshend, took over, and looked for other means of exacting tax money from the Colonies.

Agitation and resistance to the Stamp Act had been based on a logical thesis: that Parliament had no right to legislate *in*ternal taxes in the Colonies, each of which had its own government under royal charter, meaning any imposts laid on services or products originating within the respective colonies. It was conceded *ex*ternal taxation, such as customs duties, by Parliament was constitutional. Townshend, exploiting this interpretation, levied taxes on commodities for which the Colonies were dependent on English exports: glass, lead, paper, tea.

The East India Company had a monopoly on the tea. Sons of Liberty, cued by Sam Adams, looked upon British tea ships as symbols of tax tyranny, and exhorted merchants not to take the tea and citizens not to consume it. But, the East India Company agents having lowered the price as a measure against boycotting, consumption increased. The Sons of Liberty then resolved that the ships should be turned back, or the cargoes destroyed. The so-called Boston Tea Party, staged in December 1773, was only one of a series along the coast.

"Magna Britannia, Her Colonies Reduced," a cartoon for which Benjamin Franklin was said to have supplied the draft. Virginia and other colonies are the severed limbs (of commerce) cut off by Parliament.

Left: Paul Revere's fine engravings were somewhat less impressive in prints such as this one, "America in Distress." Satan is bringing the Stamp Act to bedevil the Colonies, represented by an Indian.

"Funeral Procession of the Stamp Act" has members of Parliament burying the measure after non-importation agreements in the Colonies markedly affected commerce. Idle piers are depicted in the background.

Britannia pictured being lured blindfolded into a pit dug by contending forces in French Catholic Canada and Protestant New England. Text it bore is omitted.

Redraft of cartoon by Paul Revere for the Royal American Magazine has Lord North pouring tea down Columbia's throat while Britannia (background) weeps at the outrage.

"Political Cartoon of 1775," a plate issued in London, has the German George III ("I Glory in the name of Englishman") being pulled to disaster by Pride and Obstinacy. From the Library of Congress.

A MONUMENTAL INSCRIPTION

ON THE

Fifth of March.

Together with a few LINES

On the Enlargement of

EBENEZER RICHARDSON,

Convicted of MURDER.

AMERICANS!
BEAR IN REMEMBRANCE
The HORRID MASSACRE!
Perpetrated in King-ftreet, BOSTON,
New-England,
On the Evening of March the Fifth, 1770.
When FIVE of your fellow countrymen,
GRAY, MAVERICK, CALDWELL, ATTUCKS,
and CARR,
Lay wallowing in their Gore!
Being *bafely*, and moft *inhumanly*
MURDERED!
And SIX others badly WOUNDED!
By a Party of the XXIXth Regiment,
Under the command of Capt. Tho. Prefton.
REMEMBER!
That Two of the MURDERERS
Were convicted of MANSLAUGHTER!
By a Jury, of whom I fhall fay
NOTHING,
Branded in the hand!
And *difmiffed*,
The others were ACQUITTED,
And their Captain PENSIONED!
Alfo,
BEAR IN REMEMBRANCE
That on the 22d Day of February, 1770.
The infamous
EBENEZER RICHARDSON, Informer,
And tool to Minifterial hirelings,
Moft *barbaroufly*
MURDERED
CHRISTOPHER SEIDER,
An innocent youth!
Of which crime he was found guilty
By his Country
On Friday April 20th, 1770;
But remained *Unfentenced*
On Saturday the 22d Day of February, 1772.
When the GRAND INQUEST
For Suffolk county,
Were informed, at requeft,
By the Judges of the Superior Court,
That EBENEZER RICHARDSON'S *Cafe*
Then lay before his MAJESTY.
Therefore faid *Richardfon*
This day, MARCH FIFTH! 1772,
Remains UNHANGED!!!
Let THESE things be told to Pofterity!
And handed down
From Generation to Generation,
'Till Time fhall be no more!
Forever may AMERICA be preferved,
From weak and wicked monarchs,
Tyrannical Minifters,
Abandoned Governors,
Their Underlings and Hirelings!
And may the
Machinations of artful, *defigning* wretches,
Who would ENSLAVE THIS People,
Come to an end,
Let their NAMES and MEMORIES
Be buried in eternal oblivion,
And the PRESS,
For a *SCOURGE* to Tyrannical Rulers,
Remain FREE.

AWAKE my drowfy Thoughts! Awake my mufe!
Awake O earth, and tremble at the news!
In grand defiance to the laws of God,
The Guilty, Guilty murd'rer walks abroad.
That city mourns, (the cry comes from the ground,)
Where law and juftice never can be found :
Oh! fword of vengeance, fall thou on the race
Of thofe who hinder juftice from its place.
O MURD'RER! RICHARDSON! with their lateft breath
Millions will curfe you when you fleep in death!
Infernal horrors fure will fhake your foul
When o'er your head the awful thunders roll.
Earth cannot hide you, always will the cry
Of Murder! Murder! haunt you 'till you die!
To yonder grave! with trembling joints repair,
Remember, SEIDER's corps lies mould'ring there ;
There drop a tear, and think what you have done!
Then judge how you can live beneath the Sun.
A PARDON may arrive! You laws defy,
But Heaven's laws will ftand when KINGS fhall die.
Oh! Wretched man! the monfter of the times,
You were not hung " by reafon of *old* Lines,"
Old Lines thrown by, 'twas then we were in hopes,
That you would foon be hung with *new màde* Ropes ✳
But neither *Ropes nor Lines*, will fatisfiy
For SEIDER's blood *!* But GOD is ever nigh,
And guilty fouls will not unpunifh'd go
Tho' they're excus'd by judges here below *!*
You are enlarg'd but curfed is your fate
Tho' ‖*Cufhing*'s eas'd you from the prifon gate
The ⌗*Bridge* of *Tories, it* has borne you o'er
Yet you e'er long may meet with HELL's dark fhore.

✳ "*Lins*"- the name of one of the judges
✳ Name of another judge now amena
† Do. of another of the judges
⌗ Trowbridge another judge.

Benjamin Franklin, as agent for Pennsylvania in England in 1765, had warned that if British soldiers were sent to America to enforce the Stamp Act they would *not* find a rebellion, but they might make one.

Soldiers *were* sent to Boston in 1768 in a punitive measure against violators of the customs laws, and they made troubles for themselves. Once by shooting a teenage demonstrator; again by what Sam Adams, with Paul Revere's graphic assistance, magnified into "the Boston Massacre" and made an inevitable prelude to the event at Lexington five years after.

Lexington, April 19, 1775 — A Ralph Earle on-the-scene sketch, engraved by A. Doolittle.

Opposite page: Crude woodcut simulation of Paul Revere's most famous engraving, "...the Bloody Massacre perpetrated in Kingstreet Boston on March 5th, 1770" is used as a headpiece for a broadside reminder of the unpunished perfidy of "the infamous Ebenezer Richardson, Informer, and tool to Ministerial hirelings, Most barbarously murdered Christopher Seider, An innocent youth!" Seider is a misprinting of Snider. The youth was killed in a smaller demonstration ten days before the street clash that has gone down in history as "the Boston Massacre." The anonymous chronicler, having expressed indignation over the outcome of the trial of the soldiers who fired the shots in Kingstreet, bestirs remembrance that although found guilty in the Snider death, Richardson was unhanged two years later. (Allusions in the verses were annotated by the hand of some preserver of the broadside.)

[↑] British entering Concord common 7 a.m., April 19, 1775, as shown in an old engraving. *1*. Redcoats marching onto the Common. *2*. Companies halted and drawn up in order. *3*. A detachment seizing and destroying "all the artillery and ammunition, provisions, tents and all other military stores you can find," under orders given by General Gage to Colonel Francis Smith, who led the raid. *4* and *5*. Colonel Smith and second-in-command, Major John Pitcairn of Royal Marines, viewing the positions of the militia. *6*. Court house. *7*. Meetinghouse. The British knew where rebel supplies were kept.

In October 1774, Massachusetts' provincial congress had directed the organization of a militia that would be prepared to march at a "minute's warning with a fortnight's provision, and ammunition and arms. Each town or community had to insure these 'minutemen's' being armed: stores had to be laid by. The congress professed the Province had no distant design of attacking, annoying or molesting his Majesty's troops," but had to be apprehensive of the fact that a "formidable body of troops with warlike preparations of every sort are already arrived."

General Thomas Gage, who had been sent to Boston in 1768 to quell the disturbances his Majesty's civil officials were suffering, was sent back in 1774 with four regiments to replace the now discountenanced royal governor, Thomas Hutchinson, as military governor and (as he wrote privately to a friend) "to bring the people to submission." First he tried persuasion, conciliatory gestures, futilely. He was made aware of the significance of the Stamp Act Congress at New York, where Sam Adams had made an impression on the delegates of other provinces or colonies, as a unifying force. George III had decided "The New England governments are in a state of rebellion. Blows must decide whether they are subject to this country or independent." The King and his ministers were becoming impatient with Gage: why could not the military governor of Boston seize the rebel leaders before the rebellion got out of hand? Gage's own officers were impatient with his restraint; they called him "the Old Woman."

April in 1775, when better weather came, reports from spies finally moved Gage to action.

There were muskets, powder, other military stores cached at Concord. There were good chances Sam Adams and John Hancock could also be captured: the two were known to have left Boston to attend a provincial congress thereabouts. Orders were issued for a raid the night of April 18. The secret could not be kept, one reason being the Quartering Act that had imposed British soldiers as roomers in private houses. Adams and Hancock were forewarned, as were minutemen along the planned British route, by couriers (one of whom was Paul Revere, as told in Longfellow's stirring poem).

Some seventy men formed, loose and undisciplined, at Lexington Common could not turn back the 700 drilled Redcoats led by Lieut. Col. Francis Smith. The so-called Battle of Lexington was only a skirmish in which eight Americans were killed and ten wounded. What happened when the British reached Concord and went about destroying such stores as remained and trying to get hands on Adams and Hancock, was a different story. There were trained militia among the 450, well maneuvered by officers; the British were heavily engaged at the "rude bridge" of Ralph Waldo Emerson's memorable poem and in the retreat back to Boston.

The struggle on Concord Bridge, an engraving by W. J. Edwards from a painting by Alonzo Chappel. "By the rude bridge that arched the flood,/ Their flag to April's breeze unfurled,/ Here once the embattled farmers stood,/ And fired the shot heard around the world," Ralph Waldo Emerson began his Concord Hymn, recited at dedication of the Concord Battle Monument.

"Retreat of the British from Concord," an engraving after a painting by Alonzo Chappel, a painter of Revolutionary War scenes attentive to realism in detail. The intruders are being harassed in the retirement by militia groups on both sides of the road. Major John Pitcairn's horse threw him amid the action at Concord. He lost the pair of pistols with one of which he presumably fired the shot at Lexington that started the Revolution. The pistols came into possession of Israel Putnam, who used them during his service with Washington's army, 1775-78. (A fact rarely, if ever, mentioned in accounts of Arnold's treason: An earlier attempt was made to lure Putnam over to the British side.)

Fast-spreading news of April 19 — the virtual rout of a strong force of British regulars — brought minutemen, organized militia and individual volunteers rallying in the peninsula across from Boston. When one of the couriers paused at Israel Putnam's farm near Pomfret, Connecticut, April 20, that veteran of the French and Indian War left his plow in its furrow, mounted a horse, and rode into Cambridge at sunrise the 21st. Appraising the situation, he sent back to Pomfret for the militia. Within a week he was in command of all the forces that gathered from Connecticut.

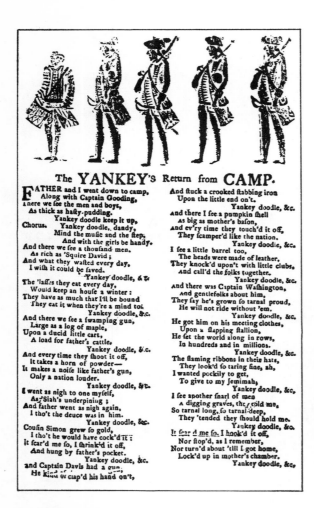

As indicated in a preceding chapter, unsoldierly turnouts of colonial militia in the French and Indian War had moved some British officers to turn an old sing-song gibe at Cromwellian troops into a gibe at the Yankeys, or Yankees. When the Yankee militiamen began beating the British, it was spontaneously adopted, with changes in verses, as a patriotic air.

Equipment with which men of the American forces were required to provide themselves varied from state to state. Facsimile of an instruction (*above*), sent one Bostonian in 1779, tells what Massachusetts men were expected to have: firearms, ramrod, bayonet, "cutting sword, or a tomahawk or hatchet," cartridge box, a hundred buckshot, jack-knife and tow for wadding, flints, powder, "forty leaden balls fitted to your gun," knapsack, blanket, "canteen or wooden bottle sufficient to hold one quart."

Artemas Ward, the commander of the Colonial forces around Boston before the arrival of George Washington at Cambridge as Congress' choice.

A view of Boston from Dorchester Heights at the beginning of the War of Independence.

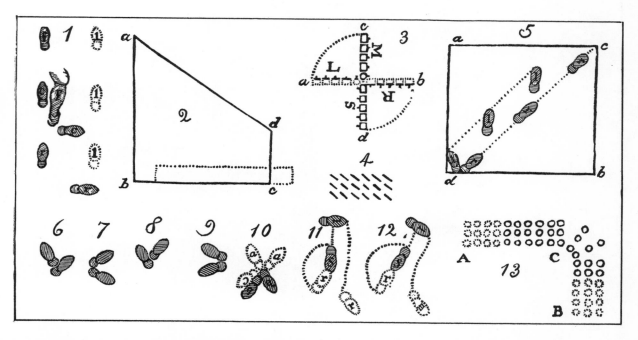

Above: One of twelve plates in "An Easy Plan of Discipline of Militia," a pamphlet published early in 1775 by Timothy Pickering, a thirty-year-old Harvard graduate who was leader of Salem's militia. Aware of the lack of knowledge of military fundamentals among officers of colonial militia, Pickering studied the writings of European professional soldiers and composed a textbook that was perhaps the manual best known in the Continental Army. Pickering applied its lessons well himself: in February 1775, the militia he commanded prevented British redcoats from crossing a drawbridge at Salem.

A more decisive blow than Concord was dealt the British after three weeks. Ethan Allen moved with some of the "Green Mountain Boys" he had collected at Castleton, Vermont, to Hand's Cove on Lake Champlain's east shore. There they met by chance a larger force from Connecticut and Massachusetts under Benedict Arnold — his entry into the war — with the same design. This was capture of Fort Ticonderoga, the strategic bastion raised by the French in 1755. Lacking boats for all the troops, Allen and Arnold packed eighty-three men into two available craft and, at dawn May 10, overwhelmed the small British garrison under Captain William Delaplane. Two days later, a detachment of reenforcements, under Seth Warner, took Crown Point, just to the north, while Arnold captured the fort at St. John's, across the Canadian border.

These coups put the patriots in possession of over eighty pieces of artillery, thousands of cannon balls, and other stores that were to be of vital importance to George Washington, who that May 10 was attending the opening of the Second Continental Congress in the State House at Philadelphia, as delegate from Virginia.

During May, the patriot forces at Cambridge multiplied to more than 15,000 under tacit leadership of Artemas Ward, who had been chosen by the Committee of Safety to command Massachusetts troops. General Gage was reenforced by arrivals of transports with regiments under Generals Howe, Clinton and Burgoyne. On June 12, Gage finally declared martial law, and ordered a movement intended to prevent further fortifications by the colonial army that could make the peninsula like a huge gun thrust at Boston's throat.

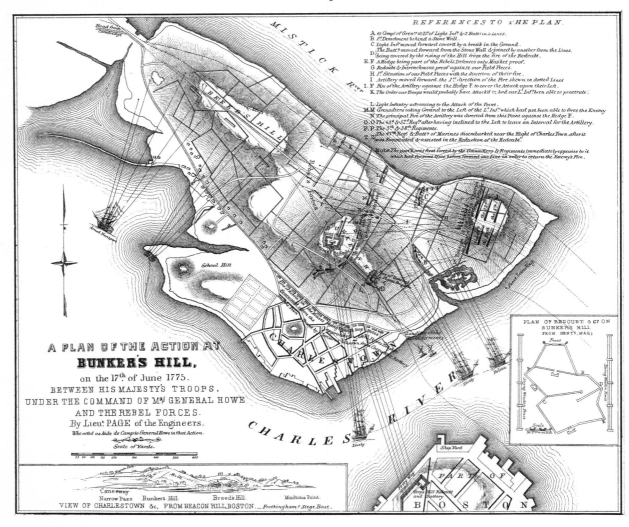

"An Exact View of the Late Battle at Charlestown, June 17, 1775, in which an advanced party of about 700 Provincials stood an Attack made by 11 Regiments and a Train of Artillery & After an Engagement of two hours retreated to their Main Body at Cambridge, leaving Eleven hundred of the enemy Killed and Wounded upon the field," was the caption on this contemporary engraving.

The resultant action, June 17, known as the Battle of Bunker Hill (actually at Breed's Hill, nearer Boston), was not the victory the Americans claimed, and not a rout for the British, though the latter's losses were heavier. But the battle made the colonies believe the British could be beaten, and — a sad mistake — without great ultimate effort. As Emory Upton was to write, "The mistaken conviction seized the public mind that . . . patriotism was the sole qualification for a soldier's calling."

"BUNKER'S HILL, or America's Head Dress," an English cartoon in 1775, when fantastically towering and ornamented hair-dos were the rage overseas. (From an original in the Library of Congress.)

The handwritten letter reads:

22ᵈ June 1775
6 o'clock PM

Sirs

The Congress just dis, below is their Determination with Respect to Superior Officers & Rank —

1ˢᵗ Genˡ Washington
2ᵈ Genˡ Ward
3ᵈ Genˡ Lee   } Major Genˡ
4 — Genˡ Schuyler
5 — Genˡ Putnam

Brigadier Generals Vizt.
1ˢᵗ Conway
2ᵈ Montgomery. For New York,
3ᵈ Wooster
4ᵗʰ Heath,
5 Spencer
6 Thomas
7 — Sullivan. member of Congress
8 — Green. Rhode Island

We have just a Report of a Battle, & that Colˡ Gardiner is mortally Wounded. We are Anxious. No Express. God Send us a good Acctˢ — I am now Signing the Commissˢ. for your whole army. The Gentˢ Setts out early in ẏ morng. I am &ᶜᵗ
J Hancock

Announcement by John Hancock, President of the Congress, giving the relative ranks of the first generals designated for the Army. Washington is followed as Major-General by Ward, Charles Lee, Schuyler, Putnam. The seniority of the Brigadiers appointed in the beginning was, as can be seen: Conway, Montgomery, Wooster, Heath, Spencer, Thomas, Sullivan, Nathanael Greene of Rhode Island (whose name was misspelled by Hancock). The latter's postscript, beginning "We have just heard of a battle," refers, of course, to the Bunker Hill struggle. John Sullivan is identified as "member of Congress."

Left: Variant type of muskets with which men supplied themselves, and a wartime sketch of one of many "Congress" soldiers who wore the deerskin or other leather hunting dress, with gaiters, of woodsmen — and often were barefoot or in moccasins. The only suggestion of a uniform was a leather cap with *Congress* burned upon it. Woodsmen from the Appalachians brought the rifle into battle for the first time during the French and Indian War, 1756-63.

IV

COMMANDER-IN-CHIEF

"It is the general's express orders, that, if any man attempt to skulk, lie down, or retreat without orders, he be instantly shot down, as an example. He hopes, no such will be found in this army; but, on the contrary, that every one, for himself resolving to conquer or die, and trusting in the smiles of Heaven upon so just a cause, will behave with bravery and resolution."

— GEORGE WASHINGTON, 1776

THE COLONEL from Virginia had been nominated by Thomas Johnson of Maryland "to command all the Continental Forces raised or to be raised for the defense of American Liberty." Washington, who was sitting near a door of the Assembly Chamber in the State House in Philadelphia, darted out as the motion was being put. It was seconded by Sam Adams. The vote, by ballot, was unanimous.

The President of the Congress went personally to escort the new general to the chamber. In a formal acceptance address, George Washington asked each member to remember that he did not consider himself equal to the great responsibility with which he had been honored. To a member of the Virginia delegation who came up to him after the ceremony, Patrick Henry, George Washington added, with a sorrowful expression, "Remember, Mr. Henry, from the day I enter upon the command of the American armies, I date my fall, and the ruin of my reputation."

A courier carried to Martha at Mount Vernon a letter which read in part:

"You may believe me, my dear Patsy, when I assure you in the most solemn manner, that, so far from seeking this appointment, I have used every endeavor in my power to avoid it, not only from unwillingness to part from you and the family, but a consciousness of its being a trust too great for my capability, and that I would enjoy more real happiness and felicity in a month with you than I have the most distant prospect of finding abroad, if my stay were to be seven times seven years."

His first act as Commander-in-Chief, on June 20, was to review several militia companies of Philadelphia: "Horse and Foot in all about 2,000," his diary said in one of the last entries until 1781. The same day he dispatched a circular letter to the Independent Companies in Fairfax County, Virginia, which he had helped to raise and drill (and equip from his pocket). He also purchased from Gibbs & Co., for forty pounds, a pumping-engine for the Friendships Fire Company of Alexandria, of which he was a member.

The Lord only knows what Washington would, or could, have done at Boston, without the cannon Ethan Allen and his Green Mountain Boys had captured at Ticonderoga, May 9, 1775. That winter of 1775-76, when Allen was suffering

Washington did not leave reconnoitering of the enemy's positions in Boston to other officers and spies. He made regular personal surveys of the situation.

Above: Field glass and casing he carried during the War of Independence, preserved at Mount Vernon. *Right:* One of his textbooks.

PROSPECT HILL.	BUNKER'S HILL.
I. Seven Dollars a Month. — —	I. Three Pence a Day.
II. Fresh Provisions, and in Plenty. — —	II. Rotten Salt Pork.
III. Health. — — — —	III. The Scurvy.
IV. Freedom, Eafe, Affluence and a good Farm.	IV. Slavery, Beggary and Want.

Attempts were made to lessen Washington's task by inducing desertions from the royal forces. This handbill was sent among the common soldiers in beleaguered Boston. "Bunker's Hill" is, of course, a reference to the battle in which the redcoats suffered such heavy casualties.

the horrors of a prison ship in New York, Washington sent for the cannon. Their weight and the lack of good roads made winter the only feasible time to try to move them overland any long distance.

Washington detailed Henry Knox to the mission. He expected Knox to use horses and sledges. The Virginian was not as well acquainted with Green Mountain winters as Knox. The erstwhile Boston bookseller wisely rounded up oxen with which to tow the cannon, which in some cases had their wheels fitted to runners and in others were stripped to the barrels, which were mounted on sledges.

Fifty-nine of the precious cannon, the good product of British arsenals, were dragged through the Green Mountains and Berkshire Hills. They weighed as much as 5000 pounds each. Passages had to be chopped through woods. Corduroy roads had to be put down across swampy places. The winding Hudson River had to be crossed four times. One or more of the forty-odd sledges or sets of runners had to be dug out of snow or set aright every day.

Fortunately, the British commander in Boston was not informed of the movement. Knox's companions, worn down by their arduous labors in keeping the cannon on the way to Dorchester

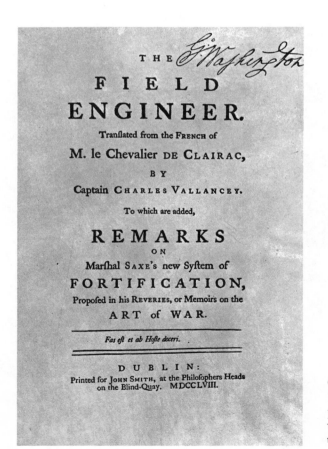

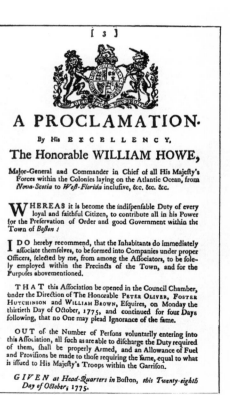

Call of British High Command for volunteers for *Tory* militia in Boston, with a promise they would "be properly armed, and an allowance of fuel and provisions be made to those requiring same, equal to those issued His Majesty's troops."

Heights, would not have been capable of protecting them from a strong British force.

Three weeks after the sledges left Ticonderoga, the cannon were unloaded at Dorchester Heights and brought to bear on the British positions.

Knox's was not the only detachment to go to Ticonderoga that autumn or winter. Brigadier General Richard Montgomery was sent as leader of one force in a two-pronged operation, designed to cut the enemy supply lines from Canada and possibly secure the French-Canadians as allies by driving the British from Montreal and Quebec. Montgomery moved up via Ticonderoga. The second detachment was under Benedict Arnold and Christopher Greene.

Montgomery captured Montreal November 12, and had to leave an occupation force when he moved to unite with Arnold against Quebec. They were repulsed December 31, with Mont-

gomery being slain in the action and Arnold wounded. Arnold, commissioned a colonel by the provincial Congress of Massachusetts, was promoted to Brigadier General for his gallantry in the Quebec attack. He maintained a siege there until April, when he was relieved by Wooster and sent to command at Montreal.

Heavily reinforced in the spring, the British were able to drive the invaders out of Canada. The hopes the New England patriots had nourished for inducing the Canadians to join the thirteen colonies in revolt faded out, as did efforts to persuade Jamaica, most productive of all Britain's New World possessions, to throw in her lot with the rebels.

In March, GW received instructions from the Congress to destroy Boston if necessary. John Hancock also wrote him that, although he — Hancock — had important property in the city, GW was "not to hesitate to fire upon it."

The arrival of Knox at the Continental Army's position outside Boston with the cannon from Ticonderoga — an engraving by Halpin from an imaginative painting by Felix O. C. Darley.

The same week the Battle of Bunker Hill was fought, the war spread to sea. The concentration of Gage's invaders in Boston necessitated construction of additional barracks. To get sufficient timber for the purpose, Howe's quartermaster sent two lumber schooners to Machias, Maine, convoyed by the cutter *Margaretta*.

The way in which demands were made upon them gave reason for an outburst by Machias townspeople, among whom news of the Battles of Lexington and Concord had been percolating. The *Margaretta*'s commander required the inhabitants to "indulge Captain Jones in carrying lumber to Boston" as a prerequisite to "their obtaining supplies of any provisions," and ordered the liberty-pole in the public square to be taken down. Quickly some forty men seized a sloop, the *Unity*, that lay in the harbor and chose Jeremiah O'Brien as captain for an attack on the *Margaretta*. Hailed challengingly, the cutter's commander turned back to sea. O'Brien drove the *Unity* in pursuit, steered it into a collision with the *Margaretta* and staged a boarding action. Beset by farmers with scythes, pitchforks and axes as well as fowling pieces, the British crewmen gave way and the captain had to surrender. The *Unity* was refitted with the *Margaretta*'s armament and renamed the *Machias Liberty*. She was the first of the privateers that did heavy damage before a navy was organized, and continued effective depredations until the end of the conflict.

The privateer, as understood at the outbreak of the war, was a ship outfitted and armed at the expense of individuals or partnerships for the business of preying on the enemy's commerce to the profit of its owners. It was necessary to obtain commissions or letters of marque from the local patriot regimes or from the Marine Committee of Congress, and abide by regulations drawn up by the latter. There usually was a governmental cut on the money realized from the sale of prizes and cargoes. Naturally the biggest share, after the distribution of portions to the captain and crew, went to the owners. However, the potential division of spoils — sometimes as much as $1000 a cruise above wages for an ordinary seaman — attracted many of the best seamen to this especially dangerous service. The privateersmen furnished the Navy with a substantial number of able officers.

Following the outrage at Machias, Royal Navy authorities sent two armed sloops, *Diligence* and *Tapanagouche*, to punish the Yankees.

Right: Formal proclamation by John Hancock of the governing rules drafted by the Marine Committee of Congress for commanders "of Private Ships or Vessels of War, which shall have Commissions or Letters of Marque and Reprisal, authorizing them to make Captures of British Vessels and Cargoes." It is stressed (Paragraph V) "You shall keep and preserve every Ship or Vessel and Cargo by you taken, until they shall by Sentence of Court properly authorized be adjudged a lawful prize, not selling, spoiling, wasting, or diminishing the same or breaking the Bulk thereof, nor suffering any such Thing..."

DONT TREAD ON ME

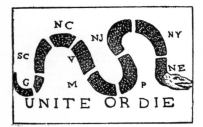

UNITE OR DIE

Later version of Franklin cartoon that inspired patriot battle flags (above and right)

DONT TREAD ON ME

Left: Beaver of New York naval ensign was suggested by beaver in coat-of-arms of New Netherland.

AN APPEAL TO HEAVEN

Above: Pine-tree flag of New England colonies was flown in variations by privateers in Revolution.

Hearing of their approach, O'Brien sailed with the *Machias Liberty* and a coasting vessel, *Portland Packet*, which had Benjamin Foster as captain. By attacking the British ships separately in the Bay of Fundy, they captured both and sailed the prizes into Watertown. O'Brien, the Revolution's first naval hero, was made a captain in the Massachusetts Marine and went out with the *Machias Liberty* and the captured *Diligence* to cruise after British prizes. They made four more captures in August.

Meanwhile the new commander-in-chief at Cambridge had, on his own initiative, purchased two schooners which he armed, officered with army captains and manned with soldiers, to serve his needs in the siege of Boston. Their orders were to take all vessels sailing to or from Boston in British-army service. Washington realized from the first how essential was sea power to military success; he did not wait for Congress to provide for the necessary naval support. Other vessels were added to the first two, Washington assigned John Manly, a real sailor, as over-all commander and within six months these ships took thirty-five prizes, including H.M.S. *Nancy*, with fifty officers and men. More importantly they supplied the Continental Army with 4000 muskets, 100,000 flints, 30,000 balls, thirty-one tons of lead, a number of barrels of powder, a large-bore brass mortar and other essential military stores.

There was need for that centuries-old marine recognition signal, a flag, to distinguish these "continental" vessels from the privateers from the respective Colonies, the neutral ships and enemy craft. The Grand Union banner — decided on by a Committee of Congress (headed by Franklin) in consultation with Washington — was the result. While not raised formally at his headquarters before January 1, 1776, it probably was at mainmasts earlier, in place of a precursor white ensign

The flag of *Bonhomme Richard* when John Paul Jones won the resounding victory over H.M.S. *Serapis*, off Scotland, in September 1779, had only twelve stripes, as shown in photograph (right above). Below it, design of flag of regiment in Continental Army at Yorktown. Numerous army units retained eagle flags up to the time of the Civil War.

"Rebellious Stripes" as transformed into Union flag with retention of British crosses of St. Andrew and St. George (Scotland and England) in a field of blue.

Right: Naval jack of Rhode Island with its thirteen stars antedated stars and stripes banner adopted by Congress in 1777. Congress did not specify a circular arrangement of the stars and there were many variations.

bearing a pine tree and the inscription *An Appeal to Heaven*. It certainly was flown by Arnold's *Royal Savage* in Lake Champlain and by Manly's squadron in 1776.

Understandably, after the Declaration of Independence, there was desire to efface from the flag the British Union, and the earlier choice by Congress was annulled by an Act of June 14, 1777. Few people realize that the Stars and Stripes flag was a substitution.

The Marquis de Condorcet, eulogizing his old friend before the Academy of Sciences at Paris in 1790, accompanied a review of the American genius' many contributions to scientific knowledge with references to Benjamin Franklin's ready, incisive wit and effective use of Socratic-method argument. As an example, he recalled how Franklin dealt with the British government's practice of consigning criminals to the Colonies.

A letter in the *Pennsylvania Gazette*, May 9, 1751, signed "Americus," began with reference to the "kindness of our mother country" in forbidding "our mistaken Assemblies" to make any law for preventing the importation of criminals on the ground "that such laws are against the

Above: Redraft of a drawing, in full colors, of the *Royal Savage*, found in the papers of Major-General Philip Schuyler. It gave positive confirmation of the design and color-scheme of the Grand Union flag. The design was said to have been suggested by Colonel Joseph Reed, military secretary to GW.

public utility, as they tend to prevent the improvement and well peopling of the colonies." Such a tender parental concern, Franklin went on, called for the highest returns of gratitude. Though recognizing that a really adequate return was impossible, he suggested a plan that might at least show a grateful disposition.

"In some uninhabited parts of these provinces, there are Numbers of these venomous reptiles we call Rattlesnakes; Felons-convict from the Beginning of the World. These, whenever we meet them, we put to Death, by virtue of an old Law. . . . But as this is a sanguinary Law, and may be too cruel; and as however mischievous these Creatures are among us, they may possibly change their Natures, if they were to change the Climate; I would humbly propose that this General Sentence of Death be changed for transportation.

"In the Spring of the Year, when they first creep out of their Holes, they are feeble, slow, heavy, and easily taken; and if a small Bounty were allow'd per head, some Thousands might be collected annually and transported to Britain. There I would propose to have them carefully distributed in St. James Park, in the Spring Gardens and other Places of Pleasure about London; in the Gardens of all the Nobility and Generally throughout the Nation; but particularly in the Gardens of the Prime Ministers, the Lords of Trade, and Members of Parliament; for to them we are most particularly obliged."

Franklin wound up his argument that rattlesnakes were the most suitable returns for the "Human Serpents sent us by our Mother-Country" with "indeed she would have the advantage of us. She will reap equal benefits without equal risk. For the Rattlesnake gives Warning before he attempts his mischief, which the Convict does not."

Newspapers whose editors read the *Gazette* perhaps even more devoutly than their Authorized Version reprinted the letter so unmistakably Franklin's, and spontaneously the rattlesnake became the most popular symbol in the Middle and Southern Colonies, and was emblazoned on patriot banners. Franklin was inspired to have engraved in wood and publish in the *Gazette*, May

9, 1754 (perhaps more than coincidentally on the third anniversary of the letter) what became the most famous and influential cartoon in American history. Showing a rattlesnake in segments, each denotive of a colony or section, it was emblazoned, "Join or die." This also appeared on patriot banners, altered to "Unite or die," as early as 1765.

Neither replaced other colonial banners: the pine tree of Massachusetts and Maine, the beaver of New York, the anchor of Rhode Island (in which thirteen stars first appeared), the palmetto of South Carolina. There was no one banner symbolizing a unity of authority before the Grand Union was adopted by General Washington in 1776, except the "Union" banner New England colonies had used in campaigns against the French.

Stripes in its substitute are traced in odd reasoning to the three stripes in the Washington coat-of-arms, which also bore three stars. Lawrence Phelps Tower had suggested, quite logically, that they derive from the Sons of Liberty flag of nine red and white stripes. (Only nine colonies took part in the Stamp Act Congress in 1765 that adopted a Declaration of Rights and Petition to the King.)

Intriguing evidence that a starred and striped flag existed before the act of Congress, June 14, 1777, specifying a naval ensign, is a reference in Isaiah Thomas' *Boston Journal, or Massachusetts Spy*, March 10, 1774: "The American ensign now sparkles a star which shall shortly flame wide from the skies." British journals had referred earlier to "the rebellious stripes." A cartoon published in France in 1775, relating to "the tea controversy" in America, showed a thirteen-stripe "rebellious flag" with the rattlesnake upon it, and the same year a British visitor in South Carolina remarked, "Even in their dress the females seem to bid us defiance — and take care to have in their breast knots, and even upon their shoes something that resembles their flag of thirteen stripes."

In ironic coincidence, the same day "the Rebellious Stripes" were raised formally at Washington's headquarters, copies of a conciliatory speech delivered in Parliament by George III were received in Boston. Copies were sent to Washington under flag of truce. Its effects were wholly misjudged by the commander of His Majesty's beleaguered forces, General Lord Howe. How much so is indicated by a note Washington penned on January 4 to Joseph Reed:

"The speech I send you. A volume of them was sent out by the Boston gentry, and, farcical enough, we gave great joy to them without knowing or intending it; for on that day, the day we gave being to the new army, but before the proclamation came to hand, we had hoisted the Union flag, in compliment to the United Colonies. But behold! it was received in Boston as a token of the deep impression the speech had made upon us and as a signal of submission. So we hear by a person out of Boston last night. By this time, I presume, they begin to think it strange that we have not made a formal surrender of our lines."

From another source, the *Annual Register*, 1776, we know "So great was the rage and indignation [of the Americans] that they burned the speech, changed their colors . . . to a flag with thirteen stripes, as a symbol of the number and union of the colonies."

WASHINGTON's little naval force, given some support by vessels Congress itself commissioned as starters of a Continental Navy, was to be instrumental in the successful movement of his army to New York after General Howe evacuated Boston. Though Howe retreated to Nova Scotia, British squadrons and single ships remained along the coast. The Continental Army's transports were in danger all the way.

With his army safely in New York, but threatened on all sides, Washington directed generals, colonels and lesser ranks in strengthening land defenses of the city, shutting off some channels with obstructions and assembling another naval force such as he had at Boston.

An innovation was the world's first combat submarine, built by David Bushnell of Saybrook, Conn. Named, appropriately, *Turtle*, it was a turtle-shaped cask about seven and one-half feet in diameter, large enough to contain a man, the working apparatus and air to sustain him thirty minutes.

The old cross-sectional drawing below was based on descriptions and is not precise in detail and proportions. The operator sat beneath the

exit-entry port, with enough work for four hands. Water had to be admitted into compartments to sink the cask to the required depth, and had to be expelled by two force pumps. (A water gauge showed the depth of submersion.) While one hand cranked the twenty-four-inch, twin-bladed propeller, the other steered the rudder. All this had to be done by "feel," for the only illumination in the darkness was a bottle of phosphorus hung by the compass and water gauge.

Above the operator's head was an auger intended to bore into the hull of the target ship to affix a 150-pound box of powder with a clockwork detonator. The detonator could be set going by lever from inside the *Turtle*, as the drawing shows.

With a sergeant from Washington's army, Ezra Lee, as operator, the *Turtle* got close enough to H.M.S. *Eagle*, flagship of Howe's fleet, September 6, 1776, to attach the bomb to the frigate's hull. However, the hull was copper-sheathed, Lee could not attach the bomb securely and it drifted from the target. Consequently, the explosion, which Lee escaped in safety, did no damage to the flagship, but it did scare the admiral into dispersing the squadron.

January 7, 1776, a pamphlet entitled *Common Sense* appeared at Philadelphia, destined to be among the most rousing publications in American history. Until that time most orators and writers for the patriot cause still spoke and wrote as if the differences with the British royal government in London could be reconciled once the king's ministers changed their policies. *Common Sense* declared unequivocally that the Colonies were qualified for independence; that their interests, current and future, demanded this.

Some other individuals had bespoken similar beliefs, but there was no open advocacy of inde-

COMMON SENSE:

ADDRESSED TO THE

INHABITANTS

OF

AMERICA,

On the following interesting

SUBJECTS.

I. Of the Origin and Design of Government in general, with concise Remarks on the English Constitution.

II. Of Monarchy and Hereditary Succession.

III. Thoughts on the present State of American Affairs.

IV. Of the present Ability of America, with some miscellaneous Reflections.

Written by an ENGLISHMAN.
By Thomas Paine

Man knows no Master save creating HEAVEN,
Or those whom choice and common good ordain.
THOMSON.

PHILADELPHIA, Printed
And Sold by R. BELL, in Third-Street, 1776.

A British printer was quick to reprint [◀—] Paine's pamphlet "with additions." It was to be followed late in 1776 by another ringing expression, *The Crisis*.

pendence in the Colonies until Thomas Paine struck a responsive chord with the arguments in *Common Sense*, which he was said to have composed at the prompting of Dr. Benjamin Rush, the eminent Philadelphia physician who himself had written stirring pamphlets on temperance, hygiene, and abolition of slavery.

The pamphlet was well timed, coming in the wake of a stubborn act of Parliament in December 1775, that forbade any nation's ships from trading with the recalcitrant Colonies. Vessels that violated this ukase were declared to be lawful prizes of war. John Adams said then, "It makes us independent in spite of our supplications and pleas," a declaration that resounded wherever *Common Sense* circulated.

Considerable credit for the pamphlet's fast-spreading, accumulative and decisive influence was due to courageous printers who brought out enormous quantities and fostered wider distribu-

tion than any previous publication had in so short a time. It was estimated that between 120,000 and 500,000 copies, many of them pirated issues, were sold within a few months, to persons who accepted its theses, "Arms must decide the contest; [they were] the choice of the king. The sun never shone on a cause of greater worth. 'Tis not the affair of a city, a province, or a kingdom, but of a continent — of at least one eighth part of the habitable globe." To Paine, "The utmost stretch of the human wisdom cannot at this time compass a plan short of separation."

In Congress in February, Benjamin Harrison spoke up: "We have hobbled on under a fatal attachment to Great Britain." His colleague from Virginia, George Wythe, said, "We must declare ourselves a free people." Then he moved a resolution "that the Colonies have a right to contract alliances with foreign powers." Delegates from seven Colonies indicated they were receptive, but

Below: Old State House, Philadelphia, in Revolutionary times when it was being transformed by what

took place there into Independence Hall. (From author's collection. Credited to John Rogers.)

assent had to come from their respective Assemblies or Conventions.

On May 15, Virginia's provincial convention decided that Richard Henry Lee, spokesman of the Virginia delegation in the Continental Congress, should propose to the Congress united separation from Britain. By coincidence, that same May 15, and before Lee received the letter of instruction from Virginia, Congress resolved "That it be recommended to the respective Assemblies and Conventions of the United Colonies, where no Government sufficient to the exigencies of their affairs has been hitherto established, to adopt such Government as shall in the opinion of the Representatives of the People best conduce to the happiness and safety of their people, and America in general." In other words, they were told to form independent governments.

June 7, Richard Henry Lee duly proposed to the Congress at Philadelphia that it resolve "These United States are, and of right, ought to be free and independent States, that they are absolved from all allegiance to the British Crown, and that all political connection between them and the State of Great Britain is, and ought to be, totally dissolved. That it is expedient forthwith to take the most effectual measures for forming foreign alliances. That a plan of Federation be prepared and transmitted to the respective Colonies for their consideration and approbation."

The result was the appointment on June 11 of a committee to draft a declaration of independence, and on the 12th another committee to draft a plan for a confederation, with John Dickinson of Pennsylvania as chairman of the latter. Richard Henry Lee having been called back to Virginia after the 7th, Thomas Jefferson was named in Lee's place to the committee that was to frame the declaration. Otherwise, some hand other than Jefferson's probably would have put it into writing.

The patriot leader who had been the most assertive in advancing independence as *the* political objective, Samuel Adams, was not put on the committee; his cousin with a milder temperament, John, was chosen, with Benjamin Franklin, Roger Sherman of Connecticut and Robert R. Livingston of New York, to draw up the draft that was submitted to the Congress on June 28.

Indisputably, the document was principally the work of Jefferson, even though the framework embodied sections from the Virginia Declaration of Rights, written by George Mason, which had been adopted in the provincial convention at Richmond on June 12. It also reflected, if it did not follow, arguments expressed in 1769 by James Wilson of Pennsylvania, who until the action on July 2, 1776, was to favor "what amounted to a dominion status, but the British statesmanship of the era was incapable of rising to the occasion as it did in the case of Canada in the next century." (The quotation is from Dumas Malone.)

Before submitting the draft to the committee as a whole, Jefferson showed it to Franklin and Adams, who were responsible for about twenty-five alterations in verbiage, and three new paragraphs. Further changes were made during consideration by the Congress, the most notable being elimination of a clause blaming George III for the slave trade and insertion in the final paragraph of phraseology of the resolution for independence upon which action was to be taken before the Declaration itself.

Above: "Resolved that copies of the Declaration be sent to the several Assemblies, Conventions, and Councils of Safety, & to the General Commanding Officers of the Continental Troops, that it be proclaim'd in each of the United States, & at the head of the Army. By order of Congress. John Hancock, Presid." — from the original record preserved.

Right: A John Dunlap broadside, with punctuation added in his printing office.

In CONGRESS, July 4, 1776.

A DECLARATION

BY THE REPRESENTATIVES OF THE

UNITED STATES OF AMERICA,

IN GENERAL CONGRESS ASSEMBLED.

WHEN In the Course of human Events, It becomes neceſſary for one People to diſſolve the Political Bands which have connected them with another, and to aſſume among the Powers of the Earth, the ſeparate and equal Station to which the Laws of Nature, and of Nature's God entitle them, a decent Reſpect to the Opinions of Mankind requires that they ſhould declare the cauſes which impel them to the Separation.

We hold theſe Truths to be ſelf-evident, that all Men are created equal, that they are endowed by their Creator with certain unalienable Rights, that among theſe are Life, Liberty, and the Purſuit of Happineſs——That to ſecure theſe Rights, Governments are inſtituted among Men, deriving their juſt Powers from the Conſent of the Governed, that whenever any Form of Government becomes deſtructive of theſe Ends, it is the Right of the People to alter or to aboliſh it, and to inſtitute new Government, laying its Foundation on ſuch Principles, and organizing its Powers in ſuch Form, as to them ſhall ſeem moſt likely to effect their Safety and Happineſs. Prudence, indeed, will dictate that Governments long eſtabliſhed ſhould not be changed for light and tranſient Cauſes; and accordingly all Experience hath ſhewn, that Mankind are more diſpoſed to ſuffer, while Evils are ſufferable, than to right themſelves by aboliſhing the Forms to which they are accuſtomed. But when a long Train of Abuſes and Uſurpations, purſuing invariably the ſame Object, evinces a Deſign to reduce them under abſolute Deſpotiſm, it is their Right, it is their Duty, to throw off ſuch Government, and to provide new Guards for their future Security. Such has been the patient Sufferance of theſe Colonies; and ſuch is now the Neceſſity which conſtrains them to alter their former Syſtems of Government. The Hiſtory of the preſent King of Great-Britain is a Hiſtory of repeated Injuries and Uſurpations, all having in direct Object the Eſtabliſhment of an abſolute Tyranny over theſe States. To prove this, let Facts be ſubmitted to a candid World.

He has refuſed his Aſſent to Laws, the moſt wholeſome and neceſſary for the public Good.

He has forbidden his Governors to paſs Laws of immediate and preſſing Importance, unleſs ſuſpended in their Operation till his Aſſent ſhould be obtained; and when ſo ſuſpended, he has utterly neglected to attend to them.

He has refuſed to paſs other Laws for the Accommodation of large Diſtricts of People, unleſs thoſe People would relinquiſh the Right of Repreſentation in the Legiſlature, a Right ineſtimable to them, and formidable to Tyrants only.

He has called together Legiſlative Bodies at Places unuſual, uncomfortable, and diſtant from the Depoſitory of their public Records, for the ſole Purpoſe of fatiguing them into Compliance with his Meaſures.

He has diſſolved Repreſentative Houſes repeatedly, for oppoſing with manly Firmneſs his Invaſions on the Rights of the People.

He has refuſed for a long Time, after ſuch Diſſolutions, to cauſe others to be elected; whereby the Legiſlative Powers, incapable of Annihilation, have returned to the People at large for their exerciſe; the State remaining in the mean time expoſed to all the Dangers of Invaſion from without, and Convulſions within.

He has endeavoured to prevent the Population of theſe States; for that Purpoſe obſtructing the Laws for Naturalization of Foreigners; refuſing to paſs others to encourage their Migrations hither, and raiſing the Conditions of new Appropriations of Lands.

He has obſtructed the Adminiſtration of Juſtice, by refuſing his Aſſent to Laws for eſtabliſhing Judiciary Powers.

He has made Judges dependent on his Will alone, for the Tenure of their Offices, and the Amount and Payment of their Salaries.

He has erected a Multitude of new Offices, and ſent hither Swarms of Officers to harraſs our People, and eat out their Subſtance.

He has kept among us, in Times of Peace, Standing Armies, without the conſent of our Legiſlatures.

He has affected to render the Military independent of and ſuperior to the Civil Power.

He has combined with others to ſubject us to a Juriſdiction foreign to our Conſtitution, and unacknowledged by our Laws; giving his Aſſent to their Acts of pretended Legiſlation:

For quartering large Bodies of Armed Troops among us:

For protecting them, by a mock Trial, from Puniſhment for any Murders which they ſhould commit on the Inhabitants of theſe States:

For cutting off our Trade with all Parts of the World:

For impoſing Taxes on us without our Conſent:

For depriving us, in many Caſes, of the Benefits of Trial by Jury:

For tranſporting us beyond Seas to be tried for pretended Offences:

For aboliſhing the free Syſtem of Engliſh Laws in a neighbouring Province, eſtabliſhing therein an arbitrary Government, and enlarging its Boundaries, ſo as to render it at once an Example and fit Inſtrument for introducing the ſame abſolute Rule into theſe Colonies:

For takin way our Charters, aboliſhing our moſt valuable Laws, and altering fundamentally the Forms of our Governments:

For ſuſpending our own Legiſlatures, and declaring themſelves inveſted with Power to legiſlate for us in all Caſes whatſoever.

He has abdicated Government here, by declaring us out of his Protection and waging War againſt us.

He has plundered our Seas, ravaged our Coaſts, burnt our Towns, and deſtroyed the Lives of our People.

He is, at this Time, tranſporting large Armies of foreign Mercenaries to compleat the Works of Death, Deſolation, and Tyranny, already begun with circumſtances of Cruelty and Perfidy, ſcarcely paralleled in the moſt barbarous Ages, and totally unworthy the Head of a civilized Nation.

He has conſtrained our fellow Citizens taken Captive on the high Seas to bear Arms againſt their Country, to become the Executioners of their Friends and Brethren, or to fall themſelves by their Hands.

He has excited domeſtic Inſurrections amongſt us, and has endeavoured to bring on the Inhabitants of our Frontiers, the mercileſs Indian Savages, whoſe known Rule of Warfare, is an undiſtinguiſhed Deſtruction, of all Ages, Sexes and Conditions.

In every ſtage of theſe Oppreſſions we have Petitioned for Redreſs in the moſt humble Terms: Our repeated Petitions have been anſwered only by repeated Injury. A Prince, whoſe Character is thus marked by every act which may define a Tyrant, is unfit to be the Ruler of a free People.

Nor have we been wanting in Attentions to our Britiſh Brethren. We have warned them from Time to Time of Attempts by their Legiſlature to extend an unwarrantable Juriſdiction over us. We have reminded them of the Circumſtances of our Emigration and Settlement here. We have appealed to their native Juſtice and Magnanimity, and we have conjured them by the Ties of our common Kindred to diſavow theſe Uſurpations, which, would inevitably interrupt our Connections and Correſpondence. They too have been deaf to the Voice of Juſtice and of Conſanguinity. We muſt, therefore, acquieſce in the Neceſſity, which denounces our Separation, and hold them, as we hold the reſt of Mankind, Enemies in War, in Peace, Friends.

We, therefore, the Repreſentatives of the UNITED STATES OF AMERICA, in General Congress, Aſſembled, appealing to the Supreme Judge of the World for the Rectitude of our Intentions, do, in the Name, and by Authority of the good People of theſe Colonies, ſolemnly Publiſh and Declare, That theſe United Colonies are, and of Right ought to be, FREE AND INDEPENDENT STATES; that they are abſolved from all Allegiance to the Britiſh Crown, and that all political Connection between them and the State of Great-Britain, is and ought to be totally diſſolved; and that as FREE AND INDEPENDENT STATES, they have full Power to levy War, conclude Peace, contract Alliances, eſtabliſh Commerce, and to do all other Acts and Things which INDEPENDENT STATES may of right do. And for the ſupport of this Declaration, with a firm Reliance on the Protection of divine Providence, we mutually pledge to each other our Lives, our Fortunes, and our ſacred Honor.

Signed by ORDER and in BEHALF of the CONGRESS,

JOHN HANCOCK, PRESIDENT.

ATTEST.
CHARLES THOMSON, SECRETARY.

PHILADELPHIA: PRINTED BY JOHN DUNLAP.

In CONGRESS, July 4, 1776.

A DECLARATION

By the REPRESENTATIVES of the UNITED STATES of AMERICA, in General Congress assembled.

WHEN, in the Course of human Events, it becomes necessary for one People to dissolve the political Bands which have connected them with another, and to assume among the Powers of the Earth, the separate and equal Station to which the Laws of Nature and of Nature's God entitle them, a decent Respect to the Opinions of Mankind requires that they should declare the causes which impel them to the Separation.

We hold these Truths to be self-evident, that all Men are created equal, that they are endowed by their Creator with certain unalienable Rights, that among these are Life, Liberty, and the Pursuit of Happiness—That to secure these Rights, Governments are instituted among Men, deriving their just Powers from the Consent of the Governed, that whenever any Form of Government becomes destructive of these Ends, it is the Right of the People to alter or to abolish it, and to institute new Government, laying its Foundation on such Principles, and organizing its Powers in such Form, as to them shall seem most likely to effect their Safety and Happiness. Prudence, indeed, will dictate that Governments long established should not be changed for light and transient Causes; and accordingly all Experience hath shewn, that Mankind are more disposed to suffer, while Evils are sufferable, than to right themselves by abolishing the Forms to which they are accustomed. But when a long Train of Abuses and Usurpations, pursuing invariably the same Object, evinces a Design to reduce them under absolute Despotism, it is their Right, it is their Duty, to throw off such Government, and to provide new Guards for their future Security. Such has been the patient Sufferance of these Colonies; and such is now the Necessity which constrains them to alter their former Systems of Government. The History of the present King of Great-Britain is a History of repeated Injuries and Usurpations, all having in direct Object the Establishment of an absolute Tyranny over these States. To prove this, let Facts be submitted to a candid World.

He has refused his Assent to Laws, the most wholesome and necessary for the public Good.

He has forbidden his Governors to pass Laws of immediate and pressing Importance, unless suspended in their Operation till his Assent should be obtained; and when so suspended, he has utterly neglected to attend to them.

He has refused to pass other Laws for the Accommodation of large Districts of People, unless those People would relinquish the Right of Representation in the Legislature, a Right inestimable to them, and formidable to Tyrants only.

He has called together Legislative Bodies at Places unusual, uncomfortable, and distant from the Depository of their public Records, for the sole Purpose of fatiguing them into Compliance with his Measures.

He has dissolved Representative Houses repeatedly, for opposing with manly Firmness his Invasions on the Rights of the People.

He has refused for a long Time after such Dissolutions, to cause others to be elected; whereby the Legislative Powers, incapable of Annihilation, have returned to the People at large for their Exercise; the State remaining in the mean time exposed to all the Dangers of Invasion from without, and Convulsions within.

He has endeavoured to prevent the Population of these States; for that Purpose obstructing the Laws for Naturalization of Foreigners; refusing to pass others to encourage their Migrations hither, and raising the Conditions of new Appropriations of Lands.

He has obstructed the Administration of Justice, by refusing his Assent to Laws for establishing Judiciary Powers.

He has made Judges dependent on his Will alone, for the Tenure of their Offices, and the Amount and Payment of their Salaries.

He has erected a Multitude of new Offices, and sent hither Swarms of Officers to harrass our People, and eat out their Substance.

He has kept among us, in Times of Peace, Standing Armies, without the Consent of our Legislatures.

He has affected to render the Military independent of and superior to the Civil Power.

He has combined with others to subject us to a Jurisdiction foreign to our Constitution, and unacknowledged by our Laws; giving his Assent to their Acts of pretended Legislation:

For quartering large Bodies of Armed Troops among us:

For protecting them, by a mock Trial, from Punishment for any Murders which they should commit on the Inhabitants of these States:

For cutting off our Trade with all Parts of the World:

For imposing Taxes on us without our Consent:

For depriving us, in many Cases, of the Benefits of Trial by Jury:

For transporting us beyond Seas to be tried for pretended Offences:

For abolishing the free System of English Laws in a neighbouring Province, establishing therein an arbitrary Government, and enlarging its Boundaries, so as to render it at once an Example and fit Instrument for introducing the same absolute Rule into these Colonies:

For taking away our Charters, abolishing our most valuable Laws, and altering fundamentally the Forms of our Governments:

For suspending our own Legislatures, and declaring themselves invested with Power to legislate for us in all Cases whatsoever.

He has abdicated Government here, by declaring us out of his Protection and waging War against us.

He has plundered our Seas, ravaged our Coasts, burnt our Towns, and destroyed the Lives of our People.

He is, at this Time, transporting large Armies of foreign Mercenaries to compleat the Works of Death, Desolation and Tyranny, already begun with Circumstances of Cruelty and Perfidy, scarcely paralleled in the most barbarous Ages, and totally unworthy the Head of a civilized Nation.

He has constrained our Fellow-Citizens, taken captive on the high Seas, to bear Arms against their Country, to become the Executioners of their Friends and Brethren, or to fall themselves by their Hands.

He has excited domestic Insurrections amongst us, and has endeavoured to bring on the Inhabitants of our Frontiers, the merciless Indian Savages, whose known Rule of Warfare is an undistinguished Destruction of all Ages, Sexes and Conditions.

In every Stage of these Oppressions we have petitioned for Redress in the most humble Terms: Our repeated Petitions have been answered only by repeated Injury. A Prince, whose Character is thus marked by every Act which may define a Tyrant, is unfit to be the Ruler of a free People.

Nor have we been wanting in Attentions to our British Brethren. We have warned them from Time to Time of Attempts by their Legislature to extend an unwarrantable Jurisdiction over us. We have reminded them of the Circumstances of our Emigration and Settlement here. We have appealed to their native Justice and Magnanimity, and we have conjured them by the Ties of our common Kindred to disavow these Usurpations, which would inevitably interrupt our Connections and Correspondence. They too have been deaf to the Voice of Justice and of Consanguinity. We must, therefore, acquiesce in the Necessity, which denounces our Separation, and hold them, as we hold the rest of Mankind, Enemies in War, in Peace, Friends.

We, therefore, the Representatives of the UNITED STATES of AMERICA, in General Congress assembled, appealing to the Supreme Judge of the World for the Rectitude of our Intentions, do, in the Name and by Authority of the good People of these Colonies, solemnly Publish and Declare, That these United Colonies are, and of Right ought to be, FREE and INDEPENDENT STATES; that they are absolved from all Allegiance to the British Crown, and that all political Connection between them and the State of Great-Britain is and ought to be totally dissolved; and that as FREE and INDEPENDENT STATES, they have full Power to levy War, conclude Peace, contract Alliances, establish Commerce, and to do all other Acts and Things which INDEPENDENT STATES may of right do. And for the Support of this Declaration, with a firm Reliance on the Protection of divine Providence, we mutually pledge to each other our Lives, our Fortunes, and our sacred Honor.

Signed by Order and in Behalf of the Congress,

     JOHN HANCOCK, President.

Attest.

CHARLES THOMSON, Secretary.

JUST PUBLISHED, AND TO BE SOLD BY HALL AND SELLERS,

At the New Printing-Office, in Market-street,

(Price Two Pounds Seven Shillings)

THE ACTS OF ASSEMBLY

Of the Province of Pennsylvania, Carefully compared with the Originals.

AND AN APPENDIX,

Containing such Acts, and Parts of Acts, relating to Property, as are expired, altered or repealed.

TOGETHER WITH

The Royal, Proprietary, City and Borough Charters; AND THE

Original Concessions of the Hon. William Penn to the first Settlers of the Province.

Published by ORDER of ASSEMBLY.

Just printed, published, and now selling by

ROBERT BELL, in Third-street,

(Price One Shilling and Threepence)

THE genuine Principles of the ancient SAXON, or ENGLISH CONSTITUTION. Carefully collected from the best Authorities; with some Observations on their peculiar Fitness for the United Colonies in general, and Pennsylvania in particular. By DEMOPHILUS.

All human Constitutions are subject to Corruption, and must perish, unless they are timely renewed by reducing them to their first Principles.   SIDNEY.

Where Annual Election ends, Tyranny begins.

HISTORICAL ESSAYS.

N. B. All the New Pamphlets may be had at said Bell's.

July 1, 1776.

WHEREAS an Advertisement, addressed to the Public, appeared in the Gazette some time past, signed *Thomas Yanney*, requesting the Favour of the Public to cross at the Old Trenton Ferry, where he now lives, and asserting that the difference of the distance between the Old and New Ferry is more than a mile in favour of the Old, whereas the true difference, on a strict survey, is no more than half a mile and forty rood, and as the subscriber hath lately come to the New Ferry, and provided a more commodious Boat than has ever been heretofore at either Ferry, as well as being the sole cause of lowering the Ferriage more than one third of the former price, which is a very great saving to the public, he flatters himself he will be indulged with their custom, which he will endeavour to merit by his particular care and attention, and is the public's most obliged humble servant,   THOMAS HARVEY.

There were those sharply opposed to the resolution and therefore to the Declaration, who believed that independence was being advocated prematurely, and virtually forced by a minority on an as yet unready, unwilling majority.

John Dickinson of Pennsylvania, a stringent critic of British policy since 1765, spoke up against the resolution as ill-timed "without some prelusory trials of our strength, and before terms of the Confederation were settled and foreign assistance made certain."

"If we are to declare a separation without waiting to hear from France, we may be overwhelmed with debt. We shall ruin ourselves and Britain will be ruined with us. France will rise on those ruins. Britain will push the war with a severity hitherto unimagined. Indians will be set loose on our frontiers."

John Adams, who had seconded Lee's resolution on June 7, rose to answer Dickinson. Jefferson was to recall years later, "He came out with a power of thought and expression that moved us from our seats." The die was cast July 2: a majority of those present voted *aye* on the resolution. John Adams wrote next day to his wife at Quincy:

"The Second Day of July, 1776, will be the most memorable Epoche in the History of America. I am apt to believe it will be celebrated by succeeding Generations, as the great anniversary Festival. It ought to be commemorated as the Day of Deliverance, by Solemn Acts of Devotion to God Almighty.... I can see that the End is more than worth All the Means...."

The action taken on July 4 was an anti-climax, with its description, "Unanimous Declaration of The Thirteen United States," a misnomer. John Dickinson was not alone in recalcitrance; unanimity was lacking in some other state delegations. Delaware's was split evenly the eve of July 2, and Caesar Rodney, who had been absent in Dover on urgent business, rode in heavy rain all night to turn Delaware to the support of the resolution. Still, the vote *for* was by *twelve* States. New York's delegates abstained because the provincial Convention at New York had delayed in sending instructions. Affirmative assent was not forwarded to Philadelphia until after the Declaration had been read to Washington's army during a brief recess in the army's effort to prepare defenses against invasion forces General Howe was assembling in New York Bay.

Upon receipt of the instructions, one New York delegate at Philadelphia, John Alsop, notified the New York Convention that inasmuch as the proposed resolution and accompanying declaration "closed the door of reconciliation" he could no longer serve as a delegate, and followed his letter back to New York. (With the fall of the city to the British, he took refuge upstate till the war was over.)

The Declaration underwent changes in punctuation and spellings at the hands of the Philadelphia printer, John Dunlap, who put it into broadside form the night of July 4-5 for distribution to the State assemblies and the armies. The document turned over to Dunlap disappeared; what survives are Jefferson draft manuscripts, some of the original broadsides, and the engrossed copy that bears signatures of fifty-six men who served in the Second Continental Congress at one time or another. Some who were members on August 2, when most of the signatures were made, had not been in Congress July 2-4. Others were not in Congress until after August 2. But all subscribed to the matchless oath of loyalty, "And for the support of this Declaration, with a firm reliance on the protection of Divine Providence, we mutually pledge to each other our Lives, our Fortunes, and our sacred Honor," at times when their lives were in danger and their fortunes at stake.

Benjamin Franklin's old paper put the Declaration on page one (*left*). John Dunlap's *Pennsylvania Packet*, "scooped" by its later press-day, ran it inside.

O N the same day, July 4, that the Congress formally adopted the Declaration, a resolution was passed directing that a committee be appointed to prepare a design for a Great Seal. Benjamin Franklin, Thomas Jefferson and John Adams were designated.

No consideration was given to a device offered in a New York newspaper in 1774 as a symbol of unity [top left]. It had twelve arms clasping a staff resting on the Magna Carta, with the whole encircled by a rattlesnake inscribed, "United now and free And thus supported everbless our land Firm on this basis liberty shall stand Till time becomes eternity."

On August 10, the Committee reported itself in favor of the design shown at left, obverse and reverse. The latter represents Pharaoh in an open chariot, sword in hand, passing through open waters of the Red Sea. This jumble of heraldic detail and Biblical legend found no favor; the recommendation was tabled.

When, after four years, the project was revived, at the insistence of the Secretary of Congress, Charles Thomson, and responsibility was shifted upon him, Thomson worked out with William Barton, an American artist, the designs for an obverse and reverse shown below at left. A counter-proposal was drafted by a Franklin protege, the young emigré French artist, Pierre du Simitiere. Its obverse is reproduced at top right. (Note the resemblance to the New Jersey State seal, which Du Simitiere designed subsequently.)

In the following two years, Thomson worked with Barton on other designs, including that at right center, in which a starred and striped shield, the eagle and the pyramid were introduced. Meanwhile, John Adams had gone to England as agent for advancement of a treaty of peace. In a conversation with Sir John Prestwich, a distinguished antiquarian, Adams mentioned his countrymen's efforts toward a suitable coat-of-arms. Sir John suggested as motto, *E Pluribus Unum:* From Many, One, as appropriate. Adams passed this on to Thomson, "who withheld this until the last, hoping something as good would be suggested by one of his own countrymen," it was recorded.

Thomson and Barton embodied and refined

ideas of others in the design finally approved by the Congress June 20, 1782. This was substantially the same as that of today, with the eagle predominant in the obverse. Franklin objected to inclusion of the eagle, for centuries a symbol of imperialism, and a robber and scavenger in nature. He proposed substitution of the turkey.

James McHenry

James McHenry (↑), a young immigrant from County Antrim, Ireland, in 1771, was studying medicine with Dr. Benjamin Rush when the second Continental Congress met. With George Washington's choice as commander-in-chief, McHenry (then twenty-two) wrote his will and followed the Washington entourage to Cambridge, to be an Assistant Surgeon. Assigned subsequently as Surgeon, 5th Pennsylvania Battalion (Col. Robert Magaw), he remained with the Army in the movement to New York and was among the garrison Magaw was forced to surrender at Fort Washington in November 1776. Formally exchanged in 1778, McHenry was chosen by Washington as military secretary and personal physician. He held this position until 1780, and was a trusted adviser and close friend of George Washington the remainder of the latter's life, despite the twenty-one-year difference in their ages.

The same day, July 2, a majority of Congress courageously approved the resolution of Congress, a dispatch from New York was at hand. "A fleet of 130 sail" had been sighted at Sandy Hook on June 30. The figure was far off: there were 400 troop transports convoyed by fifty-two ships-of-the-line, twenty-seven armed sloops and cutters.

Washington had been expecting that after the British abandonment of Boston, General Lord Howe and his brother the Admiral would strike, reenforced, at New York to secure a strategic base for operations in both the Delaware and Hudson Valleys. Ever since April he had been directing the digging of redoubts, raising of barricades, emplacement of batteries. The approximately 10,000 troops he had in the city and the

lower end of Long Island had been assembled into four brigades under Nathanael Greene (on Long Island); William Heath, Joseph Spencer, William Alexander ("Lord Stirling"). Obstacles were placed in the Hudson, and such naval auxiliaries as could be secured were placed on station. Last and not least, a spy network was woven.

Washington had a message circulated among the brigades: "The time is near at hand which must probably determine whether Americans are to be freemen or slaves . . . The fate of unborn millions will now depend, under God, on the courage and conduct of this army — We have, therefore, to resolve to conquer or die. . . ."

Passage of the troops of Generals Henry Clinton, and Charles Cornwallis, with newly arrived Hessians under De Heister, from Staten Island and transports in the Bay, to Long Island. Drawing by A. R. Waud, engraved by H. Karst, in the Bryant-Gay *Popular History of the United States*, 1879.

Opposite page: "Plan of New York Island and Part of Long Island, showing the position of the American & British armies before, at & after the Engagement on the Heights, August 27th, 1776" — an engraving by W. Kemble in the Library of Congress. Note the position of British transports at the landing, Aug. 25.

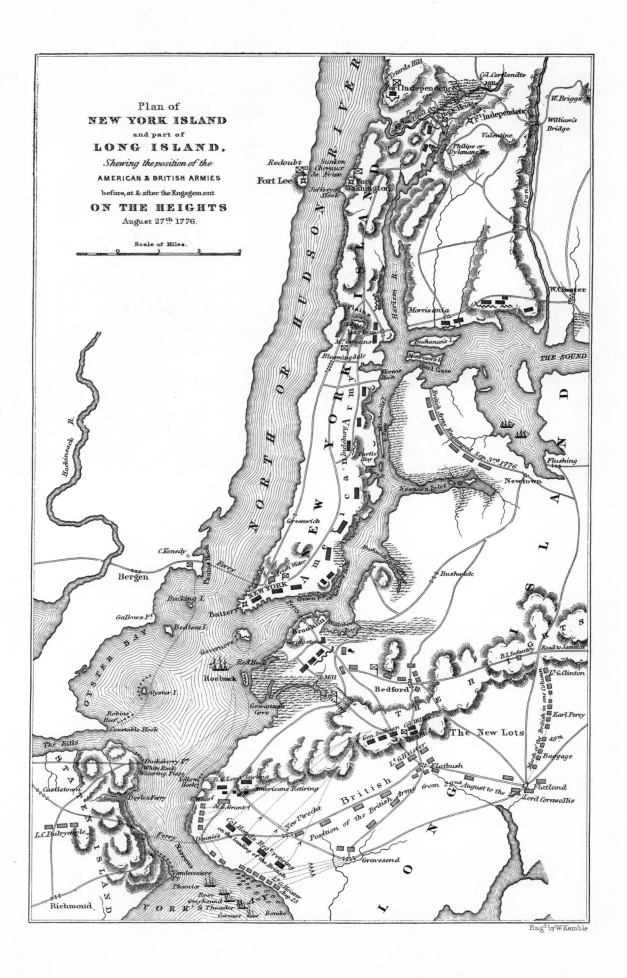

Plan of
NEW YORK ISLAND
and part of
LONG ISLAND,
Shewing the position of the
AMERICAN & BRITISH ARMIES
before, at & after the Engagement
ON THE HEIGHTS
August 27th 1776.

Scale of Miles.
0   1   2   3

Eng.d by W. Kemble

[↑] "Retreat of the Americans Under General Stirling across Gowanus Creek," engraved in 1860 from a painting by Alonzo Chappel, showing Freeke's Mill, referred to in some of the verses of John W. Palmer (1825-1906) memorializing the stand the Maryland Battalion made there:

Oh, the rout on the left and the tug on the right!
The mad plunge of the charge and the wreck of the
    flight!
When the cohorts of Grant held stout Stirling at
    strain,
And the mongrels of Hesse went tearing the slain;
When at Freeke's Mill the flumes and the sluices ran
    red,
And the dead choked the dyke and the marsh choked
    the dead!

Oh, Stirling, good Stirling! how long must we wait?
Shall the shout of your trumpet unleash us too late?

Have you never a dash for brave Mordecai Gist,
With his heart in this throat, and his blade in his fist?
Are we good for no more than to prance in a ball,
When the drums beat the charge and the clarions
    call?

Tra-la-ra, Tra-la-ra! Now praise we the Lord,
For the clang of His call and the flash of His sword!
Tralara! Tralara! Now forward to die;
For the banner, hurrah! and for sweethearts, good-
    by!
"Four hundred wild lads!" Maybe so. I'll be bound
'Twill be easy to count us, face up, on the ground.
If we hold the road open, though Death take the toll,
We'll be missed on parade when the States call the
    roll —
When the flags meet in peace and the guns are at rest,
And fair Freedom is singing Sweet Home in the
    West.

Two representations of Washington personally directing the escape of his shattered, panicky remaining forces from Long Island to New York in the boats assembled and manned by John Glover's regiment of Marblehead fishermen and whalers. Washington, who had been in the saddle all night, remained until the last company had been embarked.

Thomas Gage, an older fellow officer with George Washington in Braddock's army — and defeat, 1755 — succeeded Lord Amherst as Commander-in-Chief in North America, 1763-72, with h.q. in New York. In 1774, Thomas Hutchinson having been ineffectual in suppressing agitation against the royal government, Gage was sent to Boston to replace him as Governor and Captaingeneral of Massachusetts Bay province. The next year, Gage was redesignated C.-in-C. North America, in the expectancy that he would overcome all resistance with a strong hand. After the

reverses at Lexington and Concord, the capture of Ticonderoga from his forces, the failure to overcome the defenders of Bunker Hill and the initial success of the rebels' invasion of Canada, Gage was replaced in October 1775 by his second-in-command, Sir William Howe, and retired to England.

Sir William Howe, brother of Vice Admiral Richard "Black Dick" Howe, was joined by the latter as new commander of naval operations in America, for the conquest of New York City and the attempt to entrap and crush Washington. After a year of indecisive campaigning against Washington on land and sea, the Howe brothers resigned their commands, protesting inadequate support, and became inactive until the outbreak of the war against the French Republic and Napoleon.

Sir Henry Clinton, who arrived with Generals Howe and John Burgoyne at Boston in 1775, succeeded Howe as C.-in-C. North America after scoring successes as a division commander — notably in the storming of Forts Clinton and Montgomery in 1777. Some confusion naturally results for readers from the fact that there were Generals Clinton on each side. George Clinton

Henry Clinton (*above*), Cornwallis (*below*).

Sir William Howe: an English engraving.

was a member of a politically potent New York family for whom two Fort Clintons on the Hudson were named. His brother James served under him.

Charles Cornwallis came over with English, Scottish and Irish reenforcements for Howe at the same time the Hessians were being shipped in. He became second-in-command to Clinton after the latter succeeded Howe, and had considerable success as a commander in the South until the middle of 1781, as will be evident in later pages. Incidentally, it is incorrect for a narrator of the Revolution to refer to him as Marquis Cornwallis, as some do. He was not created a marquis until 1792, after he had won the war against Tippu Sahib in India.

Debarquement des Troupes Angloises a Nouvelle, Yorck, a French engraving *circa* 1777, of Howe's troops taking possession of New York as Washington withdrew his forces to the north. The French artist's conception bears little resemblance to the skyline of the time.

With the grouping off New York of his troops from Halifax, Hessian mercenaries from overseas and reenforcements from the South, Howe addressed a letter under flag of truce, to "Mr. Washington." Upon taking the letter from the red-coated courier, George Washington exclaimed, "Why, this is directed to a planter in Virginia. I'll keep it and deliver it to him after the war."

Then, ordering the British officer out of the lines empty-handed, he directed gunners to be alert. Washington continued to refuse to acknowledge any communications from the British commanders until they recognized his position as a legitimate officer and commander of an army, by addressing him as "His Excellency, General Washington," and adhered to military protocol in exchanges of messages relating to prisoners, removal of wounded, etc.

In taking over command at Cambridge, George Washington had to review the finding of

the military court that heard charges of derelict conduct at Breed's Hill by John Callender, captain in a Massachusetts militia regiment. Washington's General Order No. 1 said, "It is with inexpressible concern that the general upon his first arrival in the Army should find an officer sentenced by a general court-martial to be cashiered for cowardice — a crime of all others, the most infamous in a soldier, the most injurious to an army, and the last to be forgiven."

Callender did not go back home in bitterness, did not succumb to blandishments in British circulars that were being distributed around Cambridge. He found a regiment in which he could enlist as a private, inconspicuously, and was with the Army in the move to New York. In the Battle of Brooklyn, Callender's newly found obscurity ended.

When men of his company panicked and broke lines, Callender rallied them effectually to prevent an enemy breakthrough there that could have cut off any kind of retreat. Callender's conspicuous courage came to the attention of Washington, who himself rode among wavering officers and men, lashing about furiously with the flat of a sword and denouncing their cowardice profanely. Afterward GW revoked the court-martial sentence at Cambridge and restored Callender to captain's rank.

About the same time Callender was rehabilitated officially, another captain, from New England, Nathan Hale, was sent, disguised as a Dutch schoolmaster, through enemy lines to reconnoiter British positions and movements on Long Island. He was caught — denounced, it was said, by a Tory cousin. To a fellow officer who had sought to dissuade him from going on the dangerous mission, Hale had responded, "I wish to be useful, and every kind of service necessary to the public good becomes honorable by being necessary." There was no question of Hale's being a spy, and General Howe ordered him hanged without a trial. At the gallows, Hale addressed his executioners, "You are shedding the blood of the innocent; if I had ten thousand lives, I would lay them down in defense of my injured, bleeding country. ...I only regret that I have but one life to give for my country."

Hale was deserving of all the honor paid to

Above: Facsimile of a page in daybook at h.q. of a regiment in New York, with entries for September 22, 1776. The concluding lines leaves Nathan Hale unnamed: "A Spy for the Enemy (by his own full confession) Apprehended last night, was this day executed at 11 O'clock in front of the Artillery Park."

Right: Early representation of Hale, and closing lines from a letter of his that has survived.

his heroic memory. Yet he was only one of many — male and female — who served the Continental Army in espionage and counter-espionage self-sacrificially at vital times.

After a substantial portion of his forces on Long Island had been extricated from near-disaster at Brooklyn Heights, Washington's position was more dangerous than ever. The British now had the Heights from which to bombard and besiege Manhattan, where most of Washington's army remained. Howe landed troops on the island, and Washington retreated northward, fighting rear-guard actions — such as that at Harlem Heights, September 16. He eventually moved his

main force into Westchester, leaving the garrison under Robert Magaw at Fort Washington on the Hudson opposite Fort Lee. Howe followed and sharp fighting ensued at White Plains, October 28. Washington then moved part of his army across to New Jersey to dig in at Hackensack in the rear of Fort Lee. Howe turned back to Manhattan to stage the coup at Fort Washington, then sent Cornwallis across the Hudson after Washington. The Continental army melted to about 3000 in the withdrawal from Fort Lee and Hackensack toward the Delaware and a position in New Jersey to which the General now resorted in his Fabian tactics. He wrote November

British troops under Lord Cornwallis landing and filing up a trail to capture Fort Lee from Washington's defenders. They had embarked at Yonkers. The sketch is attributed to Lord Rowden, a member of Cornwallis' staff. How Cornwallis learned of the trail's existence was discovered in British archives in 1963, by Dr. Richard P. McCormick of Rutgers University. John Aldington, a New Jersey Tory who

was angered by the commandeering of his brewery by Washington's troops for a storehouse, sent word to Cornwallis and became a guide. A claim he later filed with the British Crown for services rendered in the war bore an endorsement by Cornwallis that Aldington "guided the troops under my command when I landed in the province of New Jersey."

21 to Major-General Lee, "It is of the utmost importance, that at least a show of force should be made to keep this province [New Jersey] in the connexion with the others. If that should not continue, it is much to be feared, that its influence on Pennsylvania would be very considerable. . . . Our only dependence now is upon the speedy enlistment of a new army. If this fails, I think the game will be pretty well up, as, from disaffection and want of spirit and fortitude, the inhabitants, instead of resistence, are offering submission. . . ."

Too few men of the spirit and character of James De Camp, who was to earn advancement quickly to sergeant, then captain, in Elias Dayton's 3rd New Jersey Regiment; of Daniel Bray, Jacob Gearheart, John Mott, were responding to appeals in the State. Victories of any kind, even skirmishes, were needed to spur them.

In the war there were to be about ten times as many raids and skirmishes as engagements that could be called battles. Just as single ship actions at sea were often determinant importantly, so were numerous operations on land involving no more than a company of militia. In one notable instance, a stroke by eighty-three men took Fort Ticonderoga in 1775 and secured the artillery with which Washington forced the British out of Boston.

A more typical small action, and at a crucial time in New Jersey, took place in December 1776, near a crossroads called Ringo's, after its tavern. A detachment of 500 had been drawn off the enemy forces at Trenton to reconnoiter and forage along the York Road to the east. At Pennington, a detail of twenty horsemen under Cornet Francis Geary was sent off to Flemington, a town on a branch of the Raritan River with a mill and storehouse. The movement was made through Ringo's,* where the passage was observed by informants of the militia.

While the detail was at Flemington, discovering and seizing arms hidden in the warehouse (owned by Colonel Lowrey, a militiaman), placing it under the King's seal and refreshing themselves momentarily at Fleming's Castle (the stagecoach stopping place from which the town of Flemington took its name), Captain John Schenck's militia had gathered and prepared an ambush north of Ringo's. Geary, leading the returning column, fell in the first round from the

---

* Now Ringoes, only town in U.S. of that name.

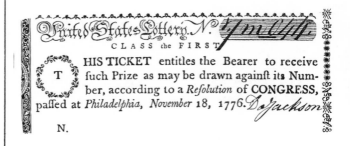

Congress' endeavors to raise money desperately needed for the war included a lottery that was poorly patronized. The prizes offered for winners in the drawing, held April 10, 1777, were Treasury notes payable at the end of five years. Some lotteries conducted in individual Colonies were better supported.

---

militia muskets. His men turned back to Flemington and forced a man to show them another route across country to the York Road. The colonel of the larger force, upon receiving the news, concluded the woods were full of rebels, and turned back to Trenton.

"This well timed ambuscade saved this part of the country from being overrun by British," a regional historian decided. With the region cleared of British, Washington was aided in staging his surprise at Trenton. Militia from the Flemington area rounded up a number of the boats in which the Delaware was crossed.

In the next two pages, Washington confides on December 23rd his intention of an "attempt on Trenton" Christmas night, one hour before day. . . .

Grave of Cornet Francis Geary, where he died in the ambuscade near Ringo's. His father, a British admiral, decided that his son should lie permanently where he fell in the service of his country. The gravesite was marked by Colonel Lowrey Chapter, Daughters of the American Revolution. (Photo by author.)

Camp above Trenton Falls
23d December 1776.

D:r Sir

The bearer is sent down to
know whether your plan was attempted last
Night — and if not to inform you that Chris
mas day at Night, one hour before day is
the time fixed upon for our attempt on
Trenton. — For heaven's sake keep this to
yourself, as the discovery of it may
prove fatal to us, our numbers, sorry
I am to say, being less than I had any
conception of — but necessity, dire neces
sity will — nay must justify any at

Prepare & in concert with Sr
tack as many of their Posts as y
sibly can with a prospect of success
— the more we can attack, at the same
Instant, the more confusion we shall
spread and greater good will result
from it — If I had not been fully
eed before of the Enemy's design I
have now ample testimony of their
Intentions to attack Philadelphia so
soon as the Ice will afford the means
of conveyance. —

As the Colonels of the Contin
tal Regiments might kick up some
dust about Command fearless Cadwal
lade.

laden is consider'd by them in the light of a Brigadier, which I wish him to be. I desired Genl. Gates, who is unwell & applied for leave to go to Philadelphia, to endeavour if his health would permit him to call and stay two or three days at Bristol in his way. —

I shall not be particular — we could not ripen matters for our attack, before the time mentioned in the first part of this Letter — so much out of sorts, & so much in want of every thing, are the Troops under Sullivan &c. — Let me know by a careful express the Plan you are to pursue. — The Letter herewith me forward on to Philadelphia — I would wish it to be in, in time for the Southern Post's departure which will be, I believe by 11 Oclock to morrow.

I am Dr Sir

Yr Most Ob. St.

Go Washington

PS

I have ordered our Men to be provided with three days Provisions ready Cook'd, with which, and their Blankets they are to March, for if we are successful which heaven grant & other Circumstances favour we may push on — I shall direct every Ferry & Ford to be well guarded & not a soul suffered to pass without an officer's going down with the permit — do the same with you. —

EXTRACT of a Letter from an Officer of Distinction in the
American *Army,*

SINCE I wrote you this morning, I have had an opportunity of hearing a number of the particulars of the horrid depredations committed by that part of the British army, which was stationed at and near Pennytown, under the command of Lord Cornwallis. Besides the sixteen young women who had fled to the woods to avoid their brutality, and were there seized and carried off, one man had the cruel mortification to have his wife and only daughter (a child of ten years of age) ravished; this he himself, almost choaked with grief, uttered in lamentations to his friend, who told me of it, and also informed me that another girl of thirteen years of age was taken from her father's house, carried to a barn about a mile, there ravished, and afterwards made use of by five more of these brutes. Numbers of instances of the same kind of behaviour I am assured of have happened: here their brutish lust were their stimulas; but wanton mischief was seen in every part of the country; every thing portable they plunder and carry off, neither age nor sex, Whig or Tory, is spared; an indiscriminate ruin attends every person they meet with, infants, children, old men and women, are left in their shirts without a blanket to cover them in this inclement season; furniture of every kind destroyed or burnt, windows and doors broke to pieces; in short, the houses left unhabitable, and the people left without provisions, for every horse, cow, ox, hogs and poultry, carried off: a blind old gentleman near Pennytown plundered of every thing, and on his door wrote, 'Capt. Wills of the Royal Irish did this.' As a notable proof of their regard and favour to their friends and well-wishers, they yesterday burnt the elegant house of Daniel Cox, Esq; at Trenton-Ferry, who has been their constant advocate, and supporter of Toryism in that part of the country: this behaviour of theirs has so exasperated the people of the country, that they are flying to arms, and forming themselves into parties to way-lay them and cut them off wherever they can meet with them: this, and other efforts which are making, I hope will so streighten them that they will soon find their situation very disagreeable in New-Jersey. Another instance of their brutality happened near Woodbridge: One of the most respectable gentlemen in that part of the country was alarmed by the cries and shrieks of a most lovely daughter; he found an officer, a British officer, in the act of ravishing her, he instantly put him to death; two other officers rushed in with fusees, and fired two balls into the father, who is now languishing under his wounds. I am tired of this horrid scene; Almighty Justice cannot suffer it to go unpunished: he will inspirit his people (who only claim that liberty which he has entitled them to) to do themselves justice, to rise universally in arms, and drive these invading tyrants out of our country.

Published by order of the Council of Safety,

GEO. BICKHAM, Secretary, pro. tem.

published also in Dunlap & Pennsylvania Packet December 27. 1776.

Printed by **JOHN DUNLAP.**

Atrocity story: An accusation by an unidentified "Officer of Distinction" of British rapine, brutality, looting, and arson, as published in broadsides and also in the newspaper of John Dunlap, official printer to the Continental Congress. "This behaviour of theirs has so exasperated people of the country, that they are flying to arms, and forming themselves into parties to waylay them," it says.

The most famous representation of the General in action, "Washington Crossing the Delaware," (*above*) is as poor as any in historical accuracy.

The German artist Emanuel Leutze (1816-1868) painted it in Dusseldorf in 1851, with no apparent attempt to obtain authentic detail. Some of its errors and anachronisms:

The boat is the wrong shape. "Durham" boats, long, canoe-shaped craft designed to carry ore down the Delaware, were used in the crossing.

The night was snowy, with visibility poor, but there were no floes in the river. Washington recorded in his report to Congress on the operation that ice was "made that night."

The Stars and Stripes flag being held by Lieutenant James Monroe, directly behind Washington, was not authorized by Congress until June 1777.

Soldiers would have carried musket barrels downward to protect them from snow and moisture. Bayonets were not fixed until after close-order fighting began in Trenton.

It is unlikely that Washington, who had crossed many a river in small boats, would have stood up and struck such a pose — especially when, as Captain Thomas Rodney recorded, "The frost was sharp and the wind high." He could not have seen any better that way in the snow-driven darkness, which required boats to follow-the-leader.

The original painting by Leutze suffered damage by fire and remained in Germany until 1942, when destroyed in an Allied raid on Bremen. What survives is a copy made by Leutze for the United States Capitol, which Congress refused to buy. It eventually passed into the hands of the Metropolitan Museum of Art for some years, after it had been made familiar to the public at large by lithographs and engravings.

To me, a far better representation of Washington's crossing of the Delaware than Leutze's was painted earlier than Leutze's by Thomas Sully. In the next two pages, an engraving of it by J. N. Gimbrede. Washington is in foreground, mounted. The original, commissioned in 1818 and measuring 17 ft. 4 in. by 12 ft. 5 in., was acquired by the Boston Museum of Arts.

Right: Map of Trenton and the order of battle, re-drafted from a sketch in a Hessian account. Broken lines indicate movement of columns of Washington and Sullivan after they emerged from woods (G) to surround positions of Rahl [Rall], Lossberg and Knyphausen. Center of village is indicated by A. Dotted lines show where Hessians attempted to make a stand. Rahl and Lossberg troops were driven back (H) while Knyphausen endeavored to reach the bridge on the Bordentown road. Sullivan cut off Kynphausen's retreat. *Below:* Part of English map of New Jersey used by Washington's army, 1778-80.

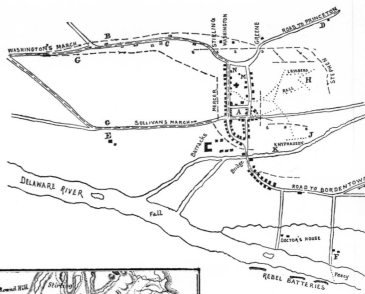

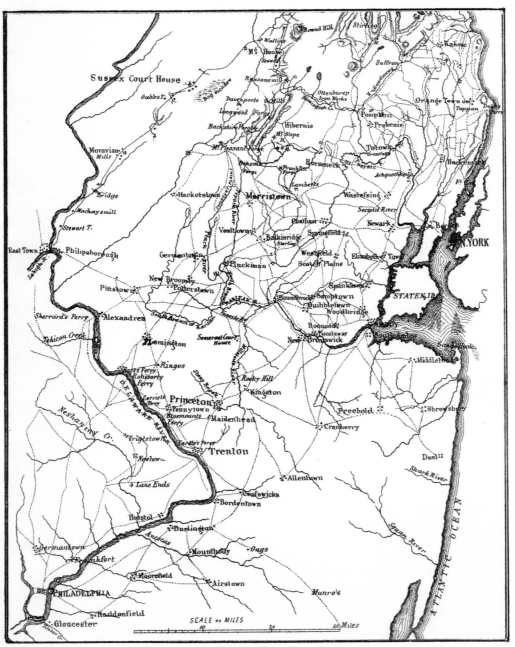

Obverse of Hessian flag captured at Trenton and (left) contemporary caricature of a Hessian grenadier. The captives taken at Trenton and elsewhere generally fared better than did the British who fell into the hands of the Continentals.

A German publisher, C. F. L. Blanckmeister, issued this engraving of the humiliating surrender of Hessians at Trenton, which was somewhat orderly, as the artist indicates. He obviously relied on imagination and popular beliefs for details.

The Stars and Stripes behind Washington and staff is one of the anachronisms: as stated previously, Washington did not have a flag of this design during the war.

The artist has a British flag among the items being surrendered. German mercenaries serving the British had banners of their respective principalities. Though generally referred to as Hessians, not all were the subjects of the Landgraves of Hesse-Cassel and Hesse-Hanau. Mercenaries also were let by contract at so much per man, by princelings of Brunswick, Anspach-Bayreuth, Waldeck and Anhalt-Zerbst, all of whom made a practice of hiring out troops, complete with surgeons, chaplains and musicians.

After 1776, the German mercenaries comprised about one-third of all the land forces fighting for George III in America. Hesse-Cassel's *Jagers* Corps were declared the best troops on the British side.

The outcome at Trenton, where the first part of the day's password for the troops, "Victory or death," had been fulfilled, did not immediately reverse Washington's fortunes. The term of service of most of the Continental Line was due to expire December 31. The hope of the Commander-in-Chief lay in persuading half-clad, half-frozen, half-starved, unpaid men to volunteer for another month. The appeals he asked Major-General Thomas Mifflin of Pennsylvania and others to make directly to groups of the troops were effective — in Mifflin's case it was assented to by "poising our firelocks on signal," a soldier recorded.

The same day, George Washington sent Captain Thomas Read, who had joined the Army early in December with a naval battery, to reconnoiter toward Princeton with six of his men.

They surprised twelve pickets of Cornwallis' army and brought them back to Washington's headquarters. Information they were made to give induced Washington to fight Cornwallis January 2 instead of turning away from the numerically superior force. His army moved in the night toward Princeton as silently as possible: gun-carriage wheels wrapped in rags to muffle sound; no talking or noise in the ranks; orders passed along in whispers. Campfires had been left burning at the abandoned position to deceive the enemy.

Cornwallis, intent on avenging Trenton and confident of catching Washington at last, was unwary. Troops he had in Princeton — three infantry regiments and cavalry under Colonel Charles Mawhood, were surprised, but Washington's brigades were too weary from the march

Below: "View of Battle of Princeton," from a painting by James Peale in the possession of the Princeton University Library.

Right: "Affair of Princeton," January 3, 1777, from a British map. The town is at top. In their retreat, the British left many wounded at the college building.

to exploit this fully. A fierce fight developed. Washington, "from his desire to animate his troops by example, rode into the very front of danger," it was recounted, "and when within less than thirty yards of the Brtish he reined in his horse, seeming to tell his faltering forces that they must stand firm or leave him to face the enemy alone. Both sides gave a volley at that moment. It was thought a miracle that Washington was untouched."

Rallied by Washington, and with added artillery support from Thomas Read's naval battery, the Rebels drove the enemy from the field. Cornwallis, outgeneraled, withdrew his entire army eastward with losses of about 500 in killed,

wounded, captured. Washington moved to Morristown, to which he had sent sick and wounded ahead of him, with fresh hopes rising among New Jersey patriots. The effect of the news in Pennsylvania was such that for a generation afterward, favorable reports, unexpectedly received, concerning any matter, were "Great news from the Jerseys."

Washington wrote to Congress from Pluckemin on January 5, 1777, "The militia are taking spirits, and are coming in fast in this state." A regional historian added, after the events of December, "The militia of New Jersey, who had hitherto behaved shamefully, from this time forward generally acquired a high reputation."

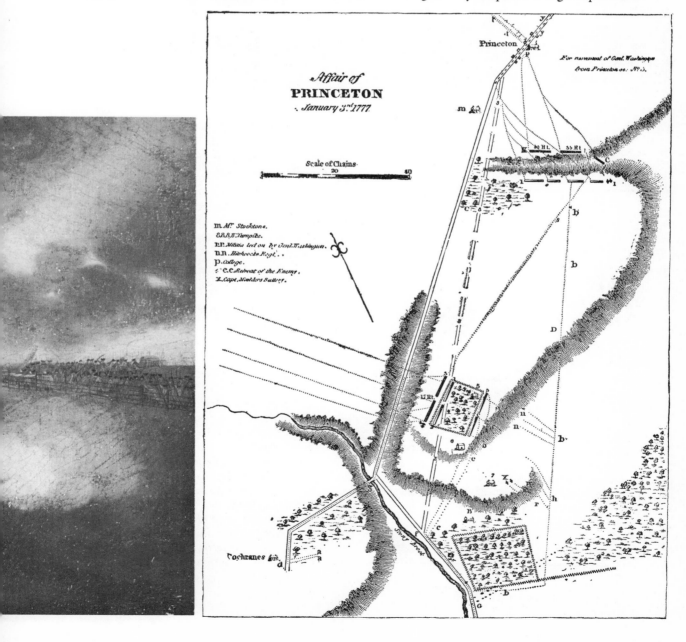

The restored mansion at Morristown where General and Mrs. Washington dwelt the winter of 1779-80, when the condition of the army was little better then it fell to in 1777 (↓).

Four days after Princeton, the Army was in winter quarters at Morristown. Before Mrs. Washington joined him, George Washington was shown a Philadelphia newspaper that insinuated he was a libertine who currently had an Irish mistress. The General sent the paper to Mount Vernon by express courier, wanting Mrs. Washington to receive it first from him. She had been aware of rumors of Washington immorality circulated when his hq. was at Cambridge, and again when the army was in New York.

Throughout the war, during periods when the army was relatively inactive, the General arranged for Mrs. Washington to be with him.

On the opposite page: Martha Washington's letter to Joseph Reed, a friend of Washington, who had offered quarters with Mrs. Reed and himself in Philadelphia when she stopped there in travels between Mount Vernon and the General's winter quarters at Morristown (where this letter was written). She declined, having previously accepted an invitation from Charles Pettit, and his wife (who was Joseph Reed's sister). Neither of the Washingtons was strong on spelling, and Mrs. Washington misspelled as Petit the name of her host to be. However, it has been suggested that this, like numerous other letters of hers, was written out by General Washington for her to copy in her hand.

Morristown In

Sir

The very polite and obliging invitation to lodge with you,— contained in your favor of the 12th Inst— came to my hands yesterday — I beg you to be persuaded sir that I should accept it with much pleasure did I not conceive myself under an engagement to Mr Pettit, who was pleased when he was here to request me to make use of his house while I stayed in Phila' which will not exceed 3 or 4 days and for which place I shall leave this to morrow —

It gives me much pleasure to hear of Mrs Reeds recovery — and that she is in a
row to receive company down
my greatful thanks and best
es attend her and you — I am sir
Your most obed.t and obliged
Martha Washington

The day before Washington crossed the Delaware, to stage the Christmas coup at Trenton, His Majesty's Minister of Foreign Affairs, Comte de Vergennes, received a letter by hand from the representatives at Paris of the Continental Congress: Benjamin Franklin, Silas Deane, Arthur Lee.

"We beg leave to acquaint your Excellency, that we are appointed by the Congress of the United States of America to propose and negotiate a Treaty of Amity and Commerce between France and the United States.

"We request an Audience of your Excellency wherein we may have an Opportunity of presenting our Credentials, and we flatter ourselves that the Propositions we are instructed to make, are such as will not be found unacceptable.

"Your Excellency's most obedient and most humble servants."

It was to prove one of the most consequential letters in the history of American diplomacy.

Above: Contemporary engraving of Charles Gravier, Comte de Vergennes, who became the French Minister of Foreign Affairs in 1774 after service as ambassador to Turkey and Sweden. A biographer comments: "His bringing France into participation in the American Revolutionary War had much to do with the subsequent French Revolution, since it drained France's resources dangerously." Vermont named a city for the Comte.

Opposite page, above: A French cartoon dated 1778 represents a French avenging angel driving the British (right) from Philadelphia. Americans (left) are dancing in glee around a flag and a liberty bonnet. This striped flag may be the earliest representation of an American flag in a foreign cartoon. (Reproduced from a print in the Library of Congress.)

Opposite page, below: Another French cartoon entitled *England At the Very End.* "1. The English, in bed, requests a remedy for his ills. 2. An American (Dr. B. Franklin), syringe in hand, is about to help him, when 3. Another American holds him back. 4. A band of doctors and pharmacists try to enter, but 5. A Frenchman, salve in hand, and 6. A Spaniard prevent them from entering. 7. Meanwhile a Dutchman profits by the mixup and gets away with the goods through the window." — Translation of the caption. (From a print in the Library of Congress.)

While Washington was at Morristown, food supply became acute. Surge of enlistments following the successes and promises of Trenton and Princeton, and reenforcements, brought his forces up to about 8000. But sorties were carried on to train and raise morale, discourage further reversions to the Tory side and seize supplies. By spring George Washington had virtually a new Army.

Except for the detachments Cornwallis had stationed at New Brunswick and the Amboys, Howe's forces spent the winter in New York, resting. At first signs of movement by Howe, Washington struck camp at Morristown in June and centered his main force at Middle Brook, near Somerville, with Sullivan on his flank toward Flemington. This put him into position to oppose Howe's striking at Philadelphia, if, as appeared logical, Howe renewed his 1776 cam-

Mansion of Judge Benjamin Chew became epicenter of the Battle of Germantown after Howe's troops turned it into a fort. Over fifty Americans were killed on the lawn in besieging the house.

paign in that direction. Howe contrived deception. After sending some 18,000 men across from New York to Amboy and on to New Brunswick, he pulled them back to transports at Staten Island. The expedition was in Chesapeake Bay before George Washington could be reasonably sure Philadelphia was the objective, and take up a defensive line close by Wilmington.

With the British disembarcation at Head of Elk [Elkton, Maryland] September 28, Washington shifted to the Brandywine. Howe outmaneuvered him and missed a great opportunity to effect a crushing victory. Colonel Louis Duportail, a volunteer French engineer with George Washington, wrote, "If the English had followed up their advantage that day [at Brandywine] Washington's army would have spoken no more; since that time, also, Howe has, in all his operations, exhibited such slowness and timidity as to strike me with astonishment."

Thanks to that slowness and timidity, Washington again escaped disaster, October 4, after Howe had taken possession of Philadelphia and

Congress was in flight (to Lancaster, then to York). The battleground was Germantown, just outside Philadelphia. Washington's daring strategy was messed up by miscalculations and mistakes of Nathanael Greene, Anthony Wayne and Adam Stephen. The latter was court-martialed and cashiered.

The good news that summer and autumn of 1777 was the surrender of Gen. John Burgoyne's army after the Battle of Saratoga, a victory made possible for Horatio Gates by the British General Henry Clinton's failure — through slowness and timidity — to join up with Burgoyne according to plan.

This was followed by news of naval warfare being carried into British home waters by Paul Jones and other daring captains.

Battlegrounds of September 19 and October 7, 1777, as mapped in Saratoga National Historical Park for tourists. The park can be approached via U.S. Highway 4 and State Roads 32, 423.

Contemporary British engraving of John Burgoyne. After the Revolution he was C.-in-C. in Ireland, and wrote a popular comedy in London, *The Heiress*.

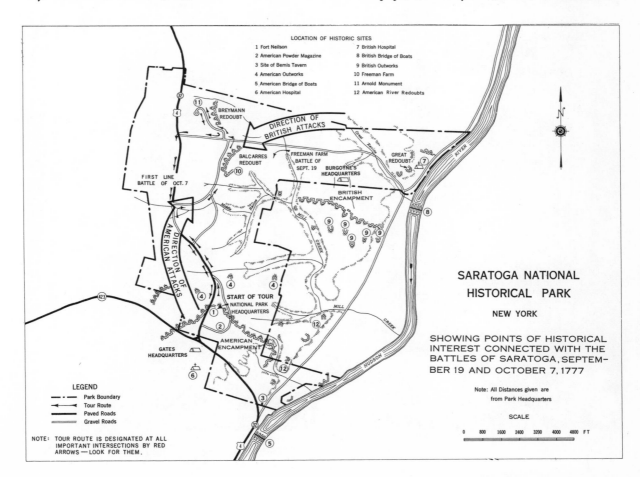

Beside this replica of a poster offering "all gentlemen seamen and able-bodied landsmen" opportunity to make their fortunes "on board the Ship Ranger, of Twenty guns (for France) . . . Commanded by John Paul Jones, Esq.," are old drawings of uniforms of a seaman and a marine. *Left and right:* Obverse and reverse design of medal struck in honor of Jones' most famous victory (see below).

Contemporary English engravings pictured Jones as a pirate and murderer. He had been involved in the killing of a crewman in the ship he commanded in 1773, and came to America under an assumed name after the incident. Note this early partial representation of the thirteen-star, thirteen-stripe flag at sea.

Jones' *Bonhomme Richard* defeated H.M.S. *Serapis* (center), despite broadsides fired blunderingly by another U.S. frigate (left) at Jones' ship.

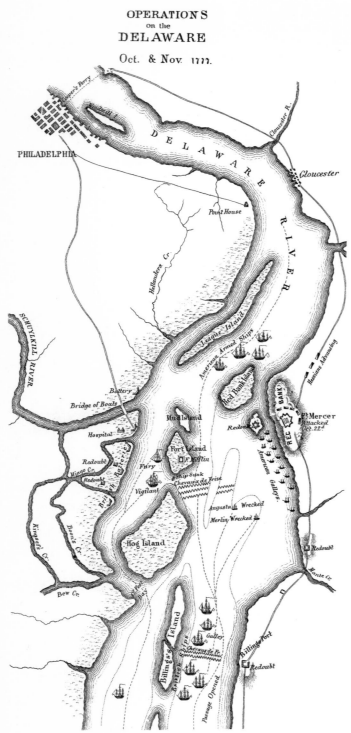

OPERATIONS
on the
DELAWARE

Oct. & Nov. 1777.

THOUGH General William Howe had beaten off Washington at Germantown, his position in Philadelphia remained highly vulnerable. The Delaware had to be opened for his brother "Black Dick" Howe's fleet. The Rebels had armed ships, fixed obstacles and two strong forts, Mercer and Mifflin, below Philadelphia.

Howe ordered Colonel Count Carl von Donop, who commanded a body of Hessian grenadiers and jägers, to cross the Delaware at Philadelphia, march down the Jersey side and take Fort Mercer by storm. Meanwhile, British vessels had reduced American works at Billingsport below and forced a narrow channel past submarine *chevaux de frise*, to cannonade the two forts in concert with Donop's attack, October 22. Before turning his own ten heavy guns upon Mercer, Donop sent a demand for its instant surrender. Colonel Christopher Greene, to whom Washington had assigned command, had only 400 men behind him when he responded, "We ask no quarter, nor will we give any."

Besiegers who pressed toward the fort under cover of Donop's cannonading were met with terrible volleys of grapeshot and musketry. Donop was one of the first to fall. His last words were quoted as "I die a victim of my ambition and the avarice of my sovereign."

The British naval attack on Fort Mifflin was also beaten off that day. But within a month the river was in control of the British. Floating batteries, four 64-gun ships and two 40-gun ships were brought to bear on Mifflin November 10. After six days, survivors of the 300-man garrison escaped at night to Fort Mercer, to which the British then turned attention. Christopher Greene held out another four days.

---

mission. De Fleury, then in his twenties, proved himself a brave and intelligent soldier in the defense of Fort Mifflin, on Fort Island (see map) where, it was calculated afterward, the garrison of 450 men sustained for six days perhaps the most concentrated bombardment of the eighteenth century — it reached an intensity of over 250 shots per minute! Lt.-Colonel Samuel Smith was among the wounded, and it remained for Major Simeon Thayer to evacuate about 300 survivors to Red Bank.

Map of operations on the Delaware, above and below the mouth of the Schuylkill, in October and November 1777, with details drawn from sketches by Major Louis de Fleury, a French volunteer trained as a military engineer, to whom Washington gave a com-

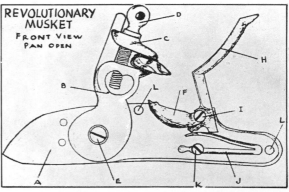

REVOLUTIONARY MUSKET
FRONT VIEW
PAN OPEN

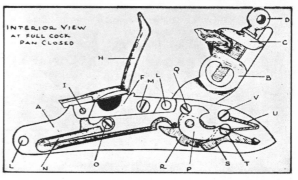

INTERIOR VIEW
AT FULL COCK
PAN CLOSED

The number and variety of weapons as well as uniforms were multiplied by the presence of foreign volunteers among the forces fighting the British, including the French troops who appeared after 1777. A drawing above illustrates some of them. *At lower right:* One mode of dress among Daniel Morgan's "Corps of Rangers," 500 sharpshooters he raised and brought into Washington's main army in April 1777, after Morgan-led riflemen had been in Benedict Arnold's abortive expedition to Quebec and Morgan had been a prisoner in Canada. Their arms, thanks to the weapons forged by hand and constantly improved by German and Swiss artisans in Pennsylvania for the needs of wilderness survival, represented an enormous improvement over the common type of musket with which most of the infantrymen were armed. Mechanism of the latter is detailed in these front and back sketches from *United States Martial Pistols and Revolvers*, by Major Arcadi Gluckman, U.S. Army.

TEUCRO DUCE NIL DESPERANDUM.

First Battalion of PENNSYLVANIA LOYALISTS, commanded by His Excellency Sir WILLIAM HOWE, K. B.

ALL INTREPID ABLE-BODIED

HEROES.

WHO are willing to serve His MAJESTY KING GEORGE the Third, in Defence of their Country, Laws and Constitution, against the arbitrary Usurpations of a tyrannical Congress, have now not only an Opportunity of manifesting their Spirit, by assisting in reducing to Obedience their too-long deluded Countrymen, but also of acquiring the polite Accomplishments of a Soldier, by serving only two Years, or during the present Rebellion in America.

Such spirited Fellows, who are willing to engage, will be rewarded at the End of the War, besides their Laurels, with 50 Acres of Land, where every gallant Hero may retire, and enjoy his Bottle and Lass.

Each Volunteer will receive, as a Bounty, FIVE DOLLARS, besides Arms, Cloathing and Accoutrements, and every other Requisite proper to accommodate a Gentleman Soldier, by applying to Lieutenant Colonel ALLEN, or at Captain KEARNY's Rendezvous, at PATRICK TONRY's, three Doors above Market-street, in Second-street.

Philadelphia, December 8, 1777.

REGULATIONS,

Under which the Inhabitants may purchase the enumerated Articles, mentioned in the Proclamation of His Excellency Sir WILLIAM HOWE, K. B. General and Commander in Chief, &c. &c. &c.

1st. NO RUM, or SPIRITS of inferior Quality, are to be sold (except by the Importer) at one Time, or to one Person, in any greater Quantity, than one Hogshead, or in any less than ten Gallons, and not without a Permit first obtained for the Quantity intended to be purchased, from the Inspector of the prohibited Articles.

2d. MOLASSES is not to be sold (except by the Importer) in any Quantity exceeding one Hogshead, at one Time, nor without a Permit as aforesaid.

3d. SALT may not be sold (except by the Importer) in any Quantity, exceeding one Bushel at one Time, for the Use of one Family, nor without Permit as aforesaid.

4th. MEDICINES not to be sold, without a special Permit by Order of the Superintendent General.

By Order of His Excellency Sir WILLIAM HOWE.

JOSEPH GALLOWAY, Superintendent General.

By His EXCELLENCY

GEORGE WASHINGTON, Esqui

GENERAL and COMMANDER in CHIEF of the For of the UNITED STATES of AMERICA.

BY Virtue of the Power and Direction to Me e cially given, I hereby enjoin and require all Pers residing within seventy Miles of my Head Quarters thresh one Half of their Grain by the 1st Day of Februa and the other Half by the 1st Day of March next ensu on Pain, in Case of Failure of having all that shall main in Sheaves after the Period above mentioned, se by the Commissaries and Quarter-Masters of the Ar and paid for as Straw

GIVEN under my Hand, at Head Quarters, the Valley Forge, in Philadelphia County, this Day of December, 1777.

G. WASHINGTO

By His Excellency's Command,

ROBERT H. HARRISON, Sec'y.

LANCASTER: PRINTED BY JOHN DUNLAP

[↑] Requisition for Washington's troops at Valley Forge published by broadside. The printer, John Dunlap, was moving his shop with the wandering Congress.

Left above: British allurement to "intrepid, able-bodied heroes" to desert the patriot forces and serve the king, for five-dollars bounty and the promise of fifty acres of land.

Below: Rationing in Philadelphia imposed by the British as a result of shortages produced by sabotage and raids by patriots and hoarding by Tories.

AFTER British military and naval forces secured control of the Delaware, with reductions of Forts Mifflin and Mercer, Washington shifted his position at Whitemarsh to Valley Forge, twenty-two miles north of Philadelphia. Howe attempted to surprise Washington as the movement was under way the night of December 6-7. A sharp engagement near Jenkintown that produced fifty British and Hessian casualties induced Howe to abandon this sortie.

Valley Forge had been well chosen from a strategic standpoint. The high ground commanded important roads west, south, north, east. Fertile farming regions were nearby for foraging. From Valley Forge scouting parties could go out covered by sloping hills and woods, to watch British movements in any direction.

But the Army was wholly unprepared for heavy snows and abnormally freezing weather that swept down Christmas week. George Wash-

Facsimile of original sketch of Valley Forge encampment, 1777-78, found in British military archives. It was attributed to "Mr. Parker," otherwise identified only as a spy for the British who visited the encampment early in 1778.

ington wrote December 23 from Valley Forge to the Congress, "Since the month of July we have had no assistance from the quartermaster-general."

The usual eastern mid-January thaw and warm spell turned roads into quagmires in which wagons of foragers were abandoned.

Officers were resigning in numbers, and not simply because of non-pay that forced them upon their own resources. Congress was bestowing high ranks on too many foreign newcomers. Washington complained, "The officers upon whom you most depend for defense of this cause, distinguished by length of service, their connections, property, and . . . military merit, will not submit, much if any longer, to the unnatural promotion of men over them, who have nothing more than a little plausibility, unbounded pride, and ambition."

Washington could have been referring in this instance to Casimir Pulaski, a troublemaker in the Army, not to Friedrich von Steuben, who had arrived with two companions at Congress in York, with papers identifying him as a "Lieutenant-General in the King of Prussia's service."

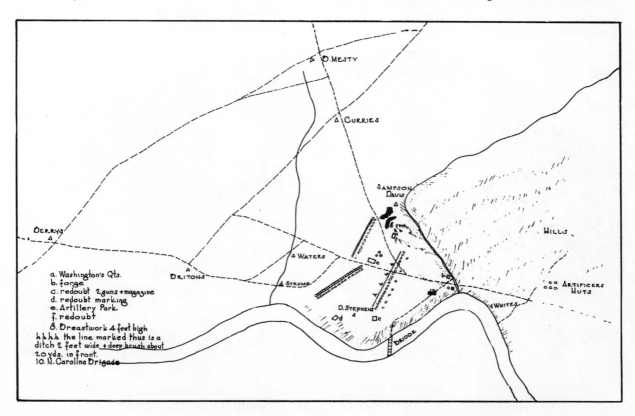

Above: Soldiers' huts reconstructed at Valley Forge (but more substantially) from descriptions by men who were there. In the originals, the "chinking" between logs was clay mud.

Below: Some habitations were dugouts similar to those of the first Jamestown settlers. Old engraving by J. McGoffin depicts Washington in a check-up round of the camp.

Factually a captain when discharged from the Prussian army, he had failed to secure an officership in the Sardinian, French and Austrian armies before offering himself to Benjamin Franklin in Paris as a volunteer.

Sent to Valley Forge, his reputation as a Prussian drillmaster impressed Washington. Assigned as acting inspector-general, Von Steuben began a transformation of the army with the training of 100-man cadres. He produced such marked improvement in discipline and efficiency before April that Washington effected Von Steuben's permanent appointment as Inspector-General, with Major-General rank.

However, the morale the army possessed in May 1778 was not solely Von Steuben's work. Washington had devised activities to raise depressed spirits — religious devotions, construction of comfortable quarters, amateur theatricals, dances and vigorous sports, one of which was rounders — direct ancestor of baseball.

In May came the biggest stimulant of all to high hopes of early victory: announcement of the French alliance.

Below: Washington dealing with one of the brawls that were recurrent as the winter of military inactivity wore on. Illustration by the nineteenth-century historical artist F. O. C. Darley. [↑] Washington's Valley Forge h.q. restored as a museum.

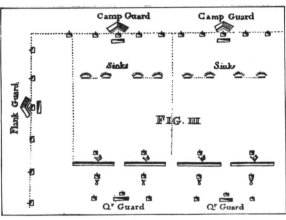

In CONGRESS, 29th March, 1779.

*C*ONGRESS *judging it of the greatest importance to prescribe some invariable rules for the order and discipline of the troops, especially for the purpose of introducing an uniformity in their formation and manœuvres, and in the service of the camp:*

ORDERED, *That the following regulations be observed by all the troops of the United States, and that all general and other officers cause the same to be executed with all possible exactness.*

By Order,

JOHN JAY, PRESIDENT.

Attest.

CHARLES THOMPSON,
Secretary.

Above: Official preface, with Washington's signature denoting this is his copy of it, to *Regulations for the Order and Discipline of the Troops of the United States,* as Approved by Congress in 1779. But Congress was laggard in providing adequate uniforms [*Above right*] to bolster discipline. [→] Diagram for laying out a camp under guard in the Von Steuben manual. "Sinks" were sanitary facilities. [↓] Details of a camp of two battalions, with their flags at tents of G and H. Sutler (at C) was seller of liquor and luxuries.

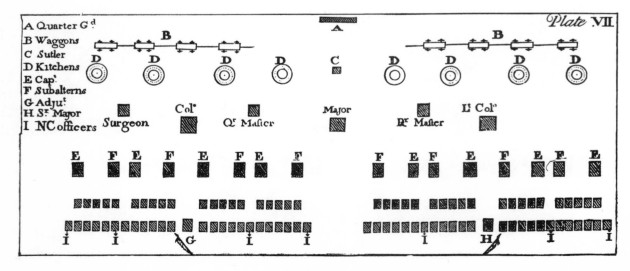

Friedrich Wilhelm von Steuben (1730-1794) as portrayed in a French engraving. Although well-trained as a Prussian staff officer, his highest rank had been captain when he represented himself to Franklin in Paris as a lieutenant-general and adviser to Frederick the Great. Impressed by Von Steuben's bearing and apparent military knowledge, and aware that Congress paid scant attention to foreign volunteers who did not claim high rank, Franklin accepted him for what he asserted he was.

The red-haired but white-wigged La Fayette arrived at Washington's h.q. with a commission as major-general, a resplendent uniform — and without ever having drilled any troops or seen a battle. He expected to lead an army division. Only nineteen, he had left his sixteen-year-old bride, who was on the verge of childbirth; had spent his own money to secure a ship for the passage for himself and other volunteers from France to Charleston, S.C.; then agreed to serve without pay.

Among other volunteers who made important military contributions were these four. Casimir Pulaski [↑], after serving at Brandywine and with Anthony Wayne, led a cavalry legion in the South. He was killed in action near Savannah in 1779.

Thaddeus Kosciusko, born in Lithuania and, like Pulaski, a veteran of the Polish army, was the engineer and artillerist who designed West Point's fortifications. He was valuable as a staff officer.

Louis LeBegue, Chevalier Duportail, was another who helped remedy a particular lack in the Continental Army: military engineers. Arriving in 1777 apart from La Fayette, he was made a brigadier.

Though he was a Bavarian by birth, Johann "Baron de" Kalb's military experience was in the French army. Arriving in the United States in 1777, he was made a major-general and had commands in both North and South before being mortally wounded.

The third, unfinished portrait by Stuart, painted in 1796, which unjustly became the most famous Washington picture. Mrs. Washington said it was *not* a "true resemblance." Stuart copied the head in the so-called Lansdowne portrait and over seventy other "originals." As he copied, he kept altering the shape of the head. (Boston Museum of Fine Arts.)

V

CHARACTER REVEALED BY ARTISTS

"I do not think vanity is a trait of my character. Any memoirs of my life, distinct and unconnected with the general history of the war, would rather hurt my feelings, than tickle my pride, while I live. I had rather glide gently down the stream of life, leaving it to posterity, to think and say what they please of me, than, by any act of mine, to have vanity or ostentation imputed to me."

— GEORGE WASHINGTON, 1784

THE spring of 1778, after that winter of ordeal at Valley Forge, the mood of the army was reflected in a letter written content if they remove most any general except His Excellency. The country, even Congress, are not aware of the Confidence the Army places in home by Elisha Sheldon of Connecticut: "I am him, or motions never would have been made for Gates to take command." Dan Morgan, the rough-and-ready colonel of the Virginia Rifles, told Gates pointedly, "Under no other man than Washington will I ever serve."

Why would the public at large have been aware of his army's confidence in Washington? There had been no news except defeat and retreat from his immediate command for nearly a year, whereas Gates had given impressive proof at Saratoga that British soldiers could be made to surrender *en masse*. The public was dependent very largely on word-of-mouth communication. The circulation of papers favoring the patriot side was under severe handicaps imposed by enemy obstacles to distribution and by shortages of paper, type, able-bodied printers. The patriot papers had to rely largely upon voluntary con-

tributions of letters, statements issued by Congress, proclamations of British commanders and pickups from other papers. They were susceptible to the impressions of Washington created by his eminent defamers and were vulnerable to rumors. Needless to say, rumor was rampant — some of it irresponsible, some concocted maliciously by Washington's detractors. Washington himself deliberately took advantage of rumor-mongers on various occasions. For example, when his army lay at Morristown in 1777, undergoing privations comparable to those it suffered at Valley Forge, Washington sent a succession of civilians into New York, primed to spread stories of the strength and readiness of his army.

At that same time, as he himself learned first from Franklin's old *Pennsylvania Gazette*, circulation was being given to a series of forged letters painting Washington as a libertine who was distracted from his duty by an Irish mistress.

The public certainly obtained a poor impression of Washington from any pictures of him exhibited or reproduced prior to about 1780.

Washington's diary entry for May 18, 1772,

says: "Went up to court and stayed all night. In the Evening Mr. Peale and J. P. Curtis came to Mount Vernon." Two days later, a Wednesday: "I sat to have my picture drawn." Friday that week: "Sat for Mr. Peale to finish my Face. Rid with him to my mill." On May 30 there was an entry in his accounts: "By Mr. Peale Painter, Drawg. my Picte. £18.4.0. Miniature Do. for Mrs. Washington. £13. Ditto Do. for Miss Custis. £13. Ditto Do. for Mr. Custis £13."

These portraits appear to have been Mrs.

First miniature of Martha Washington, by C. W. Peale, and the artist's receipt for payment.

May 30th 1772. Received Ten Guineas from George Washington for drawing Mrs. Washington's Picture in Miniature for the use of Mr. Custis, and at his desire; —

Charles W Peale

Washington's idea. That fortnight, Washington wrote to Rev. Jonathan Boucher, "Inclination having yielded to importunity, I am now, contrary to all expectations, under the hands of Mr. Peale, but in so grave, so sullen a mood, and now and then under the influence of Morpheus when some critical strokes are making, that I fancy the skill of this gentleman's pencil will be put to it in describing what manner of man I am."

Washington Irving and some other biographers referred to an earlier portrait than Peale's. The young Virginia colonel was said to have sat for John Singleton Copley at Boston in 1756 and for John Wollaston the same year.

The small oval, the portrait borne by a herald angel, is the first likeness of Washington printed in his country, and the allegorical scene is prophetic. Note in this woodcut illustration used by *Bailey's Almanac* for 1779, published in German at Lancaster, Pa., in 1778, the words issuing from the angel's trumpet: *Das Landes' Vater*, meaning "Father of the Country." This was the first instance of the phrase's application to him.

Washington's diaries for 1755-1759 are missing. Other evidence, pro or con, is inconclusive. But Washington's adopted son, George Washington Parke Curtis, termed Peale's 1772 painting as "the most ancient of the original portraits." Custis meant the life-size, three-quarter-length portrait on page 137. But there was certainly an earlier portrait, the small bust study Peale made for the painting to which Custis referred. Peale retained it and at some later date the uniform in it was changed to the Continental buff and blue.

Mrs. Washington must have approved of Peale's portraiture. The 1772 full-length picture formed the principal ornament of the parlor at Mount Vernon as long as she lived. When portraits of both the Washingtons were requested in 1776 by John Hancock, C. W. Peale was chosen to paint them. This may have been because he was at hand; he had joined the army in 1776 and became a company commander. Yet surely Mrs. Washington would not have elected to sit for an artist whose portraiture of the General she considered inadequate. In 1777, Peale did a miniature of Washington at Martha's request.

That year, Peale also received a commission from the Pennsylvania Council of State to paint a full-length, life-size portrait of the commander-in-chief. Begun at Valley Forge early in 1778, it was not completed until 1779 because of the interruptions imposed by the pursuit of Clinton through New Jersey. "He painted and fit, and painted and fit," an infantry companion of Peale's said. Peale and John Trumbull were the only artists who saw Washington in action as a general.

A note in the *Pennsylvania Packet*, Feb. 11, 1779 (Washington's birthday by the old-style calendar), said: "His Excellency General Washington set off from this city to join the army in New Jersey. During his short stay . . . the Council of State being desirous of having his picture . . . a striking likeness was taken by Mr. Peale of this city. . . . Don Juan Marrailes, the Minister of Spain, has ordered five copies, four of which, we hear, are to be sent abroad."

Peale made a first copy for Nassau Hall at Princeton, where it still hangs. The original was subjected to vandalism in 1781, when it was hanging in the Pennsylvania State House. Meanwhile.

Peale had engraved the original; in 1780, he advertised 14 x 10 mezzotint prints. "Shopkeepers, and persons going to the West Indies, may be supplied at such a price as will afford a considerable profit to them," the ad said. Copies of this print are very rare; the discovery of one can bring considerable profit to its finder.

The demand abroad for engravings of the commander-in-chief of the rebels against Britain was being catered to by an enterprising Briton, G. Shepherd, of London. On September 9, 1775, he issued the earliest images of Washington offered for public sale. They were mezzotints, one a standing figure, the other an equestrian pose purported to have been "drawn from life by Alex. Campbell of Williamsburgh in Virginia."

It is possible Campbell did sketch Washington from life on some occasion. If so, the General was unaware of it. When a friend, Joseph Reed, obtained and sent a copy of the Shepherd mezzotint to Martha Washington, the General wrote him from Cambridge in 1776: "Mrs. Washington desires I will thank you for the picture sent her. Mr. Campbell, whom I never saw to my knowledge, has made a very formidable figure of the Commander-in-Chief, giving him a sufficient portion of terror in his countenance."

In his introduction to a new edition of Leonardo da Vinci's *The Art of Painting*, Alfred Werner observed: "The men who gave us the mysterious smile of Mona Lisa knew ... that physical gestures and expressions are of interest only insofar as they express feelings, and that painting is worthless unless it is an outer projection of an inner state." By this criterion, most of the life portraiture of Washington has small value. Not much insight into his character is to be gained from them. It appears that, in general, the artists to whose scrutiny Washington subjected himself face to face either lacked divining powers or the talents to project what they perceived of the inner man.

As time went on, he seemed a more willing subject. In 1785, when asked by Francis Hopkinson to pose for Robert Edge Pine, Washington responded: " 'In for a penny, in for a pound' is an old adage. I am so hackneyed to the touches of the Painter's pencil, that I am now altogether

The earliest authenticated portrait, painted when Washington was forty by Charles Willson Peale. Canvas, 40 x 50 inches. Now owned by Washington and Lee University, Lexington, Virginia. "The bust portrait for this portrait was retained by the artist, and after finished at his leisure. It was familiar for many years to the Peale Gallery, upon the dispersion of which, this valuable *first portrait* was purchased by Charles F. Ogden of Philadelphia." Elizabeth Bryant Johnson in *The Original Portraits of Washington* (James R. Osgood and Company: Boston, 1882). Mr. Ogden presented the original to the Historical Society of Pennsylvania, which permitted it to be engraved by Max Rosenthal (*see below*) and published in a limited edition of fine prints by Dodd, Mead & Co., New York City, on May 1, 1895.

Left: French engraving of "George Washington, Esquire, Commander in Chief of the Armies of the XIII Provinces, United in America," is declared from a portrait by Alexander Campbell at Williamsburg, Virginia. Engravings of the spurious Campbell portrait had been issued earlier in England. Right: German engraving in 1777 of a Washington equestrian portrait resembles earlier engravings of Frederick the Great. Another German engraver transposed it into a standing portrait [↓].

at their beck, and sit, like Patience on a monument, whilst they are delineating the lines of my face. It is proof, among many others, of what habit and custom may effect. At first I was impatient at the request, and as restive under the operation, as a colt of the saddle. The next time I submitted very reluctantly, but with less flouncing. Now no dray-horse moves more steadily to the thrill, than I to the Painter's Chair. It may be easily conceived, therefore, that I yielded a ready obedience to your request."

He sat for at least a dozen artists after Pine, not counting silhouette cutters, and usually with good-humored toleration. Gilbert Stuart's experience with him (and vice versa!) was an exception.

Archibald Robertson, who came from Scotland in 1791 to paint Washington for the 11th Earl of Buchan, wrote: "Although familiarly accustomed to intimate intercourse with those of high rank and station in my native country, I never experienced the same feeling I did on my introduction to the American hero. The excitation in

This engraving (*above*) is stated in Washington Irving's biography to have been made from a John Singleton Copley miniature of Washington, dated 1756. Obviously, it is an engraving from the miniature shown below virtually same size as the original: one and one-fourth inches by one and one-half inches. This was painted on ivory in 1777 by C. W. Peale for Mrs. Washington's grand-daughter, Nelly Custis. The miniature is reproduced by courtesy of The Metropolitan Museum of Art, New York: Gift of William H. Huntington, 1883. There is some mystery concerning a pencil drawing at right, by C. W. Peale. I suggest this sketch, in The Historical Society of Pennsylvania Collection, was made in connection with the miniature and refutes Rupert Hughes' contention that no artist ever caught GW smiling.

the mind of the stranger was evidently obvious to Washington; for, from his ordinary cold and distant address, he declined into the most easy and familiar intercourse in conversation, with a view to disembarrass his visitor." Robertson was invited immediately to join the family at dinner where, he said, the President "engrossed most of the conversation at the table, and so delighted the company with humorous anecdotes, that he repeatedly set the table in a roar of laughter."

The Scot artist's miniature of Washington and the large oil portrait he painted subsequently do not impress the viewer as being the hero Robertson saw descend from a pedestal to be a considerate host and convivial family man. There are corresponding disparities between the written impressions and paintings of other artists for whom

→

First of three portraits by Stuart, painted in 1795. Canvas, 24 x 30 inches. Soon after completion, it or a copy was taken to England and acquired by Samuel Vaughan. From this circumstance, it became known as the Vaughan Washington. To Charles Henry Hart, who devoted years to study of Washington portraiture, this was the best of all Stuart's Washington originals and copies. (Sold to Clarke Estate.)

Washington sat. Among the life portraits there are inexplicable dissimilarities in such fundamental aspects as the shape of his head, the cast of his jaw. "His hair, eyes, complexion, apparently partook of each individual color of the rainbow," one viewer of Washington portraits remarked.

Washington was tolerant of repeated demands made upon him by the Peales, even after the whole family became engaged in wholesale copying and selling of his portraits. One day, while Gilbert Stuart was painting Washington, the patriarch of the Peales, C. W., called on the President and obtained permission to paint him again. Thereupon, James, Rembrandt and Raphaelle Peale also crowded into the Presidential presence with their equipment. Washington exclaimed lightly, "Why, gentlemen, I am being Pealed all around."

It may have been the only time he unbent while posing for Stuart. The latter, who invited himself to paint Washington in 1795, complained that the minute the President began to sit for him

This is represented as a drawing of temporary studio Gilbert Stuart used at Philadelphia for portraiture.

Martha Washington's kin did not esteem Stuart's unfinished portrait of her, painted in 1796, as the best likeness. It established itself as the No. 1 favorite as firmly with persons who never saw her as did Stuart's unfinished "Athenaeum" portrait of her husband. In copying it, Stuart followed his original concept more conscientiously than he did in copies of Washington portraits.

"an apathy seemed to seize him, and a vacuity spread over his countenance most appalling to paint."

Stuart esteemed himself as the only great artist to have painted Washington. A Rhode Island native, he had gone to England to study under another expatriate, Benjamin West. Though of military age and able-bodied, he stayed in England comfortably while the Revolution was being fought, enjoying a success as a painter of pretty portraits of fashionable folk. When it was safe for a Tory to show his head, Stuart came back to the United States to do affluent men and women at the rate of six sittings per day after giving himself prestige by painting the President.

Stuart engaged Washington in conversation about the Revolution for the purpose, he later said, of awakening "the heroic spirit in him by talking of battles." The general made it clear by his unresponsiveness that he had no wish to discuss strategy and tactics with Stuart, who once proposed, "Forget for a moment or two you are President of the United States." G. W. P. Custis said his foster father retorted tartly to Stuart, "I'll not forget that I am president; don't you forget you are a painter."

John Trumbull, who may have suffered from envy of Stuart's success in selling portraits of Washington by the dozens, remarked that Stuart had no conversation that could have interested Washington. G. W. P. Custis recalled that it took "hard begging" by Mrs. Washington to induce Washington to sit for a portrait Stuart painted in 1796. He gave in only because Mrs. Washington wanted the portrait for herself.

At that time, the President was enduring a newly made, badly fitting set of false teeth. They distorted his jowls and gave him an uncharacteristic countenance. Nevertheless, Stuart painted the misshapen jaws into the portrait. Then he played the Washingtons false. He had another client at the time of the Washington sittings and the client, upon seeing the unfinished Washington portrait in the artist's studio, commissioned a copy of it. He was only the first of many who obtained copies, for Stuart did not comply with repeated requests of the Washingtons for delivery of the portrait. He had a convenient excuse: it wasn't finished. In fact, he was using it as his

model for scores of other "original" portraits of Washington for which he received orders. Stuart called the unfinished portrait his "hundred dollar bill," for whenever he was pressed for cash, he could daub another copy and sell it. As he kept on copying, Stuart grew careless. Some of his replica portraits are scarcely distinguishable from copies by other hands. There is authentication that Stuart obtained considerably more than $100 both for originals and copies: $200, $500 and above — the equivalent of over $2000, $5000, in today's currency.

The diminished qualities of some later Stuarts inevitably invited forgeries. (Instances of forgeries of Rembrandt Peale and John Trumbull works also eventually came to light.)

The unfinished original, the "Athenaeum portrait" now deposited in the Boston Museum of Fine Arts, was the Washington image his countrymen chose to enshrine. Mark Twain remarked, "If Washington should arise from the dead and not resemble the Stuart portrait, he would be denounced as an imposter."

Irving wrote, "No artist enjoyed the opportunities of John Trumbull as portrayer of Washington," forgetting or disparaging C. W. Peale. Trumbull, the son of "Brother Jonathan," joined Washington's army at Cambridge in 1775, when he was nineteen. Through the ability he showed as a topographer, he came to the attention of the commander-in-chief, to whose staff he was attached. Though advanced to colonel and the position of deputy adjutant-general of the northern department, he left the service in 1777 — "owing to some dissatisfaction regarding rank," it was

Opposite page: A photograph of the John Trumbull portrait of Washington in the Governor's Room at New York City Hall, made especially for this book. The original is 72 x 108 inches. A writer in *Antiques Journal* estimated its market value academically at $1,000,000. Trumbull said, "I represented . . . in the background a view of Broadway in ruins, as it then was, the old Fort at the termination; British ships and boats leaving the shore, and Staten Island in the distance. Every part of the detail of the dress, horse, furniture, etc., as well as the scenery, from the real objects." It was painted from a study Trumbull made in 1790. Charles Henry Hart said it was materially altered in 1804.

said. Trumbull subsequently went to England to study art under J. S. Copley and Benjamin West. Trumbull suffered retaliatory arrest after the execution of Major John André in 1780 and spent some time in an English prison before Copley and West got him out. Trumbull resumed study under West and, while in England, began his first two paintings of Revolutionary scenes: *The Death of Montgomery* and *Battle of Bunker Hill*. He also started to make the life studies for the ambitious series now hanging in the Rotunda of the Capitol in Washington. John Adams sat for him in London and Thomas Jefferson in Paris.

Trumbull returned to the States in 1789 and during Congress' sessions in New York he drew sketches of surviving signers for his painting of the signing of the Declaration of Independence. Then, in February and March, 1790, he was given sittings by President Washington.

Washington was induced to put on his long disused Continental Army uniform and ride out on a horse with Trumbull, that the artist might make sketches for his portraits.

George Washington Parke Custis says "Trumbull, who was near-sighted, always painted his studies small."

The preliminary sketches and miniature oils which served Trumbull as notes for his pictures are deemed far better than the resultant pictures. The best collection of these and other work of Trumbull's is in the Yale University Art Gallery.

Top: Washington portrait by Charles Willson Peale from studies 1778-9. *Right:* Last portrait from life by C. W. Peale, done in 1795, during one of Washington's sittings for Stuart. Peale's two sons, Rembrandt and Raphaelle, and his brother, James, made studies of the President at the same time, in the old hall of the Philosophical Society in Philadelphia. It was purchased from Peale's Museum by an individual who presented it to the New-York Historical Society.

Left: Edward Savage's portrait in oil on canvas, 25 x 30 inches, started in December 1789, for Harvard University. *Below:* A composite by Rembrandt Peale painted after Washington's death. It was based on Peale's earlier sketches from life and studies of his father's work and Houdon's statue. La Fayette was quoted as having said on seeing it, "This, gentlemen, was the Washington I knew." Rembrandt Peale painted and sold at least seventy-five copies of it.

Above: Miniature by James Peale, done in 1788. (Owned by the Washington Grays, Philadelphia.)

The Washingtons sat for many profile artists, professional and amateur. Silhouettes of them were duplicated in quantity and peddled at large. Silhouettes, mezzotints, engravings, medallions, copy-miniatures, crude woodcuts in the press, these were the means through which the mass of Americans in the late eighteenth and early nineteenth centuries became acquainted with the features of the Father of their country.

These two pages bring together a choice of silhouettes of the Washington cut from life. *At the top, this page:* Profile by Samuel Folwell, 1795. He is sometimes confused with Samuel Powel, another artist who cut a profile in 1796. *Below:* Profiles of Mr. and Mrs. Washington traced by her granddaughter, Nelly Custis, at Mount Vernon in 1798. *Bottom:* Profile by an unidentified silhouette-cutter at Peale's Museum, Philadelphia, 1794. *Beside it:* Mechanical aid used by a professional silhouettist in Washington's time.

Opposite page, top: Silhouette by the ill-fated Major John André, who may have got a covert look at Washington at some time in Pennsylvania.

Below it: Profile of Washington in 1783, by a Miss DeHart of Elizabethtown, N.J. The full-length Washington silhouette, by an unidentified artist, was one duplicated in quantity after the Revolution.

Archibald Robertson's oil of Washington, painted in 1792, now hangs in the Washington ancestral home at Sulgrave, Northamptonshire, to which it was given by the Fifteenth Earl of Buchan. An earlier Earl be- came confused about the identity and preserved it as "Portrait of a Naval Officer." Reproduction from a color-photo, courtesy King Features Syndicate.

Left: Miniatures of the Washingtons by Archibald Robertson, in watercolor on ivory, now at Colonial Williamsburg. They preceded his oil portrait of Washington, shown in page 150. Robertson's is the least idealized portrait of Mrs. Washington.

Below: The President by Adolph Wertmüller, Swedish artist who painted him from life in 1794. Wertmüller made several copies, and the identity of the original is conjectural. Possibly the original was disposed of in an auction of the artist's effects held by his widow. A bidder got a Wertmüller portrait of Washington with some other pictures for only fifty dollars!

Justin Windsor called this life portrait [↑] "disagreeable, feeble." The painter was one William Williams. Charles Henry Hart says Williams "persecuted and persisted until he succeeded in 1794 in obtaining a sitting from Washington for a portrait now in the possession of Washington Lodge No. 22 [Freemasons] at Alexandria, Va. It is a miserable picture in every respect." Another amateur effort (*facing Williams'*) was painted in 1797 by Dr. Elisha Cullen Dick of Alexandria, one of the three doctors who attended Washington in his last illness.

At Right: The last life-portrait of Washington, drawn by Charles de Saint-Mémim in pink crayon on black paper in November 1798, at Philadelphia. The occasion was Washington's visit in the capital to confer with President Adams and others about the military preparations for the war with France. Half-inch miniatures were put in mourning rings.

[154] GEORGE WASHINGTON

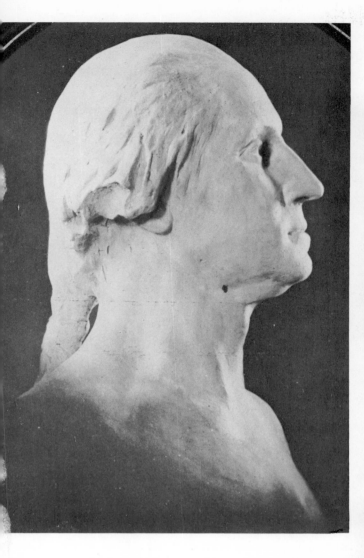

[↑] Houdon study of GW in plaster, at Mt. Vernon. *Right:* Two views of a Houdon bust, now in the Museum of Fine Arts, Boston. Washington was also sculptured from life by Joseph Ceracchi, Joseph Wright, Mrs. Patience Lovell Wright; possibly by John Echstein and others. *Opposite page:* Houdon's standing marble at the State Capitol in Richmond. The General Assembly of Virginia, having resolved June 22, 1784, that a statue of Washington should be erected as "a monument of affection and gratitude," charged Franklin and Jefferson, who were then in Paris, to order a statue from the best available European sculptor. Their choice, Houdon, was given the commission at a fee of 25,000 francs, plus 5,000 f. expenses for his trip to America, 8,800 f. for the marble, and 10,000 f. indemnity to his family in case of his death during the trip to and from America. Houdon modeled at least one bust and a life-mask at Mount Vernon in October 1785. The resultant marble statue arrived at Richmond in 1796. Houdon made other busts of GW in plaster, terra cotta, and marble, also medallions, in Paris from the originals molded at Mount Vernon.

There is insufficient space to reproduce representative examples of portraiture by all the artists who delineated Washington or his wife from life. Whole books are required to cover the subject comprehensively. An exhaustive study of all representations of GW in his lifetime, and the first century after his death, is: *Portraits of Washington,* by G. A. Eisen (Robert Hamilton & Associates: New York, 1932, three volumes.) Dr. Eisen, a professional zoologist and horticulturist, was a hobbyist water-colorist and miniaturist who became interested in Washington portraiture after emigrating from Sweden to San Francisco, where he was the Curator of the California Institute of Sciences. His exposition filled a void that existed after publication of Elizabeth Bryant Johnston's *Original Portraits of Washington* (James R. Osgood and Co.: Boston, 1882), a far less comprehensive catalogue and appraisal, became both out-of-date and out-of-print.

The most important artists known to have portrayed Washington from life are, in approximate chronological order:

Charles Willson Peale did at least fourteen large and miniature paintings in the period 1772-95. He made many copies of his originals, and engraved some of them.

Eugene Pierre du Simitiere drew a head the winter of 1778-9. It is known only from engravings; the original has been lost.

John Trumbull painted the miniature of GW (9 x 7 in.) in Washington Headquarters (Jumel Mansion) at New York. This, termed by Eisen (*see above*), "One of the most charming and convincing Washingtons," was first of Trumbull's dozen noteworthy pictures painted of GW from first-hand observations that began in 1775.

Joseph Wright painted a portrait with short, undressed hair and military garb at Rocky Hill in 1784, and also modeled a bas-relief in wax. Washington evidently liked Wright's portrait, for he paid Wright to make two formal copies for presentation to friends. Wright painted him again in 1790, and etched a small profile, said to have been the first "painter etching" made in this country. He did a third portrait in 1792.

Charles Peale Polk, nephew of C. W. Peale, who had started copying portraits at ten, obtained a sitting when 17 for a 1784 painting of GW to which his uncle might have given touches.

Robert Edge Pine painted Washington in 1785 and again in 1787.

Jean Antoine Houdon modeled a bust in 1785, from which he completed a classic full-length statue, and several busts. He also made a medallion. Numerous cast copies exist.

James Peale, younger brother of Charles Willson, painted a miniature on ivory in 1787, another on snuff-box in 1788, and another on ivory in 1795.

The Marchioness de Brehan painted a miniature, 1788, of which she made several copies; also profile heads of Washington and Lafayette in medallion form.

John Ramage, or Rammage, did miniatures, the first of them in 1789.

Edward Savage painted several portraits of Washington, 1789-91, and a family group. He engraved fine plates of his paintings.

John Trumbull made sketches beginning in 1775; went to work on oil portraits in 1790.

Archibald Robertson came from Scotland to paint the Washingtons in 1791-1792. He made miniatures in 1796 which Washington gave to his wife's granddaughters.

Adolph Wertmüller, Swedish artist, painted several portraits between 1794 and 1797 of which one or two may have been from life.

Joseph Ceracchi modeled busts 1791-95, which he cut in marble at least three or four times.

Rembrandt Peale made a portrait in 1795 and sketches which he embodied in later works.

Raphaelle Peale, another son of C. W. Peale, also made preliminary sketches in 1795 during a sitting of Washington for the elder Peales, and subsequently painted the General.

Gilbert Stuart painted Washington from life three times, 1795 and 1796, and made scores of copies of his portraits.

James Sharpless, or Sharples, made colored crayon portraits, 1796-1797. His family members made many copies.

Charles de Saint-Mémin made a crayon portrait 1798, and engraved it; painted a miniature in a gold ring.

VI

THE SEVEREST TESTS

"The General must earnestly entreat the officers and Soldiers to consider the consequences; that they can no way assist our enemies more effectually, than by making divisions among themselves; that the honor and success of the army, and the safety of our blessed country, depend upon harmony and good agreement with each other."

— George Washington, 1778

Probably few today have ever found the name of John Banister, Jr., in readings of American history. As a doctor of medicine, student of botany and author of a natural history of Virginia, Banister formed a pre-war acquaintanceship with Washington through a mutual interest in agriculture. However, Banister pursued the practice of law, a profession for which he had fitted himself in London as a more dependable source of income, when he volunteered for a regiment of the Virginia Line. He served intermittently while also a member of the Virginia Assembly and the Continental Congress. He was the member of the latter to whom Washington chose to express feelings at a crucial time for an obvious purpose.

"The enemy are beginning to play a game more dangerous than their efforts by arms. . . . They are endeavoring to ensnare the people by specious allurements of peace. . . . Whether they are sincere or not, they may be equally destructive; for, to discerning men nothing can be more evident than that a peace on the principles of dependence, however limited, after what has happened, would be to the last degree, dishonorable and ruinous. It is however much to be appre-

hended, that the idea of such an event will have a very powerful effect upon the country, and . . . will serve, at least, to produce supineness and disunion. Men are naturally fond of peace, and there are symptoms . . . that the people of America are pretty generally weary of the present war. . . .

"I have sent Congress Lord North's speech, and the two bills offered by him to Parliament. They are spreading fast through the country, and will soon become a subject of general notoriety. I therefore think they had best be published in our papers, and persons of ability set to work to counteract the impressions they may make on the minds of the people."

Henry Cinton, second in command to the British Commander-in-Chief in America since 1775, succeeded to that position in 1778. A few days after Lord Germain signed the order for Clinton to relieve Howe, London had the news of France's allying itself openly with the Rebels. An order went to Clinton to abandon Philadelphia, to send forces south to Savannah, to detail 5000 troops to West Indian islands (which France had made their first line of offense).

June 18, 1778, the British evacuated Phila-

Above: General Washington, hand raised, halts the retreating troops at Monmouth led by Charles Lee — when Washington violated his own injunction to the troops against "the foolish and wicked practice of profane cursing and swearing. . . . He hopes that officers will, by their example as well as influence, endeavor to check it." An engraving of a painting by Felix O. C. Darley.

Below: Successive positions of the contending forces at Monmouth, with Lee's original march and lines of retreat indicated, in a map prepared by a Revolutionary officer for John Marshall's biography of Washington. Individual names — Stirling, Greene, Varnum, *et al.*, designate troops of those generals' commands. Lee was suspended from duty for ordering the retreat.

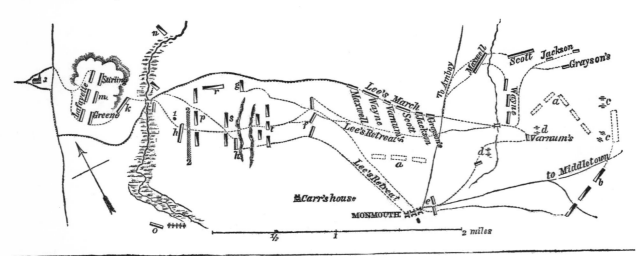

a....Position occupied by the British the night before the Battle.

b.....British detachment moving towards Monmouth.

c....British Batteries.—d. Captain Oswald's American Batteries.

e....American troops formed near the Court house.

f.....First position taken by General Lee in his retreat.

g...Attack by a Party of British in the woods.

h....Positions taken by General Lee.—i. British detachment.

k...Last position of the retreating troops.

m...Army formed by General Washington after he met General Lee retreating.

n...British Detachment.—o. American battery.—p. Principal action.

r...First position of the British after the action. s. Second position.

t...British passed the night after the battle.

1... When Washington met Lee retreating.—2. Hedge row.—3. Meeting house.

delphia and headed for New York. June 21, Washington's troops were forty miles from Valley Forge, crossing the Delaware into Jersey at Coryell's Ferry, and Clinton was trailed closely, with six brigades under Charles Lee nearest. The night of June 27-28, Clinton's army was at Monmouth Court House (Freehold) exhausted from a nineteen-mile movement, heavily burdened, in over 90-degree heat; a number had been felled by sunstroke. Opportunity was presented for an enveloping attack to destroy Clinton.

Charles Lee, who had been captured in his bed at Basking Ridge (N.J.) just before the victory at Trenton, had been exchanged in April 1778. Washington accepted him back as a ranking major general although he knew Lee had been conniving against him. Lee's having a decisive position at Monmouth proved one of Washington's worst mistakes in the war. Under orders to move against the British rear as soon as the enemy army was put in motion, Lee had not given his officers a plan of attack. When, attacked, the British swung quickly into an unyielding defensive stand, the retreat ordered by Lee became disorderly, almost panic. Washington, meeting men in flight to the rear as he advanced, dashed among them, denouncing Lee "in the most terrible manner," and with fiery orders turning the regiments back to the battleground where other units of his command were converging.

The great drama of that day, with its lost opportunity to effect a crushing blow that could have brought a negotiated peace in 1778, tended to be overshadowed by an insignificant happening: "Molly Pitcher's" becoming a spur-of-the-moment soldier.

George Washington wrote his brother, "From an unfortunate and bad beginning turned out a glorious and happy day." But Clinton's army got away in the night.

Unidealized representation of Mary Ludwig Hays ("Molly Pitcher") at Monmouth, from Headley's *Life of Washington*, 1858. Mary, twenty-four, was a camp-follower with the regiment of her husband, Sergeant John Casper Hays. Normally she did washing, sewing, cooking for the soldiers. That hot June day she carried water to the men. When her husband was overcome by heat at his gun she took his place (as Margaret Corbin had become a gunner at Fort Washington where her husband was killed.)

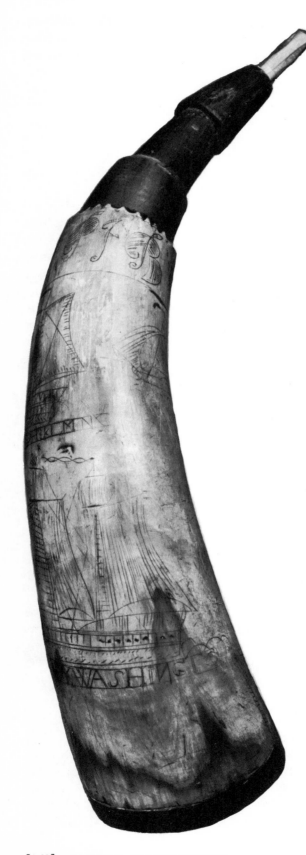

Although ships are traditionally feminine gender, relatively few vessels of war have ever been given feminine names. It appears the earliest such vessel of the United States was the flagship of the pickup squadron positioned in the Hudson by Washington to oppose penetration of the upper river by British vessels from New York City, after the king's troops obtained possession of Manhattan and mouth of the Hudson. The flagship was designated *Lady Washington* apparently by Colonel Benjamin Tupper, who commanded the squadron.

He made repeated forays against the British downriver and scored some successes. One was August 3, 1776, two days after transports brought General Sir Henry Clinton's troops from Charleston to rendezvous with reinforcements from abroad, including Hessian mercenaries, at Staten Island. The *Lady Washington* and four support vessels outfought two British ships in Tappan Zee.

There was no documentation of the appearance of this historic ship until discovery of a contemporary powderhorn bearing a picture clearly identified as the *Lady Washington*. Such a find was not unique: some of the best contemporary representatives of other engagements were engraved on powderhorns by proudly victorious participants.

The documentary powderhorn is owned by Robert Winne. The photograph and drawing of picture it bears are reproduced by courtesy of the Ulster County Historical Society, Kingston, New York, and Captain A. S. Hickey, U.S.N. (Ret.)

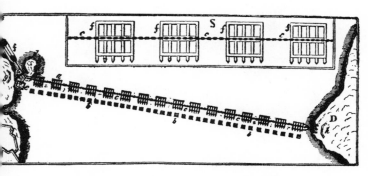

Certainly one of Washington's master tactical devices in his strategic plan for keeping the British from penetrating the Hudson full length and cutting the embattled Union in half was putting the river literally in chains. He had substantial fortifications at West Point, above the river, but the British warships running past and concentrating their cannon fire might have knocked these out. So he decided to obstruct the stream with a chain strong enough to hold back any vessel dependent on sails and wind.

The chain, weighing in all 165 tons, was forged within two weeks by Peter Townsend at his Sterling Iron Works in Orange County. Each link was about three feet in length, interlocked in 100-foot sections. The sections were joined by clevises. Swivels held them taut against log floats.* The ends — 500 feet apart — were anchored to huge blocks on each shore under cover of batteries on both sides.

The chain was out in place first in April 1778, in anticipation of a new drive up the Hudson to undo the advantage won by the Americans through forcing Burgoyne's surrender. In the autumn, before ice halted all movements in the river, soldiers went out in boats to pull the chain back to shore. Each spring thereafter, the chain was put back across the Hudson, taken in each autumn until 1783.

The British, made aware of the danger of having ships hung up by the chain while under fire of the forts at West Point, made no attempt to break through. The detection of Arnold's treason in time prevented their breaching the fortifications by baser means.

The chain at Fort Montgomery, from a cut in Ruttenber's *Obstructions to the Navigation of Hudson's River*, made from a drawing found in the papers of the secret committee. *A.* Fort Montgomery. *B.* Fort Clinton. *C.* Poplopen's Kill. *D.* Anthony's Nose. *a,* floats to the chain. *b b b,* boom in front of the chain. *c c c,* chain. Inset (S) is section showing floats and chain. *d,* rock at which chain was secured. *e,* boom anchor.

Links of the great chain with other relics at West Point — a drawing in B. J. Lossing's *Pictorial Field-Book of the Revolution.* In the center a brass mortar, mounted, taken by Anthony Wayne at Stony Point. The smaller brass mortars were in the booty surrendered by Burgoyne at Saratoga. (The links are now mounted on iron supports.)

* James Thacher recorded in 1780, "It is buoyed up by very large logs of about 16 feet long, pointed at the ends, to lessen their opposition to the force of the current at flood and ebb tide. The logs are placed at short distances from each other, the chain carried over them, and made fast to each by staples. There are also a number of anchors dropped at proper distances, with cables made fast to the chain, to give it greater stability."

In April 1778 Patrick Henry, as Governor of Virginia, had ordered Lt. Colonel George Rogers Clark (*below*) to proceed with 350 men to attack the British post at Kaskaskia, in Illinois. Embarking them at Fort Pitt (Pittsburgh), he descended to the Falls of the Ohio (Louisville). Two spies he sent on and his careful preparations enabled Clark to secure Kaskaskia by surprise in July 1778. British soon moved from Detroit under Lt. Colonel Henry Hamilton to recover the lost territory. Vincennes, French settlement on the Wabash, shifted allegiance to the U.S. upon news of the French alliance, and Hamilton, in December, forced surrender of the small garrison Clark had there. Audaciously, Clark moved with 200 men through icy "drowned lands" (*as above*) to recapture Vincennes in February 1779.

Colonel Clarks Compliments to Mr. Hamilton and begs leave to inform him that Col. Clark will not agree to any other Terms than that of Mr Hamilton's Surrendering himself and Garrison, Prisoners at Discretion ——

If Mr Hamilton is Desirous of a Conference with Col Clark he will meet him at the Church with Capt. Helms ——

Feby 24th 1779 — G R Clark

Anthony Wayne, "Mad Anthony," as engraved from a portrait study by John Trumbull. Born in Chester County, Wayne got a wilderness education in Washington's way — as a surveyor. A member of the Pennsylvania Committee of Safety in 1775, he led Pennsylvania militia in the abortive invasion of Canada and commanded at Ticonderoga in 1776. Promoted to brigadier-general, he joined Washington as a division commander. Wayne's conduct at Brandywine, Paoli, Germantown and Monmouth made him a logical choice for the operation at Stony Point.

"More active and enterprising than Judicious & cautious," was a characterization of Anthony Wayne by George Washington that proved justified in 1779. The British had taken Stony Point, on the Hudson below West Point, by surprise (without a shot) on June 1. Washington, concerned by the new menace this and enemy possession of Fort Lafayette, opposite, were to West Point, sent Allen McLane, scout for Henry Lee's Legion, to espy enemy strength at Stony Point. On the basis of McLane's finding Washington directed Wayne to make an attack. Wayne's enterprise and audacity, abetted by Lieut. Col. François Louis de Fleury, a volunteer engineer from France, brought the reduction of Stony Point the night of July 16.

Wayne was voted a gold medal by Congress for the feat, De Fleury a silver medal — the first foreigner to receive a U.S. decoration. A few weeks later, Henry Lee won a medal with a daring raid on Paulus Hook (Jersey City), across the river from British-occupied New York. Washington ordered it after the Stony Point coup as another diversionary operation while he sought to insure the impregnability of West Point, "key to the continent." He did not reckon that the most serious threat to West Point was coming from within it.

Opposite page: Facsimile of a note that anticipated by nearly a century U. S. Grant's famous demand to S. B. Buckner: "Unconditional surrender." It says: "Colonel Clark's compliments to Mr. Hamilton and begs leave to inform him that Col. Clark will not agree to any other terms than that of Mr. Hamilton's surrendering himself and garrison. . . ." Colonel Clark addressed Hamilton as 'Mr.' because the latter had denied to 'rebel' officers the courtesy of military titles. Hamilton, taken prisoner at Vincennes, was sent to confinement at Williamsburg for some months. He was eventually exchanged, although there was strong feeling against him, due to his offering bounties to Indians for scalps of patriot soldiers or settlers. However, he was not the first British officer to adopt this policy. (Engraving of George Rogers Clark from a miniature ascribed to J. W. Jarvis. "Drowned lands" illustration by F. C. Yohn, from New York Public Library.)

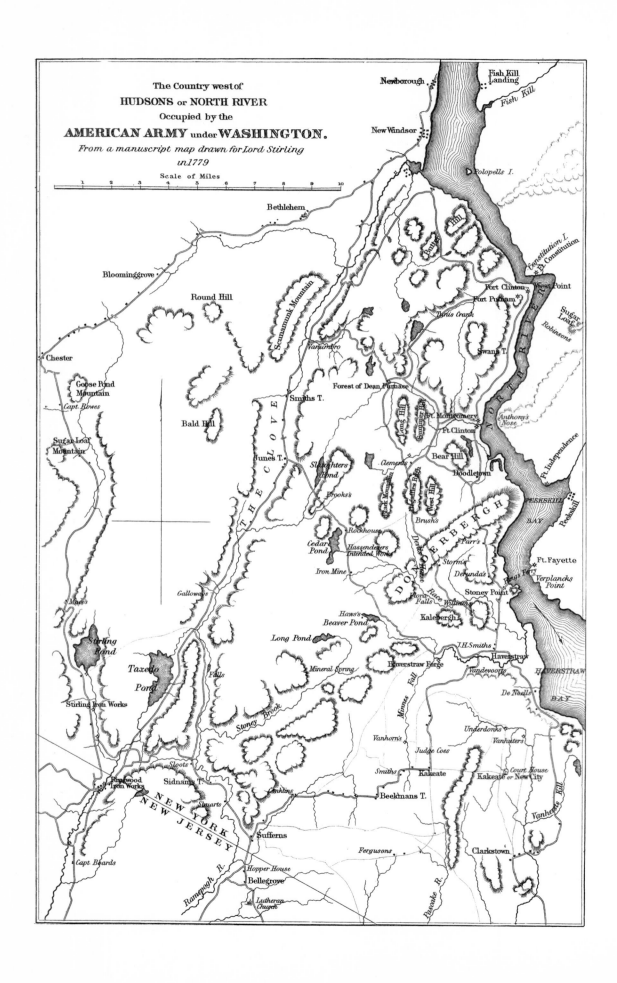

The Country west of
HUDSONS or NORTH RIVER
Occupied by the
AMERICAN ARMY under WASHINGTON.
From a manuscript map drawn for Lord Stirling
in 1779

Scale of Miles
1 2 3 4 5 6 7 8 9 10

Above: Mrs. Arnold, née Margaret Shippen, and child, from a portrait by Sir Thomas Lawrence, in the collection of the Historical Society of Pennsylvania. After his escape from arrest, Peggy rejoined him and lived with Arnold and the child in England. Her father became Chief Justice of Pennsylvania.

Benedict Arnold had apologists long after his deed. In stressing Arnold's zealous services earlier in the war — the participation in the capture of Fort Ticonderoga, the invasion of Canada, a remarkable amphibious campaign along Lake Champlain, decisive actions at Saratoga — a defender argued, "If Arnold and others, including Ethan Allen, felt that the wiser course was to go back to British rule, was his act and their contemplated ones that of capitulation or of treason?"

One could assume, to be charitable, Arnold's rationalization of his bargaining with the British was that he was helping his countrymen get out of a war they couldn't win. "By putting the British in control of the Hudson, he would give them all they had sought by campaigns of 1777-78-79; and opportunity would be created for a negotiated peace. Arnold was led to believe that the king's ministers would renew and broaden terms already offered in 1778, which conceded everything the Americans had demanded in 1775." "By rendering a cardinal service, Arnold could expect to be an influential figure in the negotiations for restoring America to its old allegiance, but with freedom from parliamentary controls," was another argument in his behalf.

Examination of his record does not generate confidence in his intentions. Arnold committed two desertions from military service in his youth. He proved a dishonest commander — juggling accounts, appropriating military stores — on more than one occasion. An aggrieved fellow officer, Lieut. Col. John Brown of Massachusetts, published an attack on Arnold in May 1777 with the characterization, "Money is this man's god, and to get enough of it he would sacrifice his country."

Silhouette of Major André, cut at Philadelphia in 1778 by Miss Rebecca Redman as a keepsake.

Right: Self-portrait by André, who was poet, musician, dramatist as well as artist.

He needed money more than ever as the husband (twice her age) of the exquisite Peggy Shippen. Officers of his rank were receiving as little as $30 month in steadily depreciating Continental currency. It was while military commander of Philadelphia in 1779 that Arnold began his secret dealings with the British that made him an informer months before the plot to turn over West Point to them. Among data Arnold sent through his British contact, Joseph Stansbury (a Philadelphia Tory storekeeper), was the scheduled arrival time of the French expeditionary force under Rochambeau. Stansbury passed Arnold's communications on to Major John André, aide-de-camp then to Maj. Gen. Charles Grey — and an admirer of Peggy Shippen. There is good reason to believe she was aware of Arnold's plotting (if she was not the instigator) during all the months various schemes for Arnold's ultimate aid to the British were under discussion.

André had advanced to adjutant-general on General Henry Clinton's staff in New York, when negotiations reached a climax. Arnold had succeeded in wangling from Washington command of West Point and surrounding fortifications (see map in preceding page) for the specific purpose of selling the key defense of the Hudson to the enemy for a top price. André's position as chief of intelligence for Clinton, as well as knowledge of Arnold, made him Clinton's emis-

Arnold's belated commission from Congress, given after five juniors had been promoted over him.

Portrait of Arnold, engraved for Washington Irving's biography of Washington.

sary to close the deal. He was taken upriver to an agreed rendezvous on the war sloop *Vulture*. The sloop was forced to depart without André and he attempted to return to New York overland, in disguise. Fortunately he was stopped by "cowboys" (irregulars), who made a practice of robbing travelers, with or without passes. They found in André's shoe the papers that were to reveal Arnold a traitor.

Above: Pass written for André as "John Anderson" by Arnold and seized with the prisoner's documents.

Above: "The Last Moments of Major André," an engraving by M. A. Wageman widely circulated in early nineteenth-century America. He had pleaded to be given a soldier's death, by shooting, but was hanged in retaliation for the unceremonious hanging of Nathan Hale.

Burning of Benedict Arnold, in effigy, with a two-faced figure representing the traitor, was carried out on occasion. Cartoon from an old print.

George Washington wrote Henry Laurens, "In no instance since the commencement of the war has the interposition of the Providence appeared more remarkably conspicuous than in the rescue of the post and garrison of West Point from Arnold's villainous perfidy."

He continued, "André has met his fate with the fortitude that was to be expected from an accomplished man and gallant officer, but I am mistaken if this time 'Arnold is undergoing the torment of a mental hell.' He wants feeling. From some traits of his character, which have lately come to my knowledge, he seems to have been so hackneyed in villainy and so lost to all sense of honor and shame, that, while his faculties will enable him to continue his sordid pursuits, there will be no time for remorse."

Arnold had to accept less than surrender of West Point would have brought him: a commission as Brigadier, about £6000 for his property losses and a pension for Peggy. He led Tories and deserters in some raids (in one of which he burned houses in his home town, New London, Connecticut), but was not trusted with higher and independent commands. After the war, when he sought to establish himself in the shipping business in Canada, Arnold was treated with hostility, and went with Peggy and their sons to England. He died in 1801 a nervous wreck, the consequence of debts, rejection and, possibly, remorse. The story that in his last hour Arnold prayed God, "Let me die in my old [American] uniform! Forgive me for ever putting on another," is of doubtful veracity.

André's last words had been, "I am reconciled to my death, but I detest the mode." The corpse was to lie at Tappan, New York, until 1821, when it was removed to a niche at Westminster Abbey. (A monument subsequently raised at the Tappan grave site was destroyed by vandals.)

Jean Baptiste Donatien de Vimeur, Comte de Rochambeau — a French engraving from a life portrait. Although his parents intended him for the priesthood, he succeeded in getting into the French army at seventeen. Four decades later he was the lieutenant-general detailed to command the 6000 troops with which the French monarch began open support of the United States. With an additional 3000 men sent in 1781, Rochambeau marched from Newport, R. I., to rendezvous with Washington's main force at Dobbs Ferry, N. Y., and proceed thence to the envelopment of Cornwallis at Yorktown.

TO ALL BRAVE, HEALTHY, ABLE BO
DISPOSED YOUNG ME
IN THIS NEIGHBOURHOOD, WHO HAVE ANY INCLINAT
NOW RAISING UNDER
GENERAL WASHINGT
FOR THE DEFENCE OF TH
LIBERTIES AND INDEPEN
OF THE UNITED STAT
Againſt the hoſtile deſigns of foreign enemies,

TAKE NOT

Poſition of a Soldier under arms — I. Poiſe Firelock. — II. Cock Firelock. — III. Take Aim — Fire — V. Half C

VIII. Shut Pan. — IX. Charge Cartridge. X. Draw Rammer. — XI. Ram Down Cartridge. — Suppo

B. Jones Sc.

THAT *tuesday, wednesday, thursday, friday*

Middlesex — *Lieutenant Reading* — with his muſic and recruiting party of
Battalion of the 11th regiment of infantry, commanded by Lieutenant Colonel Aaron O
ſuch youth of SPIRIT, as may be willing to enter into this HONOURABLE ſervice.

The ENCOURAGEMENT at this time, to enliſt, is truly liberal and generous, namely, a boun
ſupply of good and handſome cloathing, a daily allowance of a large and ample ration of pro
and SILVER money on account of pay, the whole of which the ſoldier may lay up for himſelf a
comfort are provided by law, without any expence to him.

Thoſe who may favour this recruiting party with their attendance as above, will have an op
manner, the great advantages which theſe brave men will have, who ſhall embrace this opport
different parts of this beautiful continent, in the honourable and truly reſpectable character of a
home to his friends, with his pockets FULL of money and his head COVERED with laurels.

GOD SAVE THE UNITED STATES.

ED, AND WELL

TO JOIN THE TROOPS,

NCE

CE,

VI. Handle Cartridge   VII   Prime

Arms.   Slope   Arms.   Trail   Arms.

Saturday at *Spotswood* in
.... county, attendance will be given by
.... company in *Major Shutes*
or the purpose of receiving the enrollment of

TWELVE dollars, an annual and fully sufficient
............, together with SIXTY dollars a year in GOLD
ds, as all articles proper for his subsistance and

ity of hearing and seeing in a more particular
f spending a few happy years in viewing the
, after which, he may, if he pleases return

Left: Inducements in 1781 to recruits for the decisive campaign of the Continental Army anticipated appeals in this poster in 1799, when war with France threatened and forces were collected again for George Washington's command. Aaron Ogden, commissioned in the First New Jersey Regiment, Continental Line, 1776, served subsequently on staffs of William Maxwell, William Alexander, LaFayette; he was wounded at Yorktown. With the call-up of militia in 1799, Ogden was commissioned Lieutenant-Colonel of 11th U. S. Infantry. In 1812 he was Governor of New Jersey.

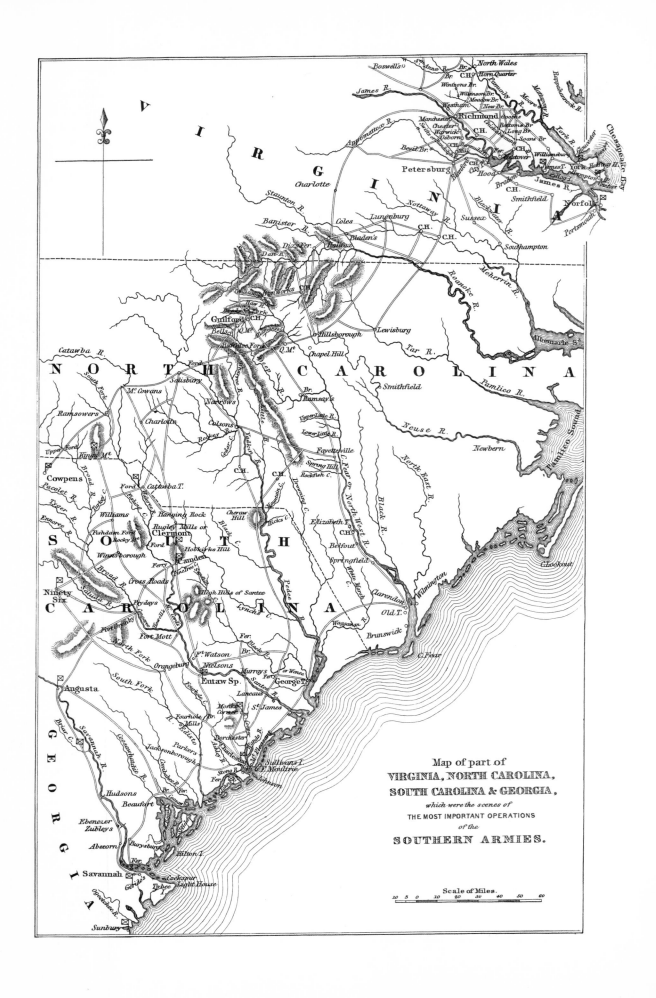

Map of part of
VIRGINIA, NORTH CAROLINA,
SOUTH CAROLINA & GEORGIA,
which were the scenes of
THE MOST IMPORTANT OPERATIONS
of the
SOUTHERN ARMIES.

Scale of Miles.

AS STATED earlier, Clinton had been ordered in March 1778 to send an expedition to Georgia. Savannah remained an American stronghold. With France having effected an alliance, Savannah was a likely entry port for French forces from the West Indies. Maj. Gen. Robert Howe (no relation of the British general Robert Howe), commanded in Georgia. His troops at Savannah numbered about 1000 Continentals and militia.

As 3500 troops detailed by Clinton under Col. Archibald Campbell sailed from New York November 27, Maj. Gen. Augustine Prevost, commander in East Florida, moved northward to join Campbell. Campbell's transports, escorted by Commodore Hyde Parker, Jr., arrived Christmas night without waiting for Prevost. After reconnaissance and contact with spies, Campbell attacked December 29. Howe had heavy losses in a brief stand before retreating to Benjamin Lincoln's camp.

Major General Benjamin Lincoln, a nineteenth-century engraving after a portrait by Henry Sargent. Lincoln, lamed for life by wounds as commander of Gates' right wing in the entrapment of Burgoyne at Saratoga and a captive of the British after the fall of Charleston in 1780, returned to duty in time to participate in Washington's advance, with French support, to surround and force the capitulation of Cornwallis at Yorktown. Washington chose Lincoln to receive Cornwallis' sword from the British general's designee to effect the surrender.

At left: The southern theater of war 1780-81, with cross flags placing such decisive scenes as Savannah, Charleston, Ninety Six, Camden, Cowpens, Kings Mountain, Guilford Court House, Eutaw Springs.

Lincoln fared no better at Savannah when he, with about 2000, joined Count d'Estaing with about 4500 French soldiers, in an attempt to retake the port city. Their assault, October 9, ended in a sanguinary repulse. Among a thousand casualties was Count Casimir Pulaski, fatally wounded in a cavalry charge.

Lincoln was to undergo defeat again the next spring, when General Clinton in person attacked Charleston. Clinton had taken a calculated risk in moving a major force south, leaving only about 10,000 at New York to cope with Washington. Disaster threatened the voyage of ninety transports and ten warships that began December 26, 1779. Storms swept ships out of contact (one of them with 200 Hessian troops was sent drifting all the way to Ireland). Thirty-seven days passed before the expedition confronted Lincoln's garrison of about 1600 Continentals plus militia. Lincoln held off the besiegers eight weeks. On March 12, he surrendered with 5466 officers and men, including seven generals — the largest number of Americans to be surrendered during the war.

Charleston was to remain in British hands in 1782, while other forces left by Clinton under Cornwallis' command were cleared out of the South and forced to surrender at Yorktown.

Seal of the Board of War and Ordnance, 1778. As its President (a position given him by Congress in a flush of gratitude for the victory at Saratoga, Horatio Gates sought to remove Washington as chief commander of the Continental Army in favor of himself. A quarrel and duel with his aide, James Wilkinson, resulted in the Gates conspiracy's being revealed. Whereupon Gates retired from his position and the Army for more than a year, and forty-nine officers of Wilkinson's grade petitioned Congress to rescind Wilkinson's promotion to brigadier-general.

Nathanael Greene, continuing hit-and-run tactics, Indian fashion, sent Daniel Morgan with his riflemen, William Washington's legion of Henry Lee's mounted corps and a regiment of Maryland Line across Broad River to operate on Cornwallis' left and rear. Informed of the movement, Cornwallis broke camp at Winnsborough and pushed northward between the Broad and Catawba Rivers to get his army between Greene and Morgan with the intention of destroying them separately. He detached Banastre Tarleton, with some 1100 dragoons and infantry, to see that Morgan didn't escape.

Morgan, detecting his danger, maneuvered to fight on ground of his choice. This was on rising ground at "the Cowpens," some thirty miles west of King's Mountain. He placed Colonel John Howard's Maryland infantry in the center, with the Virginia riflemen on the wings, and Colonel William Washington's dragoons in the rear — hidden by woods — as a reserve. Carolinians and Georgians who had rallied around Colonel Andrew Pickens, were in advance, to ambush approachers to the position, and to skirmish on the flanks.

Tarleton broke through and, seeing Morgan's troops falling back in seeming disorder, assumed victory was at hand. But Morgan had prepared a surprise: his infantry, reversing a feigned retreat, charged the British lines with volleys and bayonets. Simultaneously, William Washington's legion dashed from concealment and struck at Tarleton's horsemen, with Washington personally charging upon Tarleton. The British advance turned into a rout, and Tarleton, wounded in the onset, had difficulty in getting away with any of his men in a twenty-mile pursuit.

The British loss at Cowpens was over 200 killed and wounded, 600 captured. They abandoned in the flight some cannon surrendered by Burgoyne at Saratoga, and recaptured by the British from Gates at Camden.

Upon receipt of the news brought by courier, George Washington phrased a congratulatory letter to Congress on Morgan's victory at Cowpens over Tarleton and the flower of the British army. "It reflects the highest honor on our arms, and I hope that it will at last be attended with this advantage: that it will check

Dan Morgan

Another drawing of a Morgan rifleman (*see page 123*), and representation of banner of XI Virginia Regiment, of which he was Colonel, 1776. In 1780, Congress made him brigadier-general.

the offensive operations of the enemy until General Greene shall have collected a much more respectable force than he had under his command by the last accounts from him." Thus he chided Congress for neglect of Greene's needs in men, clothing, equipment, ammunition, food, while Greene strove to make a new army of the forces shattered under Gates at Camden.

It should be recalled in connection with Morgan's employment of his riflemen as shock troops that in 1777 Washington had suggested: "It occurs to me, that if you were to dress a company or two of the woodsmen in Indian style, and let them make the attack screaming and yelling, as the Indians do, it would have very good consequences. . . ."

It is easy to imagine the effect on British soldiers who had heard wild tales of Indian savagery when suddenly beset in a wilderness terrain.

"Conflict Between Colonels Washington and Tarleton" January 8, 1781 — an engraving after a painting by Alonzo Chappel. William Washington and Tarleton were wounded in the encounter, but both rode away uncaptured. "The wound that Tarleton received from Washington was the subject of sallies by several American ladies," it was recounted. A daughter of Joseph Montford heard the dashing ladies' man Tarleton say later, with sarcasm, "I would be happy to see this Washington," whereupon she replied, "If you had looked behind you, Colonel, at the battle of Cowpens, you would have had that pleasure." (Engraving from John Frederick Schroeder's *Life and Times of George Washington*.)

Cornwallis Retreating!

PHILADELPHIA, April 7, 1781.

Extract of a Letter from Major-General *Greene*, dated CAMP, at *Buffelo Creek, March* 23, 1781.

"ON the 16th Inftant I wrote your Excellency, giving an Account of an Action which happened at Guilford Court-Houfe the Day before. I was then perfuaded that notwithftanding we were obliged to give up the Ground, we had reaped the Advantage of the Action. Circumftances fince confirm me in Opinion that the Enemy were too much gauled to improve their Succefs. We lay at the Iron-Works three Days, preparing ourfelves for another Action, and expecting the Enemy to advance: But of a fudden they took their Departure, leaving behind them evident Marks of Diftrefs. All our wounded at Guilford, which had fallen into their Hands, and 70 of their own, too bad to move, were left at New-Garden. Moft of their Officers fuffered-- Lord Cornwallis had his Horfe fhot under him--- Col. Steward, of the Guards was killed, General O Hara and Cols, Tarlton and Webfter, wounded. Only three Field-Officers efcaped, if Reports, which feem to be authentic, can be relied on.

Our Army are in good Spirits, notwithftanding our Sufferings, and are advancing towards the Enemy; they are retreating to Crofs-Creek.

In South-Carolina, Generals Sumpter and Marian have gained feveral little Advantages. In one the Enemy loft 60 Men, who had under their Care a large Quantity of Stores, which were taken, but by an unfortunate Miftake were afterwards re taken.

Publifhed by Order,
CHARLES THOMSON, Secretary.

§†§ Printed at N. WILLIS's Office.

Major General Thomas Sumter (*left*), Major General Francis Marion (*above*) and news broadside issued at Philadelphia with supplementary information on the British reverse at Guilford Court House, in North Carolina, March 15, 1781. Greene's report was sent to the President of the Congress. Note that names of Sumter and Marion have misspellings.

THE LOSSES of Charleston and Lincoln's army left the American cause with Francis Marion and Thomas Sumter as the only effective opponents of the British in the two States. That is, until mountain men from Kentucky and Tennessee rose with their fellow frontiersmen in western North Carolina and South Carolina against Patrick Ferguson's detachment from Cornwallis' army and Tory partisans at King's Mountain, in October 1780, the same month Washington sent Nathanael Greene south with Continentals to reorganize resistance.

Marion, a veteran of Indian wars before the Revolution, played an important part in repulsing a British attack at Charleston in 1776. Transferred from the militia to the Continental Army, he continued notable service, and was a regimental commander with Lincoln at the Savannah fiasco and in the defense of Charleston.

He escaped the surrender there, and sought to join the army Washington had sent with Johann Kalb to carry on the war in the Carolinas. But finding Horatio Gates had persuaded Congress to give him Kalb's place as commander of the Southern Department, Marion returned to South Carolina to recruit a guerrilla band. The hit-and-run tactics of Marion's men, who used swamps as bases, achieved such remarkable successes that the British credited Marion with having five to ten times his actual force.

Sumter, a sergeant of Virginia troops in the French and Indian War, had a rifle regiment early in the Revolution, then fought Cherokees on the frontier. After the British had crushed organized resistance in the Carolinas Sumter raised partisan militia that paralleled in North Carolina Marion's operations to the south. The obvious inability of Cornwallis to suppress Marion and Sumter revived spirit and support for the patriot cause in the Carolinas, and set the stage for Nathanael Greene's victory at Guilford Court House (N.C.) — the turning of the tide in the South after five years of reverses.

One important battle remained to be fought in South Carolina after Cowpens, where Nathanael Greene, with Dan Morgan and William Washington, dealt 200 casualties and took 600 prisoners (with a loss of seventy-two). At Eutaw Springs, September 8, 1781, Greene had "Lighthorse Harry" Lee's cavalry as well as William Washington's, Francis Marion's legion, the militia of Thomas Sumter under substitute command (Sumter was on sick leave). The total, about 2500, gave him a numerical advantage in the fierce fighting that ensued when he attacked Colonel Alexander Stewart's detachment (estimated at 2000). Although Greene was denied a clear-cut victory, the losses he inflicted on Stewart were so heavy (approximately 700 killed, wounded, missing — the biggest percentage suffered by any force in the entire war) he forced the latter's retreat to cover at Charleston. Stewart could no longer give any support to Cornwallis, if the latter should turn back south.

An Alonzo Chappel representation of second phase of battle at Eutaw Springs, September 8, 1781. William Washington was severely wounded (see right) while leading his dragoons. He fell into British hands as the Americans, who had lost heavily in the counterattack, had to fall back before nightfall. (Engraving from author's collection.)

Nathanael Greene and, above him, obverse and reverse of medal voted him for victory at Eutaw Springs, South Carolina, September 8, 1781. Engraving by H. B. Hall, Jr., from a portrait.

While the French forces under D'Estaing were disappointingly ineffective in the South, those under Rochambeau at Newport were disappointingly inactive from the arrival in July 1780 until the next year. Washington kept the Continental Army all winter at New Windsor, New York, where concerted action could be easily taken with the French. No action was taken until, after proddings by George Washington in two conferences with Rochambeau, the decision was made for the two armies to conjoin for an attack on New York City.

After the rendezvous, reconnaissance with 5000 men against northern defenses of Manhattan Island convinced them an effective attack was beyond their means in the absence of naval superiority. Then, in August, news came that Admiral Comte de Grasse was heading for Chesapeake Bay from the West Indies with twenty-nine ships-of-war and transports with 3500 troops. Washington now had news of Cornwallis' taking up a position in the Yorktown Peninsula as a base for further operations in Virginia. Here was an opportunity! On August 20 Washington had completed disposition of troops to protect the line of the Hudson and his flank in New Jersey as the armies moved south. September 9 Washington saw Mount Vernon for the first time in six years. September 15, he was at Yorktown Peninsula, entrapping Cornwallis.

EXCERPTS from the diary GW resumed in May 1781 after a hiatus since June 1775:

Aug. 14. "Received dispatches announcing the intended departure of Count de Grasse from Cap François [San Domingo] . . . on the 3d. instance for Chesapeake Bay and the anxiety of the latter to have every thing in the most perfect readiness to commence our operations in the moment of his arrival as he should be under a necessity from particular engagements with the Spaniards to be in the West Indies by the Middle of October . . ."

Aug. 15. "Dispatched a Courier to the Marquis de la Fayette with information of this matter . . . requesting him to prevent if possible the retreat of Cornwallis towards Carolina . . ."

Aug. 16. "Letters from the Marqs. de la Fayette and others, inform that Lord Cornwallis . . . had proceeded up the York River and landed at York and Gloucester Towns where they were throwin up Works on the 6th Inst."

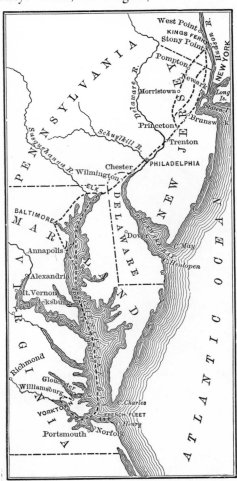

Route of Washington's troops with the reenforcements from France, in the advance from the Hudson afoot and by transport to investment of Yorktown.

Washington's traveling writing case, with compartments for paper, his pen, extra quills, sealing wax. Besides seal-ring, he had two watch-charm seals. One of latter, lost on the battlefield of Braddock's defeat in 1755, was found in 1854 and returned to the Washington family. It is at Mount Vernon.

Sept. 5. "The rear of the French Army having reached Philadelphia and the American's having passed it. The Stores having got up and everything in a tolerable Train here: I left this city [Philadelphia] for the Head of Elk [Elkton, Md.] to hasten the Embarkation at that place and on my way (at Chester) received the agreeable news of the safe arrival of the Count de Grasse wuth 28 Sail of the line and four frigates, with 3000 land Troops which were to be immediately debarked at James town and form a junction under the command of the Marqs. de la Fayette. . . . Judging it highly expedient to be with the Army in Virginia as soon as possible, to make the necessary arrangements for the siege, I . . . with the Count de Rochambeau who requested to attend me, and the Chevr. de Chastellux set out . . ."

Sept. 15. ". . . reached Williamsburg. The necessity of seeing and agreeing upon a proper

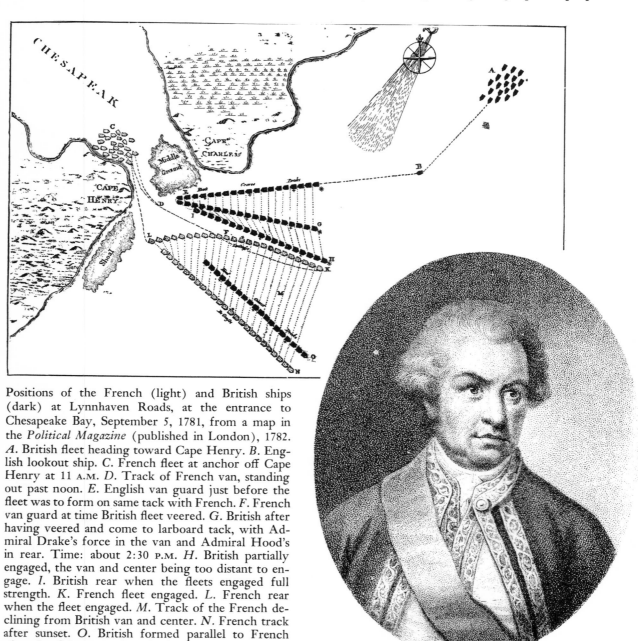

Positions of the French (light) and British ships (dark) at Lynnhaven Roads, at the entrance to Chesapeake Bay, September 5, 1781, from a map in the *Political Magazine* (published in London), 1782. *A.* British fleet heading toward Cape Henry. *B.* English lookout ship. *C.* French fleet at anchor off Cape Henry at 11 A.M. *D.* Track of French van, standing out past noon. *E.* English van guard just before the fleet was to form on same tack with French. *F.* French van guard at time British fleet veered. *G.* British after having veered and come to larboard tack, with Admiral Drake's force in the van and Admiral Hood's in rear. Time: about 2:30 P.M. *H.* British partially engaged, the van and center being too distant to engage. *I.* British rear when the fleets engaged full strength. *K.* French fleet engaged. *L.* French rear when the fleet engaged. *M.* Track of the French declining from British van and center. *N.* French track after sunset. *O.* British formed parallel to French after the firing ceased on both sides.

plan of co-operation with the Count de Grasse induced me to make him a visit at Cape Henry where he lay with his fleet after a partial engagement with the British Squadron off the Capes under the Command of Admiral Graves whom he had driven back to Sandy Hook."

Sept. 28. "Having debarked all the Troops and their Baggage, Marched and Encamped them in Front of the City [Williamsburg], having with some difficulty obtained horses and Waggons sufficient to move our artillery . . . we commenced our March for the Investiture of the Enemy . . ."

Sept. 30. "The Enemy abandoned all their exterior works and the position they had taken without the Town; and retired within their Interior works of defense in the course of last Night. . . ."

Oct. 6. "Before Morning the Trenches were in such forwardness as to cover the Men from the enemys fire. The work was executed with so much secrecy and dispatch that the enemy were, I believe, totally ignorant of our labor till the light of the Morning discovered it to them. Our loss on this occasion was extremely inconsider-

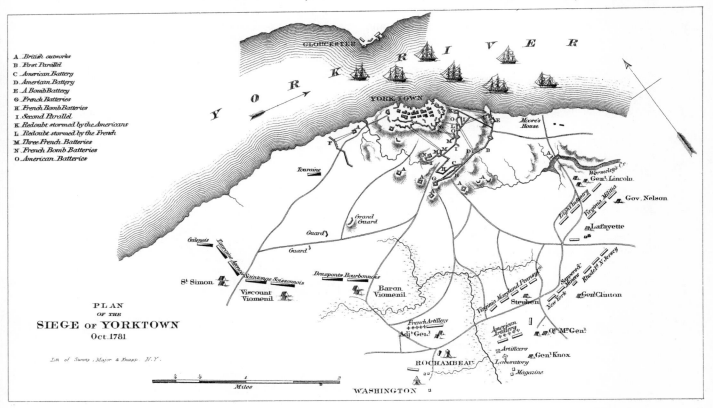

A . British outworks
B . First Parallel
C . American Battery
D . American Battery
E . A Bomb Battery
G . French Batteries
H . French Bomb Batteries
I . Second Parallel
K . Redoubt stormed by the Americans
L . Redoubt stormed by the French
M . Three French Batteries
N . French Bomb Batteries
O . American Batteries

PLAN
OF THE
SIEGE OF YORKTOWN
Oct. 1781

Lith of Sarony, Major & Knapp, N.Y.

Opposite page: Francois Joseph Paul, Comte de Grasse, an engraving by J. Chapman from a portrait for which the admiral posed. Member of one of Bourbon France's oldest aristocrat families, he entered naval school at eleven. When the American War of Independence began, De Grasse was Captain of a frigate; he was promoted to Commodore in 1778; given the rank of Admiral the day he sailed from Brest in 1781 with twenty-three warships and a convoy of some 150 ships for the West Indies — and with orders to provide the forces of Comte de Rochambeau with any feasible support. He thus was enabled to be of providential and decisive aid in the Yorktown siege.

Plan of the siege of Yorktown, September-October 1781. Note, at far right, position of home of Thomas Nelson, Jr., signer of the Declaration of Independence and at time of the siege Governor of Virginia. Cornwallis had taken over the house as his headquarters. Present at the siege as ex-officio commander of Virginia militia, Nelson had the militia's heaviest guns directed at the stone mansion and its British occupants. The residence underwent severe damage. It is tradition that Cornwallis moved to a cave for safety and attempted to arrange an escape (leaving his army to its fate) before he opened negotiations with Washington for surrender.

able, but more than one Officer (French) and about 20 Men killed and wounded; the Officer and 15 of which were on our left from the Corps of the Marqs. de St. Simond, who was betrayed by a deserter . . ."

Oct. 9. "About 3 o'clock P.M. the French opened a battery on our extreme left . . . and at 5 o'clock an American battery . . . began to play from the extremity of our right. Both with good effect as they compelled the enemy to withdraw from their ambrazures the Pieces which had previously kept up a constant firing."

Oct. 15. "Busily employed in getting the Batteries of the Second parallel compleated, and fixing on New ones contiguous to the Redoubts which were taken last Night . . ."

Oct. 17. "About ten o'clock the Enemy beat a parley, and Lord Cornwallis proposed a cessation of Hostilities for 24 hours, that Commissioners might meet . . . to settle terms for the surrender . . ."

There was no entry for Oct. 26. That day, Washington entertained his recent foe at dinner. In toasting his guest he assured him that "England would yet have reason to be proud of so gallant an officer." In reply, Cornwallis said, "When the illustrious part that your Excellency has borne in this long and arduous contest becomes a matter of history, fame will gather your brightest laurels rather from the banks of the Delaware than from those of the Chesapeake."

Before his death, Cornwallis said he personally opposed Britain's use of armed force in the America; he had accepted command against the colonists as a military duty.

Oct. 28, GW sent off a dispatch to Philadelphia, "Our operations against the Enemy in this State being concluded, it becomes my Duty to inform Congress of the future destination of the troops under my Command." In brief, a large detachment was sent to reinforce Nathanael Greene in South Carolina, and Benjamin Lincoln

Final clause of terms of capitulation, as signed by Cornwallis and aide. The cipher 1 in date October 19 is indistinct in reproduction. "No article of capitulation is to be infringed on pretense of reprisals; and if there be any doubtful expressions in it, they are to be interpreted according to the common meaning and acceptation of the words," is the phraseology. Some of preceding clauses:

Cornwallis permitted use of a sloop-of-war to send an aide-de-camp to New York with dispatches for the British c.-in-c., Henry Clinton.

Natives of the region "not to be punished on account of having joined the British army."

Both officers and soldiers to keep their private property of every kind, and no part of their baggage to be at any time subject to search or inspection.

Some 550 of the 7157 surrendered by Cornwallis were in American Tory units from North Carolina, Virginia, New Jersey, New York.

Cornwallis spent no time as prisoner. He was paroled and eventually exchanged for Henry Laurens, President of Continental Congress, 1777-8. Laurens went on a mission to the Netherlands in 1779 and captured when his ship was taken by a British man-of-war. Cornwallis was not censured in England for his surrender, and later was given high British posts in India and Ireland.

Washington at Yorktown, by Rembrandt Peale — a photograph of the original distributed by United States George Washington Bicentennial Commission in 1932. A heroic painting of the surrender scene by John Trumbull at the national Capitol has many anachronisms besides placing Cornwallis facing Washington at his ceremony, instead of his delegating surrender of his sword to General Charles O'Hara.

was sent northward with troops. "I shall myself return to my former position on the North River."

John Parke Custis had been sent ill while with his stepfather at Yorktown, as an aide-de-camp, and had been taken to the home of his aunt, Mrs. Burwell Bassett, some thirty miles from Yorktown. Martha and John's wife had gone to the bedside. Washington rode there as soon as he could leave his army. He arrived less than a hour before Mrs. Washington's last surviving child died of what was described as "camp fever" (possibly typhus), at the age of twenty-six. GW remained several days, as long as he could, superintending the funeral and sustaining his deeply stricken mother and wife. Martha left a sickbed to go with the son's wife to her beloved "Jackie," whom she had spoiled and made a continuous problem to her second husband.

Washington did not part from Martha after the funeral; he took her with him to Annapolis, where he had to endure receptions, dinners and recitations of poetry, while sharing his wife's grief, and on to Philadelphia, where there were friends to look after her while he attended to pressing business with Congress. He was fearful, as he wrote Nathanael Greene, "that Congress,

viewing this stroke [Yorktown] in too favorable a light, may think that our work is nearly closed, and will fall into a state of languor and relaxation. . . . To prevent this error, I shall use every means in my power."

There was no assurance that the British would not send more troops to America and resume the offensive. There were no signs at New York, Charleston or in the naval forces of relaxation.

Broadside circulated at Providence was typical of "extras" issued by provincial printers as rapidly as couriers brought the news to officials of the new States. Over fifteen months was to pass before ministers of George III proclaimed the effectiveness of the quadripartite treaties among Britain, U.S.A., United Provinces [Netherlands] and Spain negotiated at Paris in November 1782.

During the winter at Philadelphia, Washington talked to congressmen; he danced and exchanged pleasantries at dinner parties with ladies who had influence upon their husbands.

April 1, 1782, he was at Newburgh, the position he had chosen for the Army for a period of watchful waiting. Martha was with him. The waiting was to go on for months more. Spies he had recruited and organized efficiently in New York from 1776 onward kept him informed on whether Clinton was preparing for action; and regular dispatches from Greene were assurance that no campaign was in the making at Charleston. In September, GW felt that prospects of peace were vanishing instead of improving.

Meanwhile grievances among officers, fomented by arrears in pay and failure of Congress to make any provisions for grants or pensions, threatened another mutiny such as Washington had to deal with at Morristown in May 1780, when two Connecticut regiments were unruly, and in January 1781, again at Morristown, when there were disorders among Pennsylvania and New Jersey Line regiments who had grievances similar to those at Newburgh.

The French armies sailed away in November. Early in December the British gave up Charleston. But Washington's army had to continue to mark time at Newburgh until a stubborn George III agreed to terms reached in Paris by a British emissary, Richard Oswald, with Congress' Commissioners, Benjamin Franklin and John Jay, during discussions that began in June 1782. A provisional treaty, effective in January 1783, was followed by the final treaty signed at Paris in September and approved by Congress January 14, 1784, when Washington was already in retirement at Mount Vernon.

Washington's headquarters at Newburgh, an illustration drawn and engraved by James Smillie for Irving's *Life of Washington*. The Hasbrouck house, begun in 1725 and enlarged in 1749 and 1770, has been restored as part of a historical park that includes a museum and a commemorative Tower of Victory.

One of the original certificates of membership in the Society of Cincinnati, signed by Henry Knox as Secretary and Washington as President. It was issued in 1785 to Robert Wilson, "an Ensign in the First New York City Regt." *Below:* Seal of the organization and badge. *Right:* One of pamphlets that soon attacked the Society as a political menace.

CONSIDERATIONS

ON THE

SOCIETY or ORDER

OF

CINCINNATI;

LATELY INSTITUTED

By the Major-Generals, Brigadier-Generals, and other Officers of the AMERICAN ARMY.

PROVING THAT IT CREATES

A RACE of HEREDITARY PATRICIANS,

OR

NOBILITY.

INTERSPERSED WITH REMARKS

On its CONSEQUENCES to the FREEDOM and HAPPINESS of the REPUBLIC.

Addreffed to the PEOPLE of SOUTH-CAROLINA, and their REPRESENTATIVES.

By CASSIUS.

Suppofed to be written by ÆDANUS BURKE, Efquire, one of the Chief Juftices of the State of South Carolina.

Blow ye the Trumpet in Zion. The BIBLE.

PHILADELPHIA

Printed and Sold by ROBERT BELL, in *Third-Street.*

Price, *one-fixth of a Dollar.* M,DCC,LXXXIII.

Above: Washington leading what remained of his command into New York City, 1783. (From a print in New-York Historical Society collection.)

Right: Broadside giving the program of the reception to Governor Clinton and Washington, and expressing the hope that citizens would "conduct themselves with Decency and Decorum on this Joyful Occasion." The "Bull's Head" was a tavern.

TO Colonel Lewis Nichola's suggestion in 1782 that George Washington should take advantage of the discontent of the Army and the dilatory action of Congress and "Assume the Crown of America," Washington sent an indignant rebuke: "If you have any regard for your country . . . or respect for me, banish these thoughts from your mind." Yet in 1783, opposition arose to the Society of Cincinnati formed by officers of the Continental Army with Washington as head. The purposes were provision of aid for widows and orphans of war dead, and effecting of a closer union among the States. But it was accused of having as its design the setting up of a hereditary nobility or aristocracy.

New-York, Nov. 24, 1783.

The Committee appointed to conduct the Order of receiving their Excellencies Governor CLINTON and General WASHINGTON,

BEG Leave to inform their Fellow-Citizens, that the Troops, under the Command of Major-General KNOX, will take Possession of the City at the Hour agreed on, Tuesday next ; as soon as this may be performed, he will request the Citizens who may be assembled on Horseback, at the Bowling-Green, the lower End of the Broad-Way, to accompany him to meet their Excellencies Governor CLINTON and General WASHINGTON, at the Bull's Head, in the Bowery---the Citizens on Foot to assemble at or near the Tea-water-Pump at Fresh-water.

ORDER of PROCESSION.

A Party of Horse will precede their Excellencies and be on their flanks---after the General and Governor, will follow the Lieutenant-Governor and Members of the Council for the temporary Government of the Southern Parts of the State---The Gentlemen on Horse-back, eight in Front---those on Foot, in the Rear of the Horse, in like Manner. Their Excellencies, after passing down Queen-Street, and the Line of Troops up the Broadway, will a-light at CAPE's Tavern.

The Committee hope to see their Fellow-Citizens, conduct themselves with Decency and Decorum on this joyful Occasion.

CITIZENS TAKE CARE!!!

THE Inhabitants are hereby informed, that Permission has been obtained from the Commandant, to form themselves in patroles this night, and that every order requisite will be given to the guards, as well to aid and assist, as to give protection to the patroles: And that the countersign will be given to THOMAS TUCKER, No. 51, Water Street ; from whom it can be obtained, if necessary.

THERE were no triumphal receptions for Horatio Gates, victor over Burgoyne at Saratoga, for whom a coterie in Congress had sought to displace Washington as C.-in-C., or for Charles Lee, who earlier had sought to supplant Washington. Events had proven the likelihood of either man's being a disastrous choice for tasks Washington carried out.

The worst about Lee was not discovered until long after the war. He had sought to enter into a treasonable conspiracy with the British while their prisoner-of-war.

Almost a year and a half elapsed between Lee's capture by British dragoons at his hq., in Basking Ridge, N.J., and his exchange. There were two reasons. Inasmuch as Lee had been a lieutenant-colonel in the British army in retirement on half pay when the Revolution began, General Howe regarded him as a deserter. Lee was on a ship, ordered to London for trial, when Washington put a stop to the proceedings. He notified Howe that five Hessian field-officers were being held as hostages for Lee's personal safety. Subsequently, Howe's superior in London, informed of the situation, approved Lee's having the status of prisoner of war subject to exchange. Mean-

"Washington's Farewell to His Officers," an engraving by Phillibrown after a painting by Alonzo Chappel. The scene, "Black Sam" Fraunces' Tavern, had been one of Washington's headquarters in 1776. The old home of Etienne de Lancey, a Huguenot emigré, had been converted into a tavern in 1762. (Restored by the Sons of the Revolution, it functions today as museum and tavern open to the general public.)

while, Lee sought to make his safety more certain.

He finagled a meeting with the two Howes, general and admiral, and encouraged belief he might secure a conference with members of the Congress and initiate negotiations for a settlement of difficulties between the Colonies and the royal government. The Howes, who had a degree of sympathy for the American cause, and had sought negotiations earlier, futilely, allowed Lee to send messages to members of Congress. His proposal was refused but, oddly, did not rouse any suspicions of Lee's intentions. The Howes also continued to believe in Lee's reliability, and gave consideration to plans he drew up for a campaign in 1777 against what he considered weak positions in the American defenses. The plans were followed to some extent, but ineffectually, and General Howe consented to Lee's being exchanged in May 1777, whereupon Lee returned to Washington's command.

Obviously, if Washington had any knowledge or suspicion of Lee's dealings with the British in as treasonable a manner as Benedict Arnold's were to be, he would not have given him the command and opportunity that enabled Lee to mess up Washington's tactics at the Battle of Monmouth.

The record of Gates, also a former officer in the British regulars, has something to admire rather than to condemn, though his performance was marred by the rout at Camden, as well as by

Engraving of Horatio Gates, in *Impartial History of the War in America* (London: 1780). The scroll's heading, Articles of Capitulation, alludes to 1777.

Charles Lee. Though intended as a caricature, "it was allowed by all who knew Lee to be the only successful delineation" of him, a contemporary said.

his intrigues to take Washington's position as C.-in-C. Relieved by Nathanael Greene as commander in the South after the Camden defeat, Gates was under suspension and investigation, when victory was won at Yorktown. Acquitted in 1782 of neglect of duty (but tacitly condemned for poor judgment), Gates retired to an estate in Virginia. Unpopular among Virginians who admired Washington, he emancipated his slaves, made provision for their existence as free persons and removed to New York. There, Mrs. Gates and the General occupied themselves in alleviating the distress of soldiers who were indigent. Thaddeus Kosciusko, wounded and impoverished, lay six months at the Gates home, nursed by the Gateses themselves. Though deficient in merits as a soldier, Gates had many redeeming virtues.

A quiet evening at home in Mount Vernon.

VII

ACCOUNTS RENDERED

"I am growing old in my country's service, and losing my sight; but I never doubted its gratitude."

— GEORGE WASHINGTON, 1783

WASHINGTON, in accepting command of the Continental forces in June 1775, had told the Congress, "I do not wish to make any profit from it. I will keep an exact account of my expense . . . and that is all I desire." In four following pages are reproductions of pages from the account-book he submitted in 1783. Note in first sheet of the recapitulation, with asterisk, "Expended for secret intelligence," and the annotation in the subsequent page, "Altho' I kept mem's of these Expenditures I did not introduce them into my Public accounts as they occurred — the reason was, it appeared at first view in the commencement of them, to have the complexion of a private charge. . . ."

More than a century and a half was to pass before patient detective and deductive work was to develop comprehensive information on the persons to whom payments were made by Washington for intelligence work — Robert Townsend, Abraham Woodhull, Benjamin Tallmadge, Caleb Brewster, Austin Roe, the unforgettably named Hercules Mulligan and James Rivington were the few identified in New York, besides Nathan Hale. Rivington's double role as editor-publisher of *The Royal Gazette* and espionage operator for Washington was established clearly for the first time in *A Peculiar Service*, by Corey Ford (Little, Brown & Co., 1965.)

Accounts,
G. Washington — with the
United States,
Commencing June 1775,
and ending June
1783,
Comprehending a Space
of 8 Years.

	Dollars	Lawful		
To Household Expences (Exclusive of the Provisions had from the Commissaries & Contractors —and Liquors &c.? from them & others). viz.				
M.ʳ Austins Acc.ᵗ N.° 1 £496–19..⁹				
M.ʳˢ Smiths D.° 2				
£563.12 9 ½ C.ᵗ.eq.ᵗ to —— 422–4–				
Major Gibbs's —— 3 —483–6 & 65,990				
Cap.ᵗⁿ Colfax —— 4 –1984.15 & 3260		3387	14	4
Total H.ᵈ Expenditures — 69,250 & 3387	69,250	3387	14	4
Expended for Secret Intelligence ——* — 7617 & 1982	7617	1982	10	—
Ditto in Reconnoitring —& in travelling— sometimes with, & sometimes without the Army —but generally with a Party of Horse ———————— 42,755 ½ –1874	42,755½	1874	8	8
Miscellaneous charges amounts p.ʳ Acc.ᵗ to — 40,451½ & 2952	40,451½	2952	10	1
Total —— 160,074 10,197	160,074	10,197	3	1
To 160,074 Dollars extended in Lawful money according to the Scale of depreciation — p.ᵈ Contra		6114	14	—
Expenditures of 8 Years —— £ 16311 17 1		£ 16311	17	1

* 200 Guineas advanced Gen.ᶜ M.ᶜDougall for the like purpose is not included in this sum as I have had no controul of it & know nothing of the Application.—

Years 1775,6,7,8 &9_ and for 1780,1,2,&3

			Dollˢ._ Lawful		

1775
a
1777   By amount of several Sums received pᵉ Acct. to the date hereof._ _ _ _ _ _ _ _ _ £3126·7·9

1783 July 15   By Ditto receiv ed since to the present date_ _ _ 160,074 #6450·7·—

By 160,074 Dollars turned into Lawful money by the Scale of depreciation Adopted by Congress as. follow ~ _ viz_ _ _ _ _ _ _

When Recᵈ		Dollars		Value in Lawfˡ Monᵉʸ	When Recᵈ		Dollars		Valueiʳ Lawfˡ Money
Year	Month	Nomiaˡ	By deprekation		Year	Month	Nomˡ & By depreci		
1777	Feb.	2610	2610	£782-10-0		Broᵗ up	28710	16441	£4989-18-0
	Apr	1000	1000	300 _		Apˡ	2000	180	_54
	May	1000	1000	300 _		June	3000	220	_66-12
	July	1000	1000	300 _		Sep	2000	110	_33 _
		1000	1000	300 _		Nov	3000	129	_38-14
	Aug	_500	_500	_150 _		Dec	3000	114	_34·4
		1000	1000	300 _	1780	Jan	3000	102	30-12
	Oct.	1000	911	273·6 _		Feb.	5000	130	_39 _
		1000	_911	273·6 _		Mar	3000	_78	_23·8 _
	Dec	1000	_754	226·4 _		ᵉ	3000	_75	_22·10 _
1778	Jan	2000	1370	411 _ _		Apˡ	3000	_75	_22·10 _
		1000	_685	205·10 _		May	4000	100	_30 _
	Apˡ	1000	497	_146·2 _			4800	120	_36 _
	May	2000	868	_260·8 _		June	4300	108	_32·8 _
	June	2000	_756	_226·16 _			10,000	250	_75 _ _
	Aug	2000	_574	172·4 _		Aug	5000	125	_37·10 _
		100	_29	_8·14 _		Sep	8000	200	_60 _
	Sep.	1000	250	_75 _			5000	125	_37·10 _
	Nov	2000	366	109·16 _		Nov	1000	_25	_7·10 _
	Dec	2000	_314	_94·4 _	1781	Feb	9264	231	_69·6 _
1779	Mar	2000	_200	_60 _		May	30,000	_750	_225 _
		500	_50	_15 _		May	20,000	_500	_150 _
		28710	16441	4989-18-0			160,074	20,393	Amᵗ Jˢˡ fᵒ _6114·14·0

1783 July 15   By. Ballᵉ due G. Washington &carrᵈ to New Accᵗ folio 65 _ _ _ _ _ _ _620·8·4

£ 16,311·17·1

Note,

104,364, of the above Dollars were receivᵈ after March 1780_ and altho' credited at 40 for £ many of them did not fetch 1 for a hundᵈ Whilst 27,775 of them are returnᵈ withᵗ deductᵍ any thing from the above Accᵗ

G. Washington

1783. July.		Lawful		
1.	To Ball. bro.t from folio 50 ———	£620	8	4
	To Interest of £599.,19.,11. being the Ball. due me Dec.r 31.t 1776 — the amount having been applied to Public uses in the preceeding year — from whence to w.t July 1.st 1775 I charge Int.t at 6 p.r C.t p.r Ann ———	288	—	—
	To M.rs Washington's travell.g Exp.s in coming to & return.g from my Winter Quarters p.r Acc.ts rendered — The Money to defray which being taken from my private Purse, & brought with her from Virg. *—	1064	1	0
		£1972	9	4

* Altho' I kept Mem.ms of these Expenditures I did not introduce them into my Public Accounts as they occurred — the reason was, it appeared at first view, in the commencement of them, to have the complexion of a private charge — I had my doubts therefore of the propriety of mak.g it — But the peculiar circumstances attending my Command, and the embarrassed situation of our Public affairs which obliged me (to the no small detriment of my private Interest) to post =pone the visit I every year contemplated to make my Family between the close of one Campaign and opening of another — and as this expence was in= cidental thereto, & consequent of my self denial. I have, as of right I think I ought, upon due con= sideration adjudged the charge as just with respect to the Public as it is convenient with respect to myself; and I make it with less reluctance as I find upon the final adjustm.t of these Acc.ts (which have, as will appear, been ling unsettled) that I am a considerable looser

.—my

„Swith ___ G. Washington ___ 6" No 56

_ My disbursements falling a good deal short of my receipts, & the money I had upon hand of my own ___ For besides the sum I carried with me to Cambridge in 1775 (and which exceeded the aforementioned Ball. of £599~19-11.) I received Monies afterwards on private acc.t in 1777, and since which, except small sums that I had occasion now & then to apply to private uses, were all expended in the Public service ___ And thro hurry, I suppose, & the perplexity of business (for I know not how else to acc.t for the deficiency) I have omitted to charge — whilst every debit against me is here credited

July 1.st 1783.

G. Washington

Five-pound Virginia colonial note with John Blair, later Associate Justice of the U.S. as a signer.

"Experience has demonstrated the impracticability long to maintain a paper credit without funds for its redemption. The long depreciation of our currency was in the main a necessary effect of the want of those funds; and its restoration is impossible for the same reason, to which

Specimen of first issue, 1775, of currency authorized by Second Congress: it entitled bearer to receive "twenty Spanish milled dollars or value thereof."

Obverse of Massachusetts twenty-four-shilling note "issued in defense of American Liberty" — *Ense petit placidam sub Libertate Quietem* is added for literates.

Currency — such as this eight-dollar note — was issued in name of "United Colonies" before the Declaration of Independence. Spanish dollars specified.

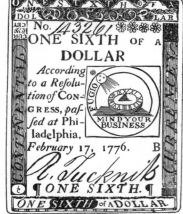 

Obverse and reverse of fractional dollar note for which Congress gave printing contract to Franklin's former partner, David Hall, and William Sellers.

Each colonial note had hand-signature of one or more officials. The J. Franklin who inscribed this six-dollar denomination was not a relative of Ben.

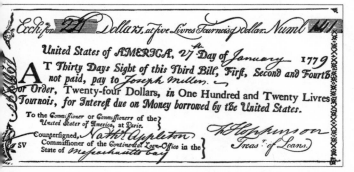

Draft of Massachusetts branch of Continental loan-office on funds held by U.S. Commissioners at Paris, for interest payment in *livres tournois*, on debts.

Although the Declaration of Independence for which Virginia called had been adopted July 4, the Virginia Convention on July 17 authorized currency in British denominations: shillings and pence.

the general diffidence that has taken place among the people is an additional and, in the present state of things, an insuperable obstacle," Washington had written to John Laurens in 1781. And now he personally, as well as the emerging nation, faced the problem of placing finances on a sound basis.

"The indisposition of the individual States to yield competent powers to Congress for the federal government, their unreasonable jealousy of that body and of one another, and the disposition, which seems to pervade each, of being

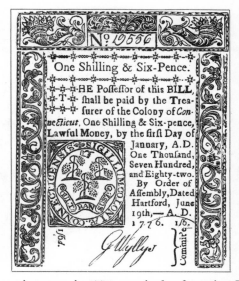

Connecticut note in 1776 promised redemption January 1, 1782. Connecticut had begun minting cents of pure copper from a mine at Granby back in 1737.

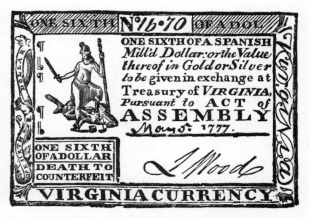

Note Virginia's change to Spanish milled-dollar base for currency issued in 1777, with warning to counterfeiters. Assembly had voted death penalty for counterfeiters. The currency still depreciated.

all-wise and all-powerful within itself will, if there is not a change in the system, be our downfall as a nation," GW wrote in 1783 to the then Governor of Virginia, Benjamin Harrison.

The States' opposition to the central government's having any standing army at its disposition was reducing the Continental forces to two batteries of artillerymen assigned to guard military stores at West Point and Carlisle (Pa.). The Continental navy was being disposed of. Britain was not retiring from the territory beyond the Appalachians, as expected; its forces were now under orders to remain at Forts Detroit and Michilimackinac, which dominated Great Lake approaches into the western lands claimed by various States under their royal charters.

Five States had withheld ratifications of the Articles of Confederation because of dissension over disposition of these western lands. Maryland was the leader in a fight for the lands' being regarded as common possessions of all the States, not preserves of a few. Ratification of the definitive Treaty of Peace with Britain was to be delayed unnecessarily for months because delegates of the nine States could not be assembled until 1784 to act on it.

"Division of the States, Ordinance of 1784," a map published at Philadelphia by Francis Bailey with the text of the Ordinance. In providing for the artificial division of the entire region between the Alleghany-Appalachian mountains and the Mississippi into sixteen districts, each eligible to statehood on attaining 20,000 population, it allocated names for them. Some not adopted by subsequent States were Metropotamia, Polypotamia, Saratoga, Pelisipia and Assenisippia. "Washington" was the designation given the district now part of western Maryland and West Virginia. The Ordinance of 1784, framed by Thomas Jefferson, was never put into effect. Ordinances in 1785 and 1787 fulfilled the purposes.

VIII

SWORD INTO PLOWSHARE

"The scene is at last closed. I feel myself eased of a load of public care. I hope to spend the remainder of my days, in cultivating the affections of good men, and in the practice of the domestic virtues."

— George Washington, 1783

AT LENGTH, my dear marquis, I am become a private citizen on the banks of the Potomac, and under the shadow of my own vine and my own fig-tree, free from the bustle of a camp and the busy scenes of public life, I am solacing myself with those tranquil enjoyments of which the soldier who is ever in pursuit of fame and the statesman whose watchful days and sleepless nights are spent in devising schemes to promote the welfare of his own, perhaps the ruin of other countries, as if the globe was insufficient for us all . . . can have very little conception. I have not only retired from all public employments, but I am retiring within myself. . . ."

GW wrote this to Marquis de la Fayette a few days before his own fifty-second birthday.

That year, 1784, was far from retiring and tranquil. He devoted himself to all-around improvements at Mount Vernon — every field, as well as house and grounds. He undertook experiments with plaster of paris, powdered stone and river-bottom mud, as fertilizers; with clover, orchard grass, guinea grass, to build up depleted soils; he inquired about every implement or machine that promised to make labor more efficient, invented one for his use. Herds of beef cattle and flocks of sheep were increased. In pasturing his stock, he moved them from field to field systematically, to manure the fields. In seeking a new farm overseer he demanded that "above all, he must be Midas-like, one who can convert everything he touches into manure as the first transmutation toward gold."

The return to Mount Vernon and its demands upon her attention relieved Martha's mind from grief over Jackie. The widow remarried, to Dr. David Stuart, but she, the children and Dr. Stuart were regular visitors. Nelly (Eleanor) and Wash (George Washington Custis) came to live at Mount Vernon. Having the grandchildren at hand was a consolation; the General accepted them as his own. While GW immersed himself in management of the estate and vast correspondence, Martha devoted attention to management of the kitchen, dairy, smoke-house, laundry and spinning-room. Typically, she insisted that the cooks try out every variety of wood on the plantation, in comparative tests of fuel-values.

1757

1776

1759

1778

1774

1787

Conjectural drawings of the development of the Mount Vernon mansion prepared by an architect, Norman M. Isham, from documentary evidence. Reproduced from *Annual Report of The Mount Vernon Ladies' Association of the Union, 1965*. Note: The Association publishes a Mount Vernon Handbook, with complete historical information and comprehensive photographic documentation of the Mansion, as well as a half dozen pamphlets of fundamental interest to visitors.

Despite all his record-keeping of agricultural experiments, returns, expenses and weather, and no let-up in correspondence (the total of all his handwritten letters was to go over 50,000 before his death) he resumed diary entries. The occasion for the new start in September 1784 was a "visit to my Landed property West of the Apalachean Mountains." For companions he had Dr. James Craik, Craik's son William and GW's nephew Bushrod (the eventual heir to Mount Vernon).

He returned fired anew with prospects of opening up the interior through improvement of navigation of the Potomac from tidewater to Will's Creek, a portage road to navigable waters of the Youghiogoheny and Monongahela, thence into the Ohio River. Learning that Pennsylvania controlled the Monongahela and its branches, and aware that Pennsylvania would be disinclined to cooperate with Virginia and Maryland in an improvement beneficial to all, he mapped for himself possible alternate routes apart from Penn-

sylvania. One was a hook-up of headwaters of the James River with the Little Kanawha, the other through Cumberland Gap into Kentucky.

He observed in a letter to Jefferson, "There is nothing which binds one country or State to another but interest. Without this cement the Western inhabitants [those beyond the Appalachians in North Carolina, Kentucky] who more than probably will be composed in great degree of foreigners, can have no predilection for us, and a commercial connection is the only tie we can have upon them."

The danger of a separation of the two populations, East and West, was indicated in 1784, when people in Western North Carolina [now eastern Tennessee] formed a temporary state and opened negotiations with Spain for an alliance, as they had no outlet to the sea except the Mississippi River, controlled by Spain.

Jefferson was to cement the Western territories to the Eastern States with the Louisiana Purchase that gave the U.S. possession of the Mississippi and its tributaries, but Arthur B. Hurlbert, author of *The Paths of Inland Commerce* (Yale University Press: 1920) names Washington as the first expansionist and declares the plan for holding the West through facilitating commercial

Samuel, the second son of Augustine and Mary Ball Washington, born in 1734. He married five times and, extravagant and irresponsible, was a trial to Washington's devotion to his family. George paid for college educations of two of Samuel's sons, supported their sister Harriot at Mount Vernon for eleven years, while a husband was being sought for her. The efforts were successful in 1796.

Bushrod Washington (1762-1829), the nephew to whom Mount Vernon was bequeathed. A graduate from William and Mary who studied law under James Wilson, a Pennsylvania signer of the Declaration of Independence, Bushrod served in Uncle George's Continental Army as a private soldier. (Wood-engraving from Benson J. Lossing's *Mount Vernon: the Home of Washington.*)

relations "a pioneer idea, instinct with genius," and that "Washington's advocacy of it marks him as the first commercial American, the first man typical of the America that was to be."

However, knowledge of a venture in 1784 of Robert Morris' might make one hesitate to declare George Washington the first great expansionist. The end of the war had not opened British ports in the West Indies or elsewhere to American commerce. Britain was determined to exclude American traders from Europe. Morris financed a challenge in another quarter of the globe. Only three months after the British surrendered New York, the 360-ton ship *Empress of China* went off to Canton with a cargo astutely chosen by Morris: quantities of ginseng roots dug along the Hudson (ginseng was in demand

among aging Chinese men as a rejuvenator) and Spanish silver dollars. The return of the *Empress of China* the following spring with an exchange cargo of silk and tea that produced $30,000 profit for Morris and associates gave decisive stimulus to American trade.

Washington's return to Mount Vernon brought family troubles closer.

Samuel, the apple of his mother's eye, continued to look to GW for support for himself and family. Mary Washington herself was no less a problem. To George's intense embarrassment and anger, she had caused the impression to spread that she was in want. GW wrote John Augustine, he learned "she is, upon all occasions, and in all companies, complaining . . . of her wants and dif-

The mansion and immediate surroundings at Mount Vernon as viewed from the air, looking back from the Potomac River. Some structural changes have been made since this photograph was taken.

ficulties.... That she can have no *real* wants, that may not be easily supplied, I am sure of. *Imaginary* wants are indefinite; and sometimes insatiable; because they sometimes are boundless, and always changing."

GW's brother-in-law, Fielding Lewis (husband to Betty), was another moneyseeker in 1784. George Washington wrote to him: "You very much mistake my circumstances when you suppose me in a condition to advance money. I made no money from the Estate during the nine

Plow of Washington's time. He effected an improvement by devising a drill-attachment that planted seed from a revolving barrel turned by a wheel that followed the plow, with a light harrow or drag behind that covered the seed. GW found it would not work well in land full of stumps or stones.

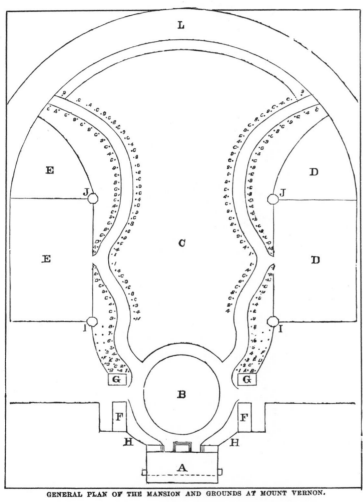

GENERAL PLAN OF THE MANSION AND GROUNDS AT MOUNT VERNON.

A The Mansion.
B Oval Grass-plot.
C The Lawn
D D Flower-garden.
E E Vegetable Garden.
F F Kitchen and Laundry

G G House-servants' Quarters.
H H Circular Colonnades.
I I Water closets.
J J Seed-houses.
K Carriage-way as finally laid out.
L Outside Road.

SECTION OF SHADED CARRIAGE-WAY.

The new plan for the grounds in front of the mansion house which Washington began laying out in 1785 and, at right, a "closeup" of the upper half of the plan as printed here — the north side geographically, next to the flower garden. He experimented with mahogany and other trees in these plantings.

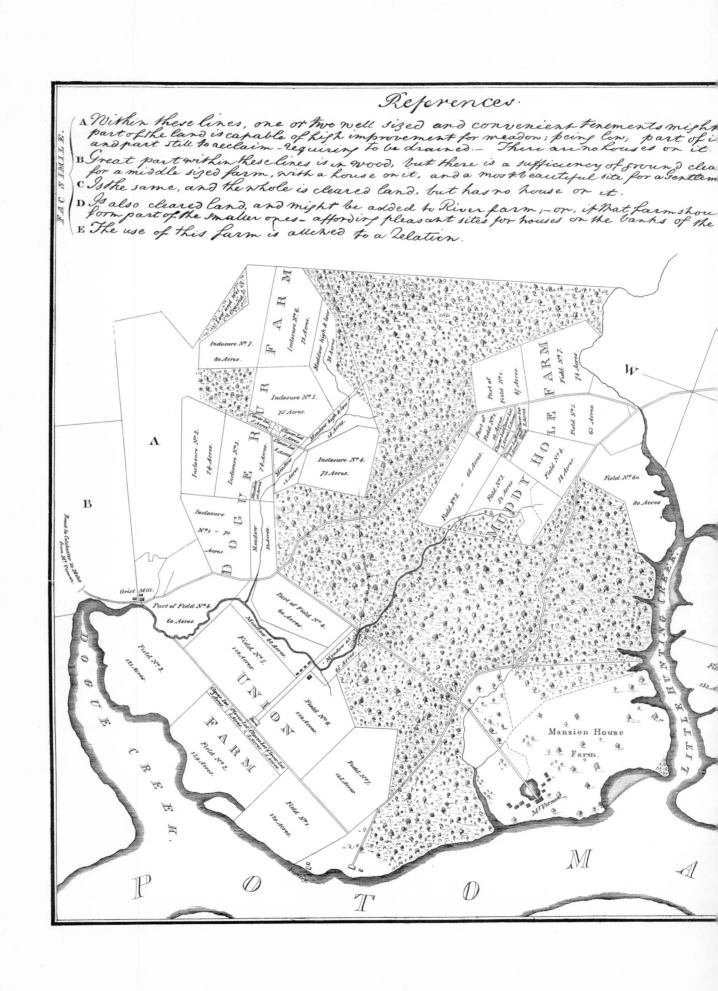

References.

A Within these lines, one or two well sized and convenient tenements might
  part of the land is capable of high improvement for meadow; being low, part of i
  and part still to reclaim—requiring to be drained.— There are no houses on it.

B Great part within these lines is in wood, but there is a sufficiency of ground clea
  for a middle sized farm, with a house on it, and a most beautiful site for a Gentlem

C Is the same, and the whole is cleared land, but has no house on it.

D Is also cleared land, and might be added to River farm;—or, if that farm shou
  form part of the smaller ones—affording pleasant sites for houses on the banks of the

E The use of this farm is allowed to a Relation.

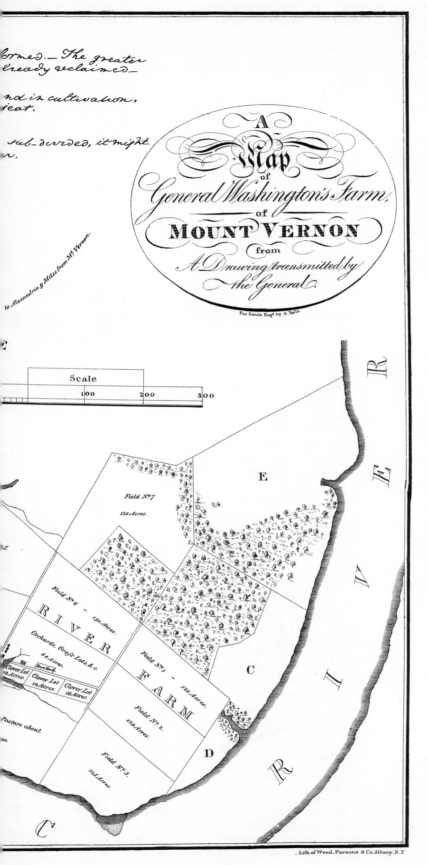

A
Map
of
General Washington's Farm,
of
MOUNT VERNON
from
A Drawing transmitted by
the General.

Fac Simile Eng.t by A. Tolle.

to Alexandria 9 Miles from Mt Vernon.

ormed. — The greater
lready reclaimed —

nd in cultivation,
eat.

sub-divided, it might

Scale
100   200   300

E

Field N.º 7
120 Acres.

R I V E R

Field N.º 6 — 130 Acres.

Orchards, Grass Lots &c.
84 Acres.

Clover Lot
Clover Lot   Clover Lot
10 Acres.   10 Acres.

Pasture about

R I V E R F A R M

Field N.º 1 — 130 Acres.

C

Field N.º 2.
120 Acres.

D

Field N.º 3.
155 Acres.

C

Lith. of Weed, Parsons & Co. Albany, N.Y.

years I was absent from it, and brought none home with me. Those who owed me, for the most part, took advantage of the depreciation and paid me off with six pence to the pound. Those to whom I was indebted, I have yet to pay . . ."

Tourists to Mount Vernon can see the so-called "kitchen gardens" George Washington laid out in 1786 in a landscaping plan that was both decorative and utile. "Kitchen" garden was largely a misnomer. For the eighteenth-century Southern plantation garden was the source of medicines for family members, guests and slaves, as well as vegetables, fruits, beverages, flowers. (A map of the household garden is obtainable by Mount Vernon visitors.)

Washington's experimental multi-sided barn (admitting light from any direction) on his Dogue Run farm.

"A view of his models, with the explanations, removed the principal doubt I ever had in mind of the impracticability of propelling against a stream by the aid of mechanical power; but as he wanted to avail himself of my introduction of it to the public attention, I chose previously to see the actual performance of the model in a descending stream before I passed my certificate; and having done so, all my doubts were satisfied."

Washington had particularized earlier, in his journal, September 6, 1784: "Remained at Bath all day and was Showed the Model of a Boat constructed by the ingenious Mr. Rumsey, for ascending rapid currents by mechanism; the principles of this were not only shown and fully explained to me, but to my very great satisfaction, exhibited in private under the injunction of Secresy, until he saw the effect of the application he was about to make to the Assembly of this State, for a reward."

Encouraged by Washington in his efforts to advance steam-powered navigation, James Rumsey, a Maryland Revolutionary soldier, kept the squire of Mount Vernon informed of progress. November 10, 1785, he reported, "I have brought it to the greatest perfection . . . the power is immense . . . boats of passage may be made to go against the current of the Mississippi or Ohio River or in the Gulf Stream from 60 to 120 miles per day."

In turn, Washington warned Rumsey January 31, 1786, against further delay in bringing his boat into usefulness, as John Fitch was "endeavoring to have something of similar nature offered to the public." He had been alerted to the Fitch steamboat experiments by Fitch's calling on him at Mount Vernon to request an introductory letter to the Assembly at Richmond. Washington had declined the request "and went on to inform him [Fitch] that though I was bound not to disclose the principles of Mr. Rumsey's discovery, I could venture to assure him that the thought of applying steam for the purpose he mentioned was not original. . . ."

Rumsey was unable to find financial backers in the United States, and went to England. His efforts there were no more successful than were Fulton's overseas at a later date. Washington was dead before practical applications were given to steam in transport, by Oliver Evans, John Stevens and Robert Fulton.

In the same period that Washington's enthusiasm for application of horsepower to navigation via steam-engine was generated, he became the first to develop mulepower for farms, mines, ferries, vehicles outside the Spanish colonies. Until 1784, exportation of full-blooded jacks from Spanish domain was prohibited. Charles III of Spain relaxed the prohibition to allow shipment

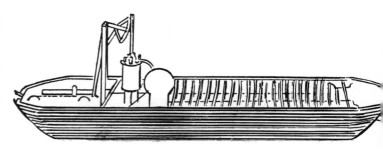

Plan of Rumsey steam-propelled boat, and (*right*) one of his bids for supporting partners in development not only of steam craft but a "machine for raising water at small expense, to be applied to the working of mills of different kinds." As a miller on Sleepy Creek, Md., Rumsey had evolved a device to lift water to run the mill, an idea that came to him in his efforts to relieve the Gnadenau Mill (*below*) from wind-wheel or, in dry seasons, upon water. *Bottom right:* Early and late examples of Fitch craft, the first having oars moved by steam, the second by buckets attached to the sides — a forerunner of the sidewheels utilized by Fulton.

of a jack and two jennies which arrived in 1785, to be followed afterward by a jack and jennies La Fayette arranged to be sent to Mount Vernon from Malta. These animals prompted some of the Washington humor cited in an earlier chapter. I suspect another example of it was a note of his:

PROPOSALS
For forming a Company, to enable
JAMES RUMSEY
To carry into Execution, on a Large and Extensive Plan, his
STEAM-BOAT
And sundry other Machines herein after mentioned.

Whereas JAMES RUMSEY, of Berkeley county, in the state of Virginia, has been several years employed, with unremitted attention and at a great expence, in bringing to perfection the following machines and engines, namely, one for propelling boats on the water, by the power of steam, which has already been accomplished in experiments, on a boat of about six tons burthen; another machine, constructed on similar principles, for raising water at a small expence, to be applied to the working of mills of different kinds, as well as to various useful purposes in agriculture; and also others, by means of which, grist and saw-mills may be so improved in their construction, by a very cheap and simple mechanism, as to require the application of much less water than is necessary in the common mode: And whereas the expenditures that the said James Rumsey has necessarily incurred in the prosecution of these important discoveries, and in endeavouring to bring the machines and engines which he has invented to perfection, have rendered him incapable, without assistance, to carry his said plans fully into effect: Therefore, he, the said James Rumsey, hereby doth, by the advice of sundry gentlemen of reputation, propose to form a company on the following plan, to enable him to complete and carry into execution his aforesaid inventions; being anxious to evince the great utility, which he is confident, will result to his country therefrom. For this purpose, he proposes.

1st. To reserve, subject to his own disposal, one moiety or half part of the interest, and property, in his said discoveries and machines.

2nd. That the other moiety of the interest and property in the same, be divided into fifty equal shares, to be disposed of to such gentlemen as may choose to encourage so laudable and beneficial an undertaking.— The purchasers to pay at the time of subscribing, twenty Spanish milled dollars, for each share, into the hands of the said James Rumsey, or of the trustees hereafter to be appointed, who will be authorized by him to receive subscriptions.

3d. The said James Rumsey, hereby engages to convey to the said, Trustees, for the use and benefit of the company, Lands, of considerable value, as a security for the faithful appropriation of the monies so to be subscribed; which monies shall be applied to the immediate purposes of perfecting the before mentioned machines, and obtaining grants from the legislatures of the several states, vesting in the said James Rumsey, his executors administrators and assigns, an exclusive right to, and interest in the said discoveries and machines, for a certain term of years.

4th The said James Rumsey farther engages, that, at the expiration of one year from the date hereof (at which time he expects to have his machines compleated) he will convey to each subscriber, his executors, administrators, or assigns, the share or shares by them respectively subscribed for, on his or their paying the said James Rumsey the additional sum of forty Spanish dollars, on each share so subscribed. And that, should any subscriber, or his legal representative, then wish to relinquish his share or shares, the money advanced by him for the same, shall be refunded to him. But should it so happen, that all, or a great number of the subscribers, or their representatives, should not be desirous of retaining their respective shares, and that the said James Rumsey should thereby, be disabled from refunding to them, out of the fund arising from the original subscriptions, the sum of twenty dollars advanced for each share; in that case he agrees that the lands, so as aforesaid to be conveyed in trust, shall be sold by the trustees aforesaid, for the express purpose of reimbursing the monies, advanced by those persons so declining to retain their shares; the surplus to be refunded to the said James Rumsey or his representatives.

5th. That those persons who may think proper to pay the additional sum of forty dollars for each share, and thereby be invested with a complete proprietorship in the concern, shall form themselves into a company, which shall hold their meetings at such times and places as may be by them agreed upon, for the purpose of promoting the interest of the proprietors, and for directing the mode, in which the business of the company shall, from time to time be conducted. That at all such meetings of the company each proprietor shall be entitled to one vote for every share he shall possess, to the number of five (inclusive) and one vote for every five additional shares. That the said James Rumsey, so long as he shall continue a proprietor of one moiety (equivalent to fifty shares) or of a lesser number, shall be entitled to a proportionable number of votes, with the other proprietors; and that every person who may purchase from the said James Rumsey a share or shares (each of which shall be one equal fiftieth part of his the said James Rumsey's proprietorship, hereby reserved) shall have the same right of voting as other proprietors.

That, so soon as twenty shares shall be subscribed for, the subscribers shall meet, in order to appoint trustees, for the purposes before specified: and that when the company shall be completely organized, every person entitled to give a vote in person, shall also, in case of absence, have a right to vote by proxy.

In Witness of the premises, We the Subscribers, have hereunto set our Names, this *first* day of *May* 1788.

"Sent my two jackasses to the election at Marlborough in Maryland that they might be seen."

Washington was to be made more aware of the seamy side of politics in the convention at Philadelphia. He had a new secretary, Tobias Lear, when he went there as a delegate from Virginia and was chosen convention President, a most trying position amidst sharp contention that developed between exponents of various replacements for the Articles of Confederation. At its precursor in Annapolis in 1786, twelve commissioners from five States had met and discussed easements of restrictions each of the States had imposed upon interstate commerce. The discussions had come to nothing except a call for the larger convention in 1787.

As a safeguard against outsiders' knowing the extent of disagreements and the compromises reached, and thus creating prejudices against the ratification of whatever document might be drafted, it was agreed to have all sessions secret. Notes or transcripts on the debates remained under suppression many years. A good reconstruction of them is in *To Secure These Blessings*, by Saul K. Padover (Washington Square Press: 1962).

Tobias Lear.

The ſenators and repreſentatives beforementioned, and the members of the ſeveral ſtate legiſlatures, and all executive and judicial officers, both of the United States and of the ſeveral States, ſhall be bound by oath or affirmation, to ſupport this conſtitution; but no religious teſt ſhall ever be required as a qualification to any office or public truſt under the United States.

VII.

The ratification of the conventions of nine States, ſhall be ſufficient for the eſtabliſhment of this conſtitution between the States ſo ratifying the ſame:

Done in Convention, by the unanimous conſent of the

States preſent, the ſeventeenth day of September, in the year of our Lord one thouſand ſeven hundred and eighty-ſeven, and of the Independence of the United States of America the twelfth. In witneſs whereof we have hereunto ſubſcribed our Names.

GEORGE WASHINGTON, Preſident,
And Deputy from VIRGINIA.

NEW-HAMPSHIRE. { *John Langdon,* / *Nicholas Gilman.*
MASSACHUSETTS, { *Nathaniel Gorham,* / *Rufus King.*
CONNECTICUT { *William Samuel Johnson,* / *Roger Sherman.*
NEW-YORK. { *Alexander Hamilton.*
NEW-JERSEY. { *William Livingſton,* / *David Brearley,* / *William Paterſon,* / *Jonathan Dayton.*
PENNSYLVANIA. { *Benjamin Franklin,* / *Thomas Mifflin,* / *Robert Morris,* / *George Clymer,* / *Thomas Fitzſimons,* / *Jared Ingerſoll,* / *James Wilſon,* / *Gouverneur Morris.*

DELAWARE. { *George Read,* / *Gunning Bedford, Junior,* / *John Dickinſon,* / *Richard Baſſett,* / *Jacob Broom.*
MARYLAND. { *James M'Henry,* / *Daniel of St. Tho Jeniſer,* / *Daniel Carrol.*
VIRGINIA. { *John Blair,* / *James Madiſon, Junior.*
NORTH-CAROLINA { *William Blount,* / *Richard Dobbs Spaight,* / *Hugh Williamſon.*
SOUTH-CAROLINA. { *John Rutledge,* / *Charles Coteſworth Pinckney,* / *Charles Pinckney.* / *Pierce Butler.*
GEORGIA. { *William Few,* / *Abraham Baldwin.*

Atteſt, *William Jackſon,* SECRETARY.

Concluding paragraphs of Constitution as printed in broadside with names of members of convention. Jackson, as Secretary of the Convention, was distinct from Charles Thomson (*above*), Secretary of Congress, who issued subsequent call (*right*) for a national election.

The Preſident

Preſents his Compliments to

Mr Broome

and requests the Favour of his Company at Dinner, on Wednesday, next at 4 o'Clock.

PHILADELPHIA, *Sept. 5th 1787.*

An Anſwer is deſired.

An invitation to dinner from Washington, as President of the Convention at Philadelphia, to Jacob Broom, delegate from Delaware (who spelled his family name without a terminal "e"). The time, four P.M., was a fashionable dinner hour then.

By the United States in Congreſs
aſſembled,

SEPTEMBER 13, 1788.

WHEREAS the Convention aſſembled in Philadelphia, purſuant to the Reſolution of Congreſs of the 21ſt February, 1787, did, on the 17th of September in the ſame year, report to the United States in Congreſs aſſembled, a Conſtitution for the People of the United States; whereupon Congreſs, on the 28th of the ſame September, did reſolve unanimouſly, "That the ſaid report, with the Reſolutions and Letter accompanying the ſame, be tranſmitted to the ſeveral Legiſlatures, in order to be ſubmitted to a Convention of Delegates choſen in each State by the people thereof, in conformity to the Reſolves of the Convention made and provided in that caſe:" And whereas the Conſtitution ſo reported by the Convention, and by Congreſs tranſmitted to the ſeveral Legiſlatures, has been ratified in the manner therein declared to be ſufficient for the eſtabliſhment of the ſame, and ſuch Ratifications duly authenticated have been received by Congreſs, and are filed in the Office of the Secretary---therefore,

RESOLVED, That the firſt Wedneſday in January next, be the day for appointing Electors in the ſeveral States, which before the ſaid day ſhall have ratified the ſaid Conſtitution; that the firſt Wedneſday in February next, be the day for the Electors to aſſemble in their reſpective States, and vote for a Preſident; and that the firſt Wedneſday in March next, be the time, and the preſent Seat of Congreſs the place for commencing Proceedings under the ſaid Conſtitution.

Cha Thomson ſecy

IX

THE PRESIDENT

"In contemplating the causes which may disturb our Union, it occurs as a matter of serious concern that any ground should have been furnished for characterizing parties by Geographical discriminations — Northern and Southern, Atlantic and Western; when designing men may endeavor to excite a belief, that there is a real difference of local interests and views. One of the expedients of Party to acquire influence, within particular districts, is to misrepresent the opinions and aims of other districts."

— George Washington, 1796

PROCEEDING from an early-morning departure from Woodbridge, April 23, Washington was met at the old East Jersey capital, Elizabethtown, by a committee of the New Congress. After a respite at the home of Elias Boudinot, he was escorted to Elizabethtown Point. A splendid barge, manned for the occasion by a symbolical thirteen harbor-pilots in white uniforms, awaited him. The craft was pulled along the shore of Staten Island, into Upper New York Bay, and up to East River. Boats of all sizes, gay with bunting and decks crowded, formed two lines between which the presidential barge and escorts slowly moved to Murray's Wharf, at the foot of Wall Street.

Guns left behind at the Battery by the departing British boomed salutes, bells pealed and cheers went up as Washington was received by the Governor, his old friend George Clinton, and the Mayor, Richard Varick.

A battalion of city militia escorted the General to the house that had been obtained for him. Carpets had been spread from the ferry to a carriage, but Washington chose to proceed on foot, perhaps to his regret. As he walked, courtesy de-

manded that he bow and doff his hat every few steps to ladies who threw flowers in his path or waved. There was barely time after he entered the residence for bathing and getting into fresh clothes before he had to go abroad again, for a dinner in his honor given by Governor Clinton. There was a display of fireworks to be witnessed before the man who had wanted to remain in seclusion and comfort at Mount Vernon was free to go to bed and try to relax.

The simple fact is that Washington's health was in decline when he became President at fifty-seven.

William Maclay, who kept detailed diaries as a Senator from Pennsylvania in the First Congress, 1789-91, saw him in 1789, "as he really is. In stature about six feet, with an unexceptional make, but lax appearance. His frame would want filling up. His motions rather slow than lively, though he showed no signs of having suffered either gout or rheumatism. His complexion pale, nay, almost cadaverous. His voice hollow and indistinct, owing, as I believe, to artificial teeth before his upper jaw, which occasions a flatness."

Washington was to prove susceptible to illnesses repeatedly throughout his Presidency. In the autumn of 1789 influenza literally laid the President so low that he pressed the attending physician for the truth about the probable outcome of the sickness. "Do not flatter me with vain hopes; I am not afraid to die, and therefore can bear the worst," it was recorded. The physician, Samuel Bard, acknowledged his apprehension. The President responded, "Whether tonight or twenty years hence, makes no difference."

Senator Maclay called at the Presidential residence to inquire about the patient, and noted in his diary, "Every eye full of tears. His life is despaired of."

Maclay earlier in 1789 had noted the decline of Washington's hearing. Of a dinner at the President's house, he recorded, "he seemed in more good humor than I ever saw him, though so deaf that I believe he heard little of the conversation." In admitting later to Thomas Jefferson that he was "sensible of a decay of his hearing," Washington remarked that "perhaps his other faculties might fall off and he not be aware of it."

His medical record in earlier years, taken from his writings, included "ague and fever"

Washington stands, hat raised in response to cheering throng, as barge is pulled to wharf in New York.

(An engraving attributed to J. Rogers, in author's collection.)

when sixteen; smallpox, which marked his face for life, at nineteen; "violent fevers and pains in my head" at one time in the campaign with Braddock; prolonged dysentery, and fever, which forced him to take leave from the Virginia Regiment on the frontier in 1757. There was an attack of "river fever," or malaria, in 1761, for which he sought a cure at Virginia Warm Springs. He wrote from there "my pains grow rather worse, and my sleep equally disturbed. What effect the waters may have upon me I can't say at present, but I expect nothing from the air — this certainly must be unwholesome."

In 1786, at Mount Vernon, there was another attack of ague, and in 1787, Washington told a correspondent of "a rheumatic complaint which has followed me more than six months, is frequently so bad that it is sometimes with difficulty I raise my hand to my head or turn myself in bed."

Plainly, the war had taken heavy toll of the vigor and health of the Virginian who in 1755 had found "I have a constitution hardy enough to encounter and undergo the most severe trials."

There was no suggestion of Washington's ever being hypochondriac. His adopted son, Washington Custis, declared that "his aversion to the use of medicine was extreme and, even when in suffering, it was only by entreaties of his lady . . . that he could be prevailed upon to take the slightest preparation of medicine." As a farmer well-informed in the doctoring of stock and horses, Washington might well have been cynical, if not contemptuous, of some treatments prescribed in his family. When poor young Martha Custis' seizures became unmistakable in causation, he noted, "Joshua Evans came here, put a ring on Patsey (for fits)."

When Dr. Laurie, at Mrs. Washington's insistence, was called in to bleed her, the physician "came here drunk," so that a night had to pass before he could render the service.

But Washington did not oppose inoculation. When smallpox was found in the army, he pleaded with Congress to repeal a law the legislators had been induced by physicians to pass against inoculation. He urged his wife to submit to the treatment (but did not succeed in inducing her to do so for four years).

What troubled him most of all, during some thirty years, was his teeth. Extractions were begun in his twenties, and from then on, his diaries had repeated variations of "Indisposed with aching tooth, and swelled and inflamed gum" and "To Dr. Watson for drawing a tooth, 5 shil." In 1789 he was wearing bridges carved out of hippopotamus tusk by John Greenwood, a craftsman in dentistry. (It was recorded that Greenwood learned the craft from his father, Isaac, and a neighbor in Boston, Paul Revere.)

Greenwood sought to save some of the teeth by capping, and this did not, of course, add to Washington's comfort. He complained frequently of being "uneasy in the mouth." All the natural teeth were gone before 1792, and the replacement dentures gave a different appearance to his mouth and jaw — a fact noted in discussion of his portraits in earlier pages.

In returning a set to Greenwood from Mount Vernon, he complained that they "bulge my lips

Washington's carriage being driven to the Federal Hall in Wall Street, New York — a redraft of a contemporary engraving at New-York Historical Society.

In the following two pages: The first Inauguration, at the Federal Hall, in Wall Street, April 30, 1789. An engraving at the New-York Historical Society.

The President [211]

out in such a manner as to make them considerably swelled."

Whatever illusions Washington may have had about the unanimity of the public expression on the occasion were shattered for him the day after his arrival in New York. A crude caricature was circulated, showing him mounted on an ass, held up by his Negro body-servant, Billy Lee. The jack was led by Colonel David Humphreys, who had accompanied him from Mount Vernon, and the "balloon" showed Humphreys was chanting hosannahs. The Devil hovered around, and from his mouth issued the lines:

The glorious time has come at last
When David shall conduct an ass.

The display of regard for the elected Chief Magistrate of the nation had aroused anew elements in New York who had fought bitterly the ratification of the Federal Constitution in that State and who voiced disapproval of every aspect of aristocracy or hero-worship that could be mistaken for an approach to a monarchial regime.

Richard Henry Lee, Washington's friend since boyhood (to whom he once penned a sort of verse), was to observe sourly in 1789, "I believe that the people of America have been guilty of idolatry, by making a man their god; and that the god will convince them that he is only man."

In the seven days between Washington's arrival in New York and the oath-taking, there were debates in Senate and House as to what titles, if any, should be adopted as honorifics for the President and Vice President. A Senate committee had reported in favor of "His Highness the President of the United States and Protector of Our Liberties." A Committee appointed in the House had offered no recommendation when the Speaker, Frederick Muhlenberg of Pennsylvania, brought up the subject with Washington at dinner, with Congressman Henry Wynkoop as a fellow guest.

"Well, General Muhlenberg, what do you think of the title of High Mightiness," Muhlenberg quoted Washington as saying. Muhlenberg knew this form of address was used for the never slender Stadtholders of the Dutch Republic, and gave a jesting reply: "Why, General, if we were certain that the office would always be held by men as large as yourself or my friend Wynkoop,

it would be appropriate enough; but if by chance a President as small as my opposite neighbor should be elected, it would be ridiculous."

The President-elect did not join in the laughter, it was stated: his evident displeasure with Muhlenberg was made manifest after Muhlenberg himself voted in the House against conferring any title on the Chief Executive other than "Mr. President."

One set of Washington's teeth carved in Ivory.

] ↑] A pair of Washington's spectacles among treasures of the Department of State. He began using glassses for reading in 1778. One of his aides, Colonel David Cobb, who rose after the war to high political office in Massachusetts, remembered that in an officers' conference in 1783, "When the General took his station at the desk, he took out his written address from a coat pocket and began, 'Gentlemen, you will permit me to put on my spectacles, for have I not only grown gray, but almost blind.' This address, with the mode of delivering it, drew tears from many of the officers." Isaac Weld recorded that Washington's eyes were of light gray color. In portraits, artists gave them varying colorations.

Two of many incidents in 1789 are indicative of Washington's extraordinary character and qualities. He wrote to Benjamin Harrison, the two-term governor of Virginia who had opposed ratification of the Constitution Washington favored: "My friendship is not in the least lessened by the differences which have taken place in our political sentiments, nor is my regard for you diminished by the part you have acted."

Similarly, Washington, with whom young Hamilton had quarreled brashly during the war in the belief he was entitled to a higher command, did not let that prevent his appointing Hamilton to the most difficult position in the administration, next to the Presidency itself: Secretary of the Treasury. And he sustained Hamilton's actions through eight years during which other members of the "Cabinet" were at odds with Hamilton — Jefferson bitterly so.

Alexander Hamilton: an engraving by H. B. Hall after a painting by Archibald Robertson.

Formal notice of Hamilton's appointment to Washington's staff, as printed and distributed to unit commanders by Alexander Scammell, of Massachusetts. Scammell was Adjutant General of the Army.

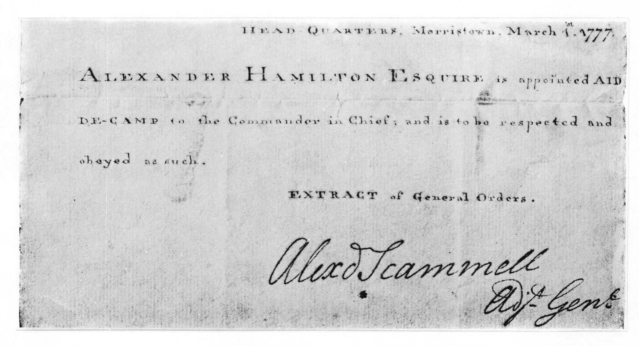

HEAD-QUARTERS, Morristown. March 1st 1777.

ALEXANDER HAMILTON ESQUIRE is appointed AID DE-CAMP to the Commander in Chief; and is to be respected and obeyed as such.

EXTRACT of General Orders.

Alexᵈ Scammell
Adjᵗ Genˡ

Next pages: An imaginative representation of Lady Washington holding a levee, a popular nineteenth-century print. The President generally stood beside Mrs. Washington, dressed plainly. At his own levees, he wore a more elaborate costume, with dress-sword at his hip and a cocked, ostrich-feathered hat.

Washington had determined to visit each of the States during his Presidency. October 15 he proceeded from New York by coach, with Major William Jackson, an aide; Tobias Lear,* secretary; and a retinue of six servants, for a tour of New England except Rhode Island. The smallest State hadn't yet ratified the Constitution. GW made a special visit to recalcitrant "Rhody" after it ratified in 1790.

Receptions at East Chester, New Rochelle, Mamaroneck, Rye, Norwalk, Fairfield, Stratford, Milford, New Haven, Middletown, Wethersfield, Hartford were described in the diary he kept. At the venturesome new woolen factory in Hartford, he ordered broadcloth "to be sent to me at New York — and a whole piece to make breeches for my servants." He continued, with receptions at each place, to Windsor, Springfield (Massachusetts), Leicester, Worcester, Middlesex, Cambridge and Boston. At the latter Washington firmly established a precedent against the will of the State's governor, John Hancock. Hancock's attempt to maintain that a State's executive had official precedence within the State over the President of the Nation met defeat from Washington. In accordance with the stand that

*GW's diary, May 9, 1786, noted that Lear, a 1783 Harvard graduate from New Hampshire, was hired at $200 a year "to live with me as a private Secretary and preceptor for Washington Custis..."

the President should pay his respects to the Governor before the Governor should call on the President, Hancock sent Lieutenant-Governor Samuel Adams to meet Washington at the town limits of the State capital. When Hancock did not call as soon as the Presidential party arrived, Washington canceled his previous acceptance to dinner at Hancock's house and dined at his own lodgings. Hancock sent a secretary with a message he was too indisposed to make the call. Washington responded, "The President of the United States presents his best respects to the Governor, and has the honor to inform him that he shall be at home until two O'clock. The President need not express the pleasure that it will give him to see the Governor; but, at the same time, he most earnestly begs that the Governor will not hazard his health on the occasion."

Hancock capitulated. October 26, he called on George Washington at the latter's chambers. The next day at 3 p.m., the President dined with Hancock "at a large and elegant dinner at Faneuil Hall," and submitted to having a portrait of him begun for Harvard by Edward Savage.

The tour was resumed on the 29th, via Charlestown, Cambridge, Mystic, Malden, Lynn, Marblehead, Salem, Newburyport, Beverly, (with a visit to the Cabots' cotton mill), Ipswitch, Salisbury and into New Hampshire. Visits to a dozen other places were recorded by GW with such comments as "It being disagreeable to the People of this State (Connecticut) to travel on the sabbath day, I stayed at Perkins' tavern (which, bye the bye is not a good one,) all day — and a meeting-house being within a few rods of the door, I attended morning and evening service and heard very lame discourses..."

November 13 he was back in New York. On the 26th, the day appointed for observance of the first Presidential Thanksgiving Proclamation, he "went to St. Paul's Chapel, that it was most inclement and stormy but few people at Church."

Opposite page: Mr. and Mrs. John Hancock from life: oil on canvas portrait by Edward Savage in the Corcoran Gallery of Art at Washington, D.C. Mrs. Hancock was Dorothy Quincy of Fairfield, Conn. Their only child, born in 1778, and named John George Washington Hancock, died at age of nine.

One action of Hamilton's that produced strained relations between Washington and his Secretary of the Treasury took place on that first Thanksgiving, when the administration overrode protests that setting apart an occasion for religious devotions was in conflict with the constitutional purpose to separate state and church.

Hamilton had prompted celebration, with pageantry and parade. Washington chose to hold a public levee at the Presidential mansion, in Franklin Square, after his attendance at church. Hamilton, not discouraged in the least by this and rain, reviewed the parade from the front of Fraunce's Tavern, where he had arranged a banquet for his friends. Hamilton absented himself immediately after the procession to make an appearance at the Presidential levee, and his friends proceeded to dine and wine without him. By the time he arrived the banquet was a brawl, with bottles and crockery littering floors before the turkey arrived.

News of the unholy goings-on reaching Washington's ears at the levee, he held his temper with difficulty and absented himself from the visiting line when Hamilton was summoned to

Desk Washington used as President in New York. Preserved in the New York City Hall.

Washington's lepine watch, the key with which its mainspring had to be wound, and the personal seal that he carried on the same ribbon, handily for correspondence. The reproduction is larger than the originals. The watch is preserved among the Washington relics. The case is of gold-copper alloy; the dial of white enamel; the hands of carmine red. Stones adorning the seal are polygonal cornelian.

his presence. As furious as he had been with Hamilton on an occasion during the war, he denounced the whole proceedings as an outrage and disgrace.

No Washington proclamation of Thanksgiving was issued again for five years. Two days earlier, Washington had noted in his diary, "Went to the play in the evening. Sent tickets to the following ladies and gentlemen, and invited them to sit in my box, viz: Mrs. Adams (lady of the Vice President), General Schuyler and lady, Mr. King and lady, Major Butler and lady, Colonel Hamilton and lady, Mrs. Greene — all of whom accepted and came except Mrs. Butler, who was indisposed." Upon the President's entering the stage-box with his guests, the orchestra struck up "The President's March," a composition by an erstwhile German bandmaster. Applause accompanied the President's entrance, and this provoked a few in the audience to demonstrate newly aroused feelings in some quarters against Washington by getting up noisily and leaving the theater. Understandably, the President was in no mood on Thursday for such a provocative scene as took place through Hamilton's misarrangement.

The Washington levees, at which David Humphreys presided as major-domo, were open on occasion in a republican manner, but did not necessarily improve the President's popularity. He was insistent on punctuality on all social occasions and was recorded as producing his watch and ordering dinner begun at the appointed time regardless of whether guests had been delayed by carriage traffic or miscalculation.

Mrs. Washington confided her displeasure with "court life" to intimates. She wrote a friend, "I think I am more like a state prisoner. There are certain bounds which I may not depart from; and, as I cannot do as I like, I am obstinate, and stay home a great deal."

Thomas Jefferson as painted by Bass Otis (1784-1861) in 1816 for Delaplaine's Repository of the Lives and Portraits of distinguished American Characters. Of the portrait, Jefferson wrote a friend, " . . . I am not qualified to say anything, for this is a case where the precept of Know Thyself does not apply. The ladies from their studies of their looking glasses may be good judges of their own faces, but we see ours only under a mask of soap suds and the scraping of the razor." The original hangs at Monticello, a gift of Mrs. Elizabeth M. Bolles, into whose family it came from the artist's son.

PICTURE ON A PANEL OF WASHINGTON'S COACH.

Mary Washington lived to be honored by her neighbors in Fredericksburg (Va.) as mother of the President. GW made a last filial visit before he rode north for the inauguration. She died August 25 at the home to which, in 1781, her son had taken Count Rochambeau and other French officers during the march to Yorktown, and where Marquis de la Fayette had visited her after the victory. "Never have I felt such veneration," he said.

She was eighty-three, and forty-six years a widow. The interment was within what was then the estate of Fielding Lewis, husband of her daughter Betty. (Andrew Jackson laid the cornerstone for a marble shaft that, never completed, was scarred in the Civil War.) (Another monument now standing was dedicated by President Cleveland in 1894.)

The President was informed of his mother's death days later, while proceeding with the necessary organization of administrative departments — Treasury and Customs, Foreign Affairs, War, Justice [Attorney-General], Post Office — and selection of Justices of the Supreme Court. The influx of settlers begun with establishment of Marietta at the mouth of the Muskingum by Rufas Putnam's company from Massachusetts and Connecticut had stirred Indian trouble on another front. Southern Indians had risen, too.

Hysac, one of twenty-eight chiefs and sub-chiefs of the Creek tribe and their allies, the Seminoles and Chickamaugas, brought to New York in 1790 for a conference with President Washington. This is one of the sketches made on the occasion by the eminent artist John Trumbull. They accompanied Alexander McGillivray, the Scot-French-Spanish quarter-bred Creek who had made himself a despotic ruler of the tribe. His siding with the British in the Revolution led to seizure by Georgia of Creek lands after the war and this in turn produced a long war by Creeks against the white settlers. McGillivray would not respond to any overtures for peace until invited to New York by Washington. Then, having secured a treaty under which the United States restored much territory to the Creeks, paid him $100,000, and gave him a commission as Major-General, U.S. Army, McGillivray sought to make a deal with the Spanish in Florida against the United States.

Fort Washington, the most extensive military works in the Northwest Territory when it was erected in the autumn of 1789. Lieutenant-Colonel Harmar marched from it in 1790 for his ill-fated campaign against the Miami Indians. Major General St. Clair, Governor of the Territory, also marched from there for his disastrous campaign. About half the inhabitants of the town of Cincinnati that was rising around the Fort marched with St. Clair and many died.

An actual gown worn by Martha Washington during her husband's Presidency. Handed down through her granddaughter's family, it was eventually obtained for the collection of gowns of First Ladies exhibited at the Smithsonian Institution.

John Jay, enrobed as Chief Justice of the United States, another engraving after a painting by Alonzo Chappel. A graduate of King's College (Columbia) at twenty-one, and admitted to the Bar at twenty-three, he was a delegate to the first Congress and member of succeeding sessions until 1779 (president of the body 1778-9); Colonel of New York Militia; Minister to Spain; co-negotiator of the peace with Britain; Secretary of Foreign Affairs for the Congress, 1784-9. All his prestige was at stake in his struggle to secure New York ratification of the Constitution. Jay co-authored the Federalist Papers.

TH: (TH: is the form he always used) Jefferson, chosen as Secretary of Foreign Affairs in September 1789, did not serve until he ended his five-year tour as Minister to France and returned to New York in March 1790. Meanwhile, the position, changed in title to Secretary of State, was occupied by John Jay of New York. Jay, the Secretary of Foreign Affairs under the Confederation Congress from 1784 on, was Washington's choice for Chief Justice. He organized the Court before turning over the State Department to Jefferson — and before the capital was removed to Philadelphia. Alexander Hamilton and Jefferson swung a trade between Southern States and Northern States in Congress. Southern Congressmen wanted the national capital moved southward. Northern States favored assumption by the central government of the individual States' war debts. Votes were swapped, and it was provided that the national capital be transferred to Philadelphia for ten years, while a new site was being laid out, and suitable buildings constructed, beside the Potomac. Robert Morris, a party to the deal, was attacked in the press as engineering it for his own profit as a speculator.

Hamilton made the Federal Government the beneficiary. Holders of the obligations of the States had to look to the Federal Treasury for payment, and thus had to give stronger support to the new government. Consonant with this, he induced Congress to incorporate in 1791 a Bank of the United States, with the government providing twenty per cent of the capital and private investors the remainder.

"View of Congress on the Road to Philadelphia," a caricature in 1790 of Robert Morris, large money-bag in hand, dragging Congress from New York. "Small" minority is represented (A) climbing the "ladder of money and preferment," "large" majority (B) follows tamely. Figure at bottom of ladder, with small money-bag, is saying, "This is what is influencing me." One of the trailers is remarking, "I hope the Philadelphians will not serve us as they once did," an allusion to happenings during Congresses there.

The first Christmas after the surrender at Yorktown, while the General and Martha were staying the winter in Philadelphia, GW chose to have dinner with Robert and Mary Morris* at the Morrises' splendid home on the Schuylkill River. (Washington had spelled it the *School Kill* in writing to Martha in 1775 of the visit to Philadelphia during which he formed this friendship.)

Earlier in 1781, Washington was in desperate need of money with which to pay the troops. Morris, on his personal obligation, to make the amount good — not as Superintendent of Finance for the bankrupt treasury of the newly legitimized Confederation — "raised $1,400,000 to assist Washington in the movement that resulted in

*Robert Morris, born in England 1734 and an immigrant to Philadelphia at thirteen, was only twenty when he earned a partnership in an old Philadelphia mercantile house. Though an early supporter of the patriot cause, he voted against the Declaration of Independence, believing it premature. He was not related to the Morrises of New York — Gouverneur, Lewis, Richard, Staats, etc.

the capture of Yorktown," it was recorded. His fellow Philadelphia banker, Haym Solomon, deserved a share of the credit for the accomplishment.

In December, when the Washingtons were the Morrises' guests, the financial difficulties of the central government had not lessened despite the victory at Yorktown; it was $2,500,000 in

Above: A money chest of Robert Morris that is preserved at Philadelphia.

Contemporary woodcut of the mansion that brought Morris into bankruptcy.

$ _5000_ Dollars. Philadelphia 21 December 1795

Nine Months after date, I promise to pay to the order of James Greenleaf Five Thousand - - - - - - - - - - - - - - Dollars, for Value received.

Robt Morris

a·d

arrears in payments for war supplies. Morris organized the Bank of North America, with $400,-000 capital, to facilitate financing of government obligations.

Morris nominated Washington as President of the Constitutional Convention. With the establishment of the Federal Government, Washington sought him as Secretary of Treasury and organizer of Federal finances, but Morris declined, recommended Alexander Hamilton and kept the position of Senator from Pennsylvania. He was speculating in huge tracts of land. Those acquisitions and construction of a marble palace in Philadelphia — designed by Pierre L'Enfant — induced a financial collapse, and his sentencing under debtor laws. The principal financier of the Revolution was left in Prune Street Prison for three years, until his release was secured under a new Federal bankruptcy law.

Meanwhile, the Washingtons invited Mary Morris and children to stay under "our roof as long as you shall find convenient." Gouverneur Morris obtained an annuity for Mary, who was sister of William White, first Episcopal Bishop of Pennsylvania.

Washington's tour of the Southern States occupied him from April 7 to June 12, 1791, after he had met at Georgetown [Maryland then] the commissioners he had appointed to lay out the new Federal District. He personally inspected

Facsimile of one of promissory notes Morris gave.

Below: Certification by Notary Public that at the request of a debtor he "went with original promissory note of which the above is a true copy to the dwelling house of Robert Morris and presented the same for payment when I received for answer that Mr. Morris was not there and had left no orders for the payment of same. The nonpayment of which I duly notified the endorser." (Original preserved in the collection of the author.)

The first Cabinet: Washington with the Secretaries of State (Jefferson), Treasury (Hamilton), War (Knox) and, in background, Attorney General (Randolph), an engraving from a painting by Alonzo Chappel (1828-1887). Originals of Chappel's works are in the collections of the New-York and Chicago Historical Societies. The figurative first meeting, February 25, 1793, was at Mount Vernon.

the land and talked to the landholders about terms for the acquisition before proclaiming from Georgetown the fixed boundary lines of a ten-mile-square preserve.

The official trip southward, proceeding from Mount Vernon, almost came to disaster quickly. In the ferrying of Washington's carriage at Colchester (Va.), one of the four horses "by the neglect of the person who stood before them," got overboard when the ferry was fifty yards from the shore. Its struggling while still hitched to the others frightened them. "Providentially, indeed miraculously, by the exertions of people who jumped in the river," no harm was done to

GEORGE WASHINGTON
PRESIDENT.
1792.

Obverse design of the Peace Medal given in the name of the President to a tribal head chief with whom a treaty was effected. Of solid silver, and with the national emblematic eagle on the reverse, it was intended to be worn proudly as a symbol of association with the President in treaty-making. The first of the medals was struck in 1792 for presentation to Sagoyewatha, or Red Jacket, of the Senecas, when a treaty was made with the Six Nations.

the horses, the carriage or its distinguished passenger. From Fredericksburg, and a reunion with his sister Betty, George Washington's route was to Richmond, New Bern, Wilmington, into South Carolina, Georgia. At Charleston, "There were a great number of Boats with Gentlemen and ladies in them; and two boats with music." At a reception in the evening, "There were at least 400 ladies the number & appearance of which exceeded anything of the kind I had ever seen."

He went out of the way near Savannah to call on Mrs. Nathanael Greene, widow of the General, at the plantation where, within a year, the young Yale tutor to the Greene children, Eli Whitney, was to invent the cotton gin that revolutionized the South's agricultural economy.

The tour could have been considered politicking: the second national election was coming up in 1792. If he was not desirous of a second term, as appears likely, he let himself be persuaded. Opposition arose, with Jefferson as its mastermind, but Washington was re-elected unanimously. Adams received only half as many for Vice President, most of the others going to a New York foe of Hamilton, George Clinton.

Washington's acceptance of a second term was regrettable from the standpoint of what he had to endure in the following four years, and the damage done to his reputation. The French Revolution and its brash envoy, Citizen Genet; the ensuing hostilities of France and England; Washington's policy of neutrality; the Jay Treaty with England on the Northwest boundaries and other controversial issues remaining from the Revolution were exploited by a pro-Jefferson press for purposes of vilifying Washington. The Philadelphia *Aurora*, owned by Benjamin F. Bache (Franklin's grandson) declared, "If ever a nation was debauched by a man, the American nation has been debauched by Washington." Vile, compromising letters were forged and attributed to Washington in one paper. When the fraud was exposed, Washington observed, "Falsehood can wound a man, but truth strikes the final blow."

The political and military revolution, 1774-1788, in which Washington played so decisive a part was followed by events that produced an industrial revolution with profound effects. They were to shape American society over a century.

That revolution is stated by some historians to have begun with the textile works Samuel Slater erected for Moses Brown at Pawtucket, R.I., to utilize a waterwheel for spinning cotton yarn. Induced by bounties, advertised by spinning houses in the new country for workable improvements, Slater got around English law forbidding export of the Arkwright machines he had learned to operate. Slater simply memorized every detail of the machinery. He put the specifications on paper when safely beyond British jurisdiction.

Alexander Hamilton, in his report as Washington's Secretary of the Treasury for 1791, referred to the result of Slater's piracy of Arkwright's invention: "The manufactory at Providence has the merit of being the first in introducing into the United States the celebrated cotton mill, which not only furnishes materials for the manufactory itself but for the supply of private families, for household manufacturing." Home spinning, a domestic duty of housewives and servants for centuries, was soon to end.

Of more immediate consequence was an invention made the next year, 1792, by Eli Whitney: the cotton gin. Before the Whitney gin, a man could clean seeds from five pounds of cotton a day. With the gin, a slave could clean over 1000 pounds daily, and leave the fibers in finer condition than the old process did. Consequently, raw-cotton exports from the U.S. were to rise from 190,000 pounds in 1791 to more than 40,-000,000 pounds a year within a single decade. Lord Macaulay was to observe, "What Peter the Great did to make Russia dominant, Eli Whitney's cotton gin has more than equalled in its relation to the power and progress of the United States."

Whitney was to broaden the industrial revolution in 1798 when hostilities were thrust on the U.S. by the French Directory. Whitney, realizing there was urgent need of arms for the men George Washington had been summoned from retirement to lead, wrote to Adams' Secretary of the Treasury, Oliver Wolcott: "I should like to undertake the manufacture of ten to fifteen thousand stand of arms. I am persuaded that machinery moved by water, adapted to this business would greatly diminish the labor. . . . Ma-

Whitney cotton gin. The original was devised on the Georgia plantation of Mrs. Nathanael Greene, widow of the General, where young Whitney had gone as a tutor for youths in the household.

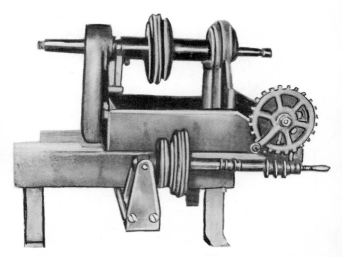

[↑] A Whitney milling machine for arms.

chines for forging, rolling, floating, grinding, polishing, etc., may all be made use of to advantage."

Whitney had some difficulty selling his idea, but Jefferson and Washington were perceptive of its merits, and the military emergency promoted acceptance. Whitney's introduction of production-line assembly of standardized and interchangeable parts, each produced by semi-automatic machinery, changed the whole economic history of the United States. Fortunately there was no such opposition in the country as organized craftsmen in England interposed there to mechanization. The Whitney system took manufacture away from farms and firesides, and signaled the end of individuality in craftsmanship.

Washington, who had seen the advent of Rumsey's steamboat, and with it application of the principle of jet-propulsion, was a witness to a beginning of airborne transport in North America. A breezy morning in January 1793, he wrapped himself warmly and took members of the official family to Germantown. Promoters of exhibitions by Jean Pierre Blanchard, eminent aeronaut from France, had obtained the yard of the Germantown prison for the occasion. The high walls enabled the promoters to exact fees from those who wanted to be close by the take-off spot and see the preparations and farewells. The giant yellow varnished silk bag was in process of inflation with hydrogen for an hour. Then Blanchard, whose fashionable attire was topped with a cocked hat adorned with white feathers, stepped into the car suspended from the netting covering the bag. His lone companion there was his little black dog.

A band played and cannon were fired as Blanchard pulled up his ground anchor and started dumping ballast. The balloon rose straight up before it started swinging southeastward. Blanchard doffed his hat in acknowledgment of cheers that rose to him, and unfurled two flags: the Stars and Stripes and the French tricolor.

The yellow bag passed over Philadelphia at twenty miles an hour, quickly outdistancing men who tried to follow Blanchard on horseback.

The balloon hurdled the Delaware in the first crossing of that river ever made by a man without swimming or ferrying.

Blanchard carried food for several days and the first and only passport ever issued personally by the President of the United States. Over his signature President Washington asked "To all whom these presents shall come" that Blanchard be allowed "to pass in such direction and to descend in such places as circumstances may render most convenient." Compliance with this request, the President said, was "justice to an individual so distinguished by his efforts to establish and advance an art."

Blanchard may have thought or hoped that he was going a long way on that flight. Eight years earlier, he had accomplished the first international journey by air: he crossed the English channel from France to England, with a Boston-born physician as a passenger. But on January 9, 1793, he was able to stay up only about forty-five minutes. Circumstances forced him to land near Woodbury in Gloucester County, New Jersey. His "passport" proved its worth immediately. "How dear is the name of Washington to these people!" he exclaimed concerning the New Jerseyites who bade him welcome, then returned him to Philadelphia that evening in a carriage for a cheering reception.

"His face is handsome, noble and mild," Blanchard wrote of Washington. "He is tall (at least five feet eight inches). In the evening I had supper with him; I mark it as a fortunate day, that in which I had been able to behold a man so truly great."

A cloak worn on a chilly January day in the open, and a tendency to stoop in addressing shorter men who stood with him, could have deceived Blanchard concerning Washington's stature. He was six feet, two inches — tallest of Presidents except Lincoln (six feet, four) before Lyndon Johnson (also six feet, two).

Other events before Washington bowed out of the Presidency require a book in themselves for exposition. Notably so, the "Whisky Insurrection" of 1794, when organized resistance in western Pennsylvania to Federal excise taxes was broken up by force.

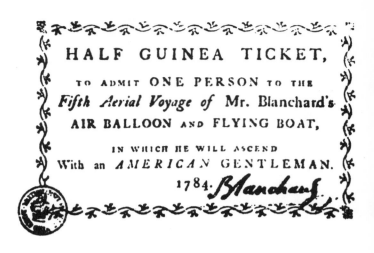

Left: Contemporary woodcut of J. P. Blanchard ascension from Germantown, January 9, 1793, witnessed by President Washington. [↓] Ticket sold in England to witness takeoff nine years earlier of Blanchard with passenger, Dr. John Jeffries, in preliminary to first flight across the English Channel.

Old representation of Blanchard-Jeffries aerial voyage from France to England, in 1785, an exploit for which he was granted a pension by Louis XVI.

Vision in 1790s of an aerostatic warship, such as Ben. Franklin had prophesied when he witnessed, back in 1784, as U.S. envoy at Paris, flight in Montgolfier hot-air balloon.

A twentieth-century liberal, Thurman Arnold, was to write, in *The Symbols of Government* (1935), "The principles of Washington's Farewell Address are still sources of wisdom when cures for social ills are sought. The methods of Washington's physician, however, are no longer studied. Only political and legal science look to the past."

The Farewell Address was never uttered publicly. An actual farewell address *was* spoken by George Washington to a joint session of Congress, December 7, 1796. The so-called Farewell Address had been given to the people through publication in the *American Daily Advertiser* at Philadelphia the previous September 19, in accordance with a suggestion of James Madison's: for the mode of the announcement there was "none better than a simple publication in the newspapers," directed "to the people," who were his "only constituents."

The announcement Washington had determined to make was his disinclination to have a third Presidential term. In those days before press associations, political correspondents in capitals and news-feature syndicates, newspapers gathered information from each other and reprinted freely. Madison's advice was sound. Editors and pamphleteers all through the States, territories and Great Britain told readers within a month or so after that September 19 of Washington's declining to be considered as a candidate again for "first magistrate of the United States," or "resignation of the Presidency." The latter was the phrase in Glasgow, Scotland, where it was declared "an event which must be deeply deplored, not only by every friend to America, but by every man who feels himself interested in the general welfare of Europe." The Scot editor concluded the address "contains much salutary advice."

The announcement was a statement with three sections: 1) the reason for retiring; 2) "disinterested warnings of a parting friend" of the urgency of stronger unity among the States and advocacy of principles upon which internal felicity could be achieved and maintained; and 3) Washington's justification of his policy of neutrality in the Franco-British struggle. "Against the insidious wiles of foreign influence, I conjure

you to believe me, fellow citizens, the jealousy of a free people ought to be *constantly* awake, since history and experience prove that foreign influence is one of the most baneful foes of Republican government.... Excessive partiality for one foreign nation and excessive dislike of another, cause those whom they actuate to see danger on only one side, and serve to veil and even second the arts of influence on the other ..."

George Washington had planned retiring at the end of his first term. He called upon James Madison in 1792 to help him in the preparation of a valedictory. Madison prepared a draft that was filed away when Washington was persuaded to continue. Upon deciding firmly in 1796 to retire, he embodied Madison's draft in the structure of a valedictory. After this was completed, a conversation he had with Alexander Hamilton moved GW to ask Hamilton to go over the address and advise on eliminations and additions. The claim that Hamilton was the chief author is disposed of in a study, *Washington's Farewell Address*, by Victor Hugo Paltsits, published by the New York Public Library (which owns Madison's original draft, a Hamilton revision of Washington's first draft and Washington's final manuscript in his own hand, from which the *American Daily Advertiser* set type). That pa-

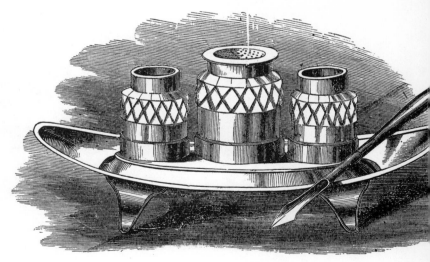

Washington's inkstand, carried from Philadelphia back to his desk at Mount Vernon. The middle piece held fine sand that, sifted across the ink, had a blotting action on what had been written.

per's front page was regularly filled with announcements of patent medicines, ship sailings, land estate sales and the like. Washington's historical announcement was printed inside.

Monarchist France had been less desirous of insuring establishment of a free republic by England's rebellious thirteen colonies than of striking a blow at its old enemy, Britain. There was reason for France to hope that the revolt against George III would help it recover part of the possessions lost in the 1754-1763 warfare. Richard Morris, great historian of the peacemaking between Britain and the United States in 1783, found evidence that France, while acting as an ally of the Americans, attempted undercover negotiations with Britain to end the war short of independence for the colonies.

The treaty that came out of the long, arduous deliberations at Paris in 1783 was inconclusive: Britain intended to confine the new nation east of the Alleghanies or the Ohio. She held on to Fort Detroit, Fort Mackinac and other strongholds until Washington sent John Jay to London to dicker.

The French revolutionary regime that uprooted the Bourbons, just as empire-minded as its predecessors, was displeased by the treaty Jay made as Washington's legate. It engaged in un-

Crude cartoon representation of the brawl in Congress, 1798, of Matthew Griswold and Matthew Lyon over the latter's criticisms of actions of the Federalist administration.

declared hostilities against United States commerce; in 1797 alone thirty-two merchant ships flying the United States flag were taken by French privateers — some of them in our own harbors — and their captured crews treated inhumanely.

President Adams sought to appease the French Directory and was confronted with demands for "loans." Congress ordered preparations for war, and Adams turned to General Washington to direct defensive measures. The Secretary of War, James McHenry, went to Mount Vernon bearing a commission signed July 4, 1798. McHenry found the retired President riding in a field, superintending haymaking.

"War is on again, General," McHenry said; "this time with France. I bring you the will of the nation."

Washington, well aware of the onset of troubles with the land of La Fayette, led his visitor to the mansion for a recital of details. Finally, with Adams' letter in hand, he told McHenry that as long as he was able he would never refuse a call to duty, but he was willing to accept the commission only on condition that Alexander Hamilton be appointed his chief aide. So at sixty-five, Washington rode north again in uniform. His new service was to be brief.

Adams secured Congressional authorization for a Navy, had a Navy Department organized and had the satisfaction of receiving news of victory by the U.S. *Constellation* over the French frigates *La Vengeance* and *Insurgente* in single-ship actions, and of large numbers of captures or sinkings by the privateers that went out from United States ports. There was no French military threat to these shores. Napoleon, who came to power in 1799, was faced with struggles in Europe and directed that peace be made with the U.S. It was effected by treaty in 1800.

President John Adams: a life-mask. In sending Washington the appointment as "Lieutenant-General and Commander-in-chief of the Provisional Army," he expressed regret he couldn't have the pleasure of tendering it in person.

Philadelphia July 7. 1798

Dear Sir

Mr McHenry the Secretary at War, will have the Honor to wait on you in my behalf to impart to you a Step I have ventured to take and which I should have been happy to have communicated in person, if such a journey had been, at this time, in my power. As I said in a former letter, if it had been in my power to nominate you to be President of the United States, I should have done it with less hesitation and more pleasure. My reasons for this measure, will be too well known to need any explanation to the public. Every Friend and every Enemy of America will comprehend them, at first blush. To you, Sir, I owe all the Apologies I can make. The urgent necessity I am in, of your advice and assistance indeed of your Conduct and Direction of the War is all I can urge; and that is a sufficient Justification to myself and the world. I hope it will be so considered

The bearer, Secretary of War James McHenry, had been secretary to General Washington 1778-80 and Maryland delegate to the Constitutional Convention of 1787. Fort McHenry of Star-Spangled Banner fame has his name. (See page 93.)

On Washington's sixty-seventh birthday **by** the new calendar — the last one of his life — his adopted daughter, and his wife's granddaughter, Nelly Custis, was married at Mount Vernon to Major Lawrence Lewis. The Major was the son of Washington's only sister, Betty, and Colonel Fielding Lewis.

A pen picture of Nelly was given by Benjamin Latrobe, just arrived from the capitals of Europe: "She has more perfection of form, of expression, of color, of softness, and of firmness of mind than I have ever seen before."

(See engraving of portrait on opposite page.)

Washington wrote to one friend, Charles Cotesworth Pinckney, "Mr. Lewis and Nelly Custis fulfilled their matrimonial engagement the 22nd of February. In consequence, the former, having relinquished the lap of Mars for the sports of Venus, has declined military appointment."

Washington's wedding gift to the bride was a harpsichord, a royal gift for those days, for it cost a thousand dollars. To her and her husband jointly he gave, conditionally, 1000 acres of his land holdings adjoining Mount Vernon. The condition was that if the Lewises (meaning the husband) did not attend properly to the management and development of the property, the donor could reclaim the farm, paying for such improvements as might have been made thereon.

The Lewises erected a home on the place, named Woodlawn, and passed all their married life there. Four children were born under its roof: Agnes, who died young; Frances, who married E. G. W. Butler; Lorenzo, who married Esther Coxe, of Philadelphia; and Eleanor, who married C. M. Conrad of Louisiana.

Major Lewis died in 1839. Nelly had a widowhood of thirteen years; she died at seventy-four and was buried from the parlor of Mount Vernon — the room in which she became a bride fifty years before.

Some of Washington silver-plate, with family coat of arms, at Mount Vernon.

Specimens of dinner set presented to Mount Vernon with names of states in chain-link design encircling each piece.

Wedding gift of Washington to Nelly Custis Lewis. It is at Mount Vernon, playable.

Recreation that Washington had to forego for duty, as depicted in a popular lithograph print of the 1800's, "Washington and Friends After a Day's Hunt." The General sits, back to tree, with "Mad Anthony" Wayne at his right and Nathanael Greene at his left. The hunt is shown to have brought down a deer and many birds.

A son born to Adrienne la Fayette after the young General spent a furlough from Washington's army in France, was named for George Washington. G.W. la Fayette, who served in his twenties under Napoleon, visited Mount Vernon with his father in the 1820's.

X

WASHINGTON'S WIT AND WISDOM

"I can hardly refrain from smiling to find you caught at last...."

— GEORGE WASHINGTON (to a bridegroom).

THE assumption that Washington was a staid, somber, unbending individual is supported by the portraits reproduced or simulated most often. He is made to appear consciously heroic or self-satisfied, unyielding, stuffy, unhappy, through no fault of his own. His wit and humor were often evident publicly. His laugh rose unmistakably in gatherings with men, and at theaters in Williamsburg, New York and Philadelphia, where he was a constant attendant.

That he could be amused by caricatures of himself was apparent when Thomas Wignell played William Dunlap's comedy, *Old Soldier*, at Philadelphia. Wignell, in the part of "Darby," a clownish veteran of the Continental Army, gave a ludicrous account of his experiences at the first Inauguration, and, when asked by another character, "How looked he, Darby?" spluttered a description. Washington went to see a performance, and audience eyes naturally turned to his box as Darby gave a soldier's exaggerated impression of the general. There were hundreds of witnesses of Washington's hearty laughter; a Philadelphia newspaper reported this in its next issue.

The Virginian's sense of humor was in evidence early. He joked about having been reported a casualty with Braddock. He wrote his brother John, "As I have heard since my arrival at this place, a circumstantial account of my death and dying speech, I take this early opportunity of contradicting the first, and assuring you that I have not yet composed the latter."

The names given the hounds in the hunting pack of the young master of Mount Vernon are indicative of his humor: Chloe, Tipler, Truelove, Sweetlips, Juno, Singer, Music, Trial, Taster.

The illusion that Washington never told a joke or laughed at one was propagated by such basic biographers as Sparks and Irving who rejected any anecdotes of Washington that cast contrary reflections on the man's image that they felt necessary for the country's appreciation of him.

Washington's risibility responded often to stimuli deemed too earthy or off-color for reportage in recollections of the great man. A jackass was shipped to him in 1785 as a gift of the Spanish monarch, who had been made aware of the likeness of Washington to the Cincinnatus of Latin tradition. The beast was the object of much joking by Washington. Perhaps due to the long, uncomfortable ocean voyage the jack was sluggish and of no use for some time. Washington wrote La Fayette of the animal that had been given the aged Spanish king's name facetiously in the privacy of the Mount Vernon stables, that "his late royal master ... cannot be less moved by female allurements than he is." Washington's comment to a nephew was, "He seems too full of Royalty to have anything to do with a plebeian race."

Wayne Whipple recorded that during one of the winter encampments at Morristown, Washington, a good judge of the qualities of horses, bought a well formed colt that evidenced strong spirit. A prideful young officer, vain of his horsemanship, asked the privilege of "breaking" the horse to a saddle for the General. Washington gave his consent and, with some of his officers, went to see the horse receive its first lesson. A moment after the assumed master of equitation mounted into the saddle, the colt planted his forefeet, threw up his heels, and gave the presumptive rider a somersault over his head. Showing no sympathy for the youth who, fortunately, suffered only a shaking up, Washington was so convulsed with laughter that, it was declared, tears ran down his cheeks.

As indicated in an earlier page, Washington had detailed to himself the task of breaking all the colts and fillies at Mount Vernon and had won praise from Jefferson, Henry Lee and others as a "very excellent and bold horseman, and the most graceful figure that could be seen on horseback."

"Lighthorse Harry" Lee recalled that at a neighborly dinner at Mount Vernon, Washington mentioned his need of another pair of carriage horses, and asked if Lee knew where he could get a pair.

"I have a fine pair, General," Lee replied, "but you cannot get them."

Washington responded, testily, "Why not?"

"Because you will never pay more than half price for anything; and I must have full price for my horses."

This bantering reply set Mrs. Washington laughing. Her parrot, perched as usual beside the lady, imitated her laugh.

Washington smiled and said, "Ah, Lee, you are a funny fellow. See, that bird is laughing at you!"

Gilbert Stuart once remarked to Lee that Washington had a tremendous temper, but that

Washington frontispiece which Noah Webster inserted in 14th edition of his *The American Spelling Book*, issued in 1791, probably was the most familiar single picture of Washington for many years. The Speller, the most extensively used textbook in American history, went through successive editions until its total printings were over a hundred million. The portrait was cut by Alexander Anderson in type-metal. Anderson subsequently introduced wood-engraving in the United States and improved the quality of the frontispiece, but continued to represent a Washington less stern and humorless than the image represented in portraiture that was being exhibited in public buildings. Anderson could have been influenced by anecdotes reflective of Washington's lighter side that were being circulated.

he had it under wonderful control. Lee repeated the first part of the remark while dining with the Washingtons. Mrs. Washington flushed, and said Mr. Stuart took a great deal upon himself. General Lee then repeated the second part of the remark, that the President had his temper under control. After a pause, Washington smiled and said, "Mr. Stuart is right."

Washington penned numerous jocular letters that survive. Upon learning that the Marquis de Chastellux, one of the French officers who served with the Continental Army, was a bridegroom, Washington wrote him, "I can hardly refrain from smiling to find you are caught at last . . . now you are well served for coming to fight in favor of the American rebels, all the way across the Atlantic ocean, by catching that terrible contagion — domestic felicity — which same, like the smallpox, a man can have only once in his life . . ."

Chevalier de Pontigibaud, another of the French volunteers in the Revolutionary Army, recounted, "One day at dinner at General Washington's headquarters, an Indian entered the room, walked round the table and, then stretching forth his long, tattooed arm, seized a large joint of hot roast beef in his thumb and fingers, took it to the door, and began to eat it. We were all much surprised, but General Washington gave orders that he was not to be interfered with, saying laughingly, that it was apparently the dinner hour of this Mutius Scaevola of the New World."

On another occasion, while the headquarters was at Newburgh and Washington was sailing in a boat on the Hudson for fishing, he was so overcome by the drollery of a story told by a companion that "he fell back in the boat in a paroxysm of laughter."

Instances of Washington's actually collapsing in mirth were attested more than once. One attestant was John Marshall, who told of a predicament he and Bushrod Washington got into one day as they rode to Mount Vernon to pay a call on the General.

They knew how expectant Washington was of neatness and cleanliness and, quite dusty from their ride, they stopped in a grove by the Potomac for a bath and change of clothes. After they had stripped, bathed in the river and climbed ashore for a body-servant to hand them towels and clean garments, they found the servant staring in distress at the contents of the valises he had taken from the carriage and opened. The bags were filled with peddler's wares — thimbles, thread, scissors, etc. At the last inn at which the travelers had stopped, the servant had unwittingly exchanged luggage with a peddler.

The servant's spluttered explanations and the state in which the exchange left them moved Marshall and Bushrod Washington to laughter. This attracted General Washington, who was making his almost invariable daily ride over his plantation. Marshall related that when Washington took in their dilemma, he was so overcome by the ludicrousness of the two men that he actually rolled on the ground in merriment.

There were badinage and joking exaggeration in his exchanges with the ladies but no vulgarity. (Washington once decided Sheridan's *School for Scandal* an unsuitable attraction to which to take ladies because of some of the verbiage in it.)

To Annie Boudinot Stockton,* one of the ladies who composed poems about the victorious General and sent him a copy, Washington responded in 1783, "Fiction is to be sure the very life and soul of poetry. All poets and poetesses have been indulged in the free and indisputable use of it, time out of mind. And to oblige you to make such an excellent poem, on such a subject, without any material but those of simple reality, would be as cruel as the Edict of Pharaoh, which compelled the children of Israel to manufacture bricks without the necessary ingredients."

A tantalizing fragment of a story with which the President animated conversation among the male guests at a dinner is in William Maclay's memoirs:

"The ladies sat a good while, and the bottles passed about; but there was a dead silence almost. Mrs. Washington at last withdrew with the

---

* She was the wife of Richard Stockton, of Princeton, N.J., a signer of the Declaration of Independence. She also wrote the stanzas sung by young ladies of New Jersey while strewing flowers before Washington on his passage through Trenton to New York for his inauguration in 1789.

ladies. I expected the men would now begin, but the same stillness remained. The President told of a New England clergyman who had lost a hat and wig in passing a river called the Brunks.

"He smiled, and everybody laughed." Seemingly, Maclay assumed his readers knew the allusion.

"Much as he tried, however, at Mount Vernon to be a simple farmer and no better than his neighbors, he had still to suffer many of the miseries of greatness," Wayne Whipple stressed. "His mere presence overawed many people with whom he came in contact, so when he wanted to enjoy the spectacle of a merry company he frequently had to keep himself behind a door and peer through the crack, so to speak. With those who knew him well and familiarly, he was not treated as an idol but was allowed to behave as a human being and be treated as one, and numerous letters and other records prove that in such circumstances he could be jolly good company. It was impossible for him not to be thoughtful — not to be silent when he had anything to think about, but he was among the first to be infected by any merriment about him."

Thomas Jefferson and James Madison remarked the animation with which Washington entered into conversation in the circle of friends, "where he might be unreserved in safety." The story of his never laughing Madison said was "wholly untrue; no man seemed more to enjoy gay conversation. He was particularly pleased with the jokes, good humor and hilarity of his companions."

The Prince de Broglie recorded after being a guest at the Washington table that "at desserts he eats an enormous quantity of nuts, and when the conversation is entertaining he keeps eating through a couple of hours, from time to time giving sundry healths, according to the English and American custom. It is what they call 'toasting.'" (Hazelnuts and black walnuts were brought to his residence by the barrel. Any toasting was probably with Madeira wine, homemade beer or punch. These were commonly mentioned Washington potables, although he was a moderate drinker of alcohol. He took cups of tea in quantity.)

Among Washington dinner-table badinage recorded in memoirs was an occasion when there was reference to a duel. Washington commented, "They say the shot Jones fired at his opponent cut a piece off his nose. How could he miss it? You know Mr. Livingston's nose and what a capital target it is."

He recalled stopping on a Sunday in York, Pennsylvania. Finding no Episcopal clergyman conducting services, he "went to hear morning service in the Dutch Reformed Church, which, being in that language not a word of which I understood, I was in no danger of becoming a proselyte to its religion by the eloquence of the preacher."

More than one lady wrote a correspondent of how utterly charming the General was informally. A Virginia woman confided in a letter that when "General Washington throws off the Hero and takes up the chatty agreeable Companion — he can be downright impudent sometimes — such impudence, Fanny, as you and I like."

William Sullivan said, "the young ladies used to throng around him, and engage him in conversation. There were some of the well-remembered belles of the day who imagined themselves to be favorites with him. As these were the only opportunities which they had of conversing with him, they were disposed to use them." But the sharply observant Sullivan detected a Washington characteristic that many others missed: Washington had an uncommon faculty of associating a person's name and personal appearance so durably in his memory, as to be able to call one by name in a second meeting. No wonder ladies were flattered into believing themselves favorites!

Nelly Parke Custis, his adopted daughter, said, "I have sometimes made him laugh most heartily from sympathy with my joyous and extravagant spirits."

Washington's own puckish impulses on occasion could be credited with originating all the jokes about voracious New Jersey mosquitoes. He told Isaac Weld, an Irish journalist who visited the President in the 1790s, "the mosquitoes of New Jersey bite through the thickest boots."

Weld, taking Washington's hyperbole too literally, elaborated himself on the size and rapaciousness of New Jersey mosquitoes in his subsequent book, *Travels Through the States of*

I am now, by desire of the General to add a few words on his behalf; which he desires may be expressed in the terms following, that is to say, — that despairing of hearing what may be said of him, if he should really go off in an apopletic, or any other fit, (for he thinks all fits that issue in death are worse than a love fit, a fit of laughter, and many other kinds which he could name) that he is glad to hear beforehand what will be said of him on that occasion; — conceiving that nothing extra: will happen between this and then to make a change in his character for better, or for worse. — And besides, as he has entered into an engagement with Mr. Morris, and several other Gentlemen, not to quit the theatre of this world before the year 1800, it may be relied upon that no breach of contract shall be laid to him on that account, unless dire necessity should bring it about, maugre all his exertions to the contrary. — In that case, he shall hope they would do by him as he would by them, — excuse it. At present there seems to be no danger of his giving them the slip, as neither his health nor spirits, were ever in greater flow, notwithstanding he is descending, & has almost reached, the bottom of the hill; — or in other words, the shades below

Washington as both wit and prophet. On December 17, 1797, he enabled his wife to catch up in neglected correspondence by phrasing a letter for her to send in response to Mrs. Samuel Powell of Philadelphia. He included this fifth paragraph, reproduced from the original draft in his distinctive script:

"I am now, by desire of the General to add a few words in his behalf; which he desires may be expressed in the terms following, that is to say, — that despairing of hearing what may be said of him, if he should really go off in an apopletic, or any other fit, (for he thinks that all fits that issue in death are worse than a love fit, a fit of laughter, and many other kinds which he could name) — he is glad to hear *beforehand* what will be said of him on that occasion; — conceiving that nothing extra: will happen between *this* and *then* to make a change of his character for better, or for worse. — And besides, he has entered into an engagement with Mr. Morris, and several other Gentlemen, not to quit the theatre of *this* world before the year 1800, it may be *relied upon* that no breach of contract shall be laid to him on that account, unless dire necessity should bring it about, mangre all his exertions to the contrary. — In that case, he shall hope they would do by him as he would by them, — excuse it. At present there seems to be no danger of his giving them the slip, as neither his health nor spirits, were ever in greater flow, notwithstanding, he adds, that he is descending, & and has almost reached, the bottom of the hill; — or in other words, the shades below." (Facsimile from Harper's New Monthly Magazine in the New York Public Library Collection.)

He was to "quit the theatre of *this* world" only seventeen days before the year 1800. The Morris to whom he referred was Robert.

North America. This was popular reading for a generation, and made the New Jersey mosquito as well known by exaggerated reputation as the Abominable Snowman of later day.

Though often infuriated by criticisms of him and his Administration in the press and the rantings of anti-federalists in the Congress, his sense of humor never corroded completely. Once, when the Federalists were being accused of stealing from the public treasury, Washington wrote facetiously to a member of the Cabinet:

"And pray, my good sir, what part of the $800,000 have come to your share? As you are high in office, I hope you did not disgrace yourself in the acceptance of a paltry bribe — $100,000 perhaps!"

He needed his sense of humor to survive eight years as President.

XI

THE END
AND A BEGINNING

"Doctor . . . I die hard . . . but I am not afraid to go."

— GEORGE WASHINGTON, 1799

TUESDAY, December 19, 1799, as we know from his journals, Washington completed a general plan of several years' duration for the management, profitably, of the properties centered at Mount Vernon, which had been made a thousand acres less by the gift to his adopted daughter and her husband. Thursday that week he rode in alternately snowy, misty rain over the properties. He came home chilled but stayed up attending to correspondence. He wrote Alexander Hamilton that the establishment of a military academy in America "upon a respectable and extensive basis, has ever been considered by me as an object of primary importance to this country; and while I was in the Chair of Government, I omitted no opportunity of recommending it, in my public speeches and other ways, to the attention of the Legislature."

Friday he was abed at Mrs. Washington's insistence, nursing a cold, but used the time to catch up on reading newspapers and hearing Tobias Lear read the printed debates in the Virginia legislature. He lay awake unusually late.

Saturday morning he could barely speak, and submitted to bleeding by one of his overseers,

Rawlings, who practiced this allopathy among the plantation people. Mrs. Washington sent for Dr. James Craik, who drew more blood, ordered inhalation of vinegar and hot water, and tried to get the patient to gargle vinegar and sage tea. Washington was almost suffocated by the gargle. Whereupon, Craik sent for two consultants, Dr. Gustavus Brown and Elisha Dick, at Alexandria. (Bleeding was a universal specific, comparable to psychiatry, in those days.) Brown bled him again, despite a demur by Dr. Dick.

Washington sensed the end was at hand. He said with difficulty to Lear, "Arrange my accounts and settle my books." To Craik he murmured, "Doctor, I die hard, but I am not afraid to go." Recognizing the body servant Christopher, who Washington realized had been standing in attendance at the bedside for hours, he thoughtfully commanded in a whisper, "Sit down."

That was about 4:30 P.M. There are conflicting versions of what transpired in the next six hours. At 10:30 P.M. he expired, with Mrs. Washington, Tobias Lear and Drs. Craik and Elisha Dick as witnesses.

Mrs. Washington, unwilling to believe her eyes, asked, "Is he gone?"

Upon hearing the affirmative response, she was quoted as saying, "'Tis well . . . I shall soon follow him."

As the news went forth, a French frigate in the Potomac opposite Mount Vernon gave the earliest reaction: its bells sounded a muffled knell.

Washington had wanted to be interred without fanfare within three days of his death. Dr. Dick hastened to convoke a special meeting of Alexandria Lodge to arrange a Masonic funeral rite. The body was laid away in the old family vault at Mount Vernon with the Reverend Thomas Davis of Christ Church, Alexandria, reading the service. The coffin bore a silver plate engraved with the dates of birth and death, plus the inscription *Glorio deo* and *Surge ad judicium*.

Mrs. Washington was not at the committal. She stood with Nelly Lewis at a window in the mansion house and watched.

Billy Lee was at the entombment, of free choice; the contents of Washington's will were known.

At Philadelphia, "Lighthorse Harry" Lee announced the doleful news to Congress, and proposed a public memorial service in a church.

Washington's will had been executed five months before his death. After devising to his wife the use, for the whole of her survivorship, the major part of his estate, he stipulated the following solicitude:

"Upon the decease of my wife, it is my will and desire that all the slaves whom I hold in my own right shall receive their freedom. To emancipate them, during her life would, though eminently wished by me, be attended by insufferable difficulties, on account of their intermixture by marriage with the dower Negroes, as to excite the most painful sensations, if not disagreeable consequences to the latter, while both descriptions are in the occupancy of the same proprietor, it not being in my power, under the tenure by which the dower Negroes are held, to manumit them. And, whereas, among those who will receive their freedom according to this device, there may be some, who, from old age or bodily infirmity and others, who, on account of their infancy, will be unable to support themselves, it is my will and desire that all . . . shall be comfortably clothed and fed by my heirs while they live. . . . The Negroes thus bound, are to be taught to read and write, and to be brought up in a useful occupation. . . . And I do most

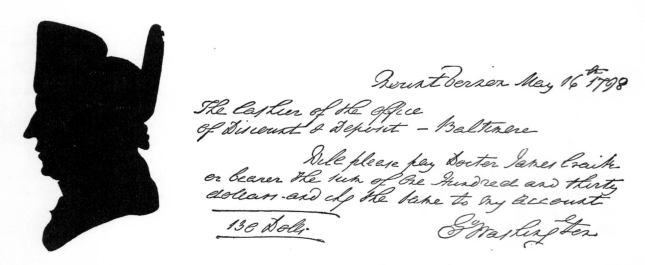

Silhouette portrait of Dr. James Craik cut from life, and facsimile check for $130 written for the physician by Gen. Washington at Mount Vernon in 1798.

Henry Lee as soldier, from a portrait by Alonzo Chappel.

pointedly and most solemnly enjoin it upon my executors, to see that this clause respecting slaves, and every part thereof, be religiously fulfilled at the epoch at which it is to take place, without evasion, neglect or delay. . . . And as to my mulatto man, William [Lee], I give him immediate freedom. . . . I allow him an annuity of thirty dollars during his natural life . . . as testimony of his attachment to me, and for his faithful services during the Revolutionary War."

Other bequests, besides relics or mementos to nephews:

Twenty shares which he held in the Bank of Alexandria, to the support of a free school at Alexandria.

One hundred shares in the James River Company and 100 shares in the Potomac River Company, toward the establishment of a university "in a central part of the United States, to which youths . . . from all parts thereof may be sent for the completion of their education."*

Fifty shares of the Potomac Company toward the endowment of a university within the limits of the District of Columbia.

One hundred shares of the James River Company for Liberty Hall Academy, in Rockbridge County, Virginia.

A schedule of property attached to the will listed items throughout the house, including these in the front parlor:

Elegant looking glass	60.00
5 China flower pots	50.00
Likeness of General Washington	50.00
Likeness of Mrs. Washington	50.00.

U.S. Bonds were evaluated at $6,246. (The U.S. Bonds had been authorized in 1790.)

Martha Washington, G. W. Parke Custis and his nephews Lawrence Lewis and William, Richard, and George Stephen Washington, were appointed executors.

Nine months after her husband's death, Mrs. Washington drew up her own will.

With her death, two and a half years after him, in pursuance to a clause in his will, Mount Vernon and the General's books, pamphlets and papers remaining at the residence passed to his nephew Bushrod.

---

* See quotation of his letter to Hamilton, page 245.

This principal heir, son of the General's younger brother Augustine, was a graduate of William and Mary College in 1778 who served as a private in the Continental Army, studied law after the war with James Wilson (a signer of the Declaration of Independence) and practiced law at Richmond until 1798. He was appointed then by John Adams to the Supreme Court, on which he served as Associate Justice until his death in 1829.

At his death, childless, Mount Vernon passed to his nephew, John Augustine Washington.

The day after Christmas, Henry Lee spoke his eulogy to a joint meeting of the two Houses. The best remembered phrase in his review of Washington's illustrious career came near the end of the more than 3000 words:

"First in war, first in peace, and first in the hearts of his countrymen, he was second to none

Modern view of the Washington tomb, visited by hundreds of thousands annually.

in the humble and endearing scenes of private life. Pious, just, humane, temperate, and sincere; uniform, dignified and commanding, his example was edifying to all around him as were the effects of that example lasting . . ."

Significant tributes came from abroad. An obituary editorial in *The Courier*, published in the capital of the empire from which the thirteen States had been wrested: "General Washington is not the idol of the day, but the hero of the ages . . . The whole range of history does not present to our view a character upon which we can dwell with such pure and entire admiration." Naturally, it had not forgotten he was of British ancestry.

Though well aware that Washington had been summoned from retirement to direct an army against the French, Napoleon Bonaparte, as First Consul, ordered crepe to be suspended for ten days from all flags and standards in the French service, and directed that a Washington funeral oration be pronounced before him and the civil and military authorities. (This was done at the Temple of Mars, at Paris, February 8, 1800.)

Clearly, it was George Washington's desire to be buried at Mount Vernon. The wish was disregarded quickly by the Congress. Presumably stirred to act by the effect of Henry Lee's eulogy, a joint resolution written by John Marshall was adopted by the Senate and House of Representatives "that a marble monument be erected by the United States, in the Capitol at the City of Washington, and that the family of George Washington be requested to permit his body to be deposited under it; and that the monument be so designated as to commemorate the great events of his military and political life."

Early engraving of the tomb, with the mansion the background (author's collection). Washington had chosen the site long before, and superintended the construction. The mahogany coffin made for the corpse was lined with lead and soldered at the joints. A cover of lead was soldered on after the corpse was in the coffin, the whole then being put into a case covered with black cloth. This lay on a draped bier on the veranda fronting the Potomac — a view he loved in life — for servants, neighbors and friends to file by before it was borne to the tomb by eight men who had been officers in the Revolutionary Army. Horse and foot militia from Alexandria formed a guard-of-honor.

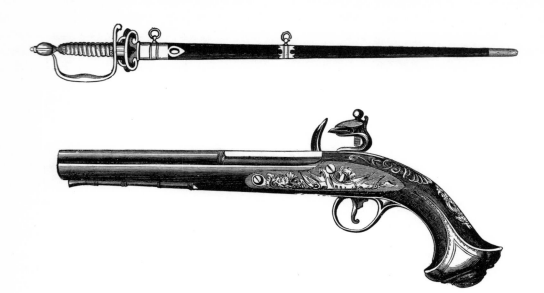

—— To each of my Nephews, William Augustine Washington, George Lewis, George Steptoe Washington — Bushrod Washington and Samuel — Washington, I give one of the Swords or Cutteaux of which I may die possessed; and they are to chuse in the order they are named. — These Swords are accompanied with an injunction not to unsheath them for the purpose of shedding blood, except it be for self defence, or in defence of their Country and its rights; and in the latter case, to keep them unsheathed, and prefer falling with them in their hands, to the relinquishment thereof

G:o Washington

Proviso in General Washington's will which provided for choice by five of Washington's nephews of "swords or cutteaux of which I may die." He enjoined them "not to unsheath them for the purpose of shedding blood, except it be in self defense, or in defense of their country and its rights." Above it,

Washington's dress-sword which he wore at levees as President, and one of a pair of his flintlock pistols, presented by the French Minister, Comte de Moustier, as a token of personal regard. They were presented by Washington in turn to Colonel Samuel Hay of the Tenth Regiment, Virginia Line.

Mrs. Washington reluctantly granted the request. It was envisioned that when the central unit of the Capitol was built, the tomb should be placed under the Rotunda. One of her last days, the widow told her grandson, G. W. P. Custis, "Remember, Washington, to have my remains placed in a leaden coffin, that they may be removed with those of the General at the command of the Government."

When the Rotunda was completed in 1827, the Washington descendants were requested formally to permit removal of the coffins to Washington. G. W. P. Custis was prevented from granting permission by John Augustine Washington, as the new owner of Mount Vernon. (The tomb at the Capitol remained empty, except for a simple catafalque subsequently used in funeral rites of Lincoln and other Presidents.)

All attempts to secure Congressional action on a monument were fruitless until 1848. Then a private organization, Washington National Monument Association, headed by Chief Justice John Marshall, succeeded in inducing Congress to approve allocation of a site from the public preserve. This site was within a hundred feet of the location Pierre L'Enfant had indicated for a pantheon in his original plan for the City.

The cornerstone was laid with ceremony July 4, 1848, with the Grand Master of Masons using the identical trowel with which Washington himself had officiated at the cornerstone-setting of the Capitol in 1793.

The funds collected by the Monument Association for construction were exhausted before it had taken the form the architect, Robert Mills of South Carolina, had designed: an Egyptian shaft 700 feet tall with a circular Greek temple at its base adorned by a colossal figure of Washington in a Roman toga. Mills' grand plan was denuded as raising of funds proceeded with increasing difficulty until onset of the Civil War brought a halt to the building. It stood as a virtually square stub, a little over 150 feet high, until public sentiment generated by the Centennial of the Declaration of Independence moved Congress to authorize the Army Corps of Engineers to take over the work and to allocate $200,000 for expense. The engineers found the substructure to be inadequate; the monument was tilting.

Roscoe Conkling of New York complained in the Senate, "The mammoth chimney called the Washington Monument is a meaningless and unsightly thing; its foundations are insecure; and we have buried a hundred thousand dollars in the ground. Assuming that we succeed in founding or establishing the foot of the monument so that it will not give way, it will still remain as I have described it."

Work went on anyway and the tons of concrete poured to form a base under the old foundation corrected the fault. Other problems had to be solved and additional appropriations wheedled from Congress. The capstone was finally put in place the end of 1885. Interior finishing and landscaping remained to be done, and the structure was not opened to the public until 1888.

WestFord, one of the last surviving Mount Vernon slaves, as sketched by Benson J. Lossing and autographed by the subject. WestFord was a skilled artisan, a plowmaker and repairer.

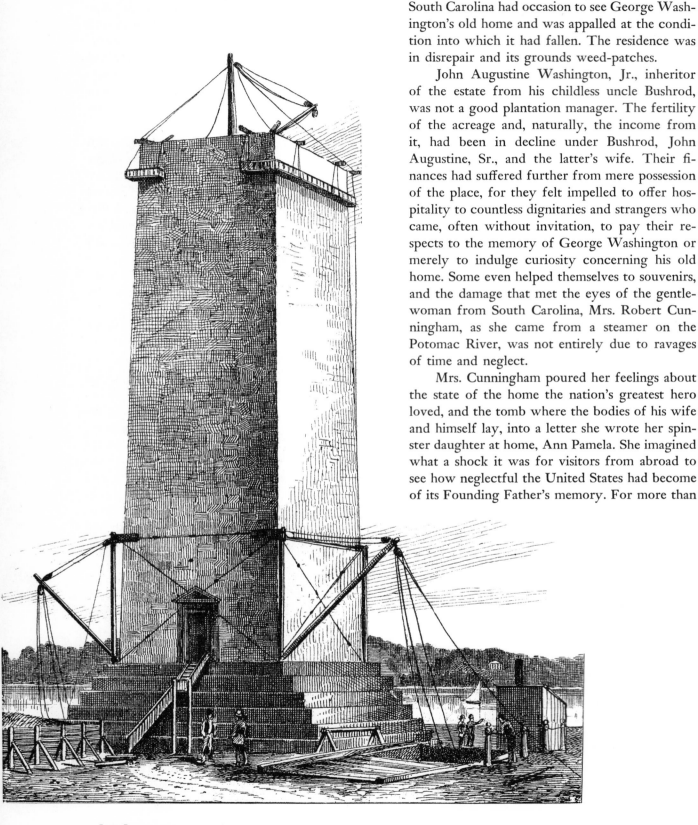

In the autumn of 1853, a gentlewoman from South Carolina had occasion to see George Washington's old home and was appalled at the condition into which it had fallen. The residence was in disrepair and its grounds weed-patches.

John Augustine Washington, Jr., inheritor of the estate from his childless uncle Bushrod, was not a good plantation manager. The fertility of the acreage and, naturally, the income from it, had been in decline under Bushrod, John Augustine, Sr., and the latter's wife. Their finances had suffered further from mere possession of the place, for they felt impelled to offer hospitality to countless dignitaries and strangers who came, often without invitation, to pay their respects to the memory of George Washington or merely to indulge curiosity concerning his old home. Some even helped themselves to souvenirs, and the damage that met the eyes of the gentlewoman from South Carolina, Mrs. Robert Cunningham, as she came from a steamer on the Potomac River, was not entirely due to ravages of time and neglect.

Mrs. Cunningham poured her feelings about the state of the home the nation's greatest hero loved, and the tomb where the bodies of his wife and himself lay, into a letter she wrote her spinster daughter at home, Ann Pamela. She imagined what a shock it was for visitors from abroad to see how neglectful the United States had become of its Founding Father's memory. For more than a decade the remains of Napoleon, who himself had paid impressive tribute to Washington, had been lying in a splendid tomb in Paris for all to see, through action by a Bourbon successor. The Congress of the United States and the Legislature of Virginia had refused to do anything toward preserving Mount Vernon and enshrining George Washington. The Monument in Washington, as indicated in an earlier section, was a half shell, due to lack of funds.

Left: Monument as it appeared when construction was resumed. A sketch by Miss C. A. Northam for the *New York Graphic*, October 16, 1879, in author's collection. *Above:* Capstone being set, December 6, 1884, a drawing in *Perley's Reminiscenses* by Ben Perley Poore, Philadelphia, 1886.

John Augustine, Jr., conscious of the sad state George Washington's heirs had let the property get into, proposed to sell the mansion and some 200 acres around it to the nation for $200,-000. Congress refused the offer. It was confronted with a legal opinion that the United States Government could not buy any land lying within an organized State from an individual; acquisition would have to be made from the State itself.

The Virginia Legislature, duly approached by John Augustine, Jr., was no more receptive to his proposition. Spend $200,000 for a property without any absolute assurance that the Federal Government would take the property off Virginia's hands and repay the $200,000? No, sir! (As Gerald W. Johnson and Charles Cecil Wall remarked in *Mount Vernon: The Story of a Shrine*, no one familiar with the record of Congress in financial matters could blame the Virginia legislators for their skepticism.)

Hence the condition of Mount Vernon when Ann Pamela Cunningham, a recluse at the family plantation in South Carolina because of invalidism, read her mother's indignant letter. She was moved to address an open letter "to the Ladies of the South," which the Charleston, S.C. *Mercury* published December 2, 1853. The *Mercury*, founded and given prestige by Henry Laurens Pinckney, was read by important Southern editors who often appropriated contents or quoted them. Miss Cunningham's summons to women to aid in securing funds for the purchase of Mount Vernon was reprinted widely in the South and eventually got into Northern papers.

"A spontaneous work like this would be such a monument of love and patriotism as never has been reared to mortal man; and while it would save American honor from a blot in the eyes of the gazing world, it would furnish a shrine where at least mothers of the land and their children might make their offering in the cause of greatness, goodness, and prosperity of the land, . . . " Miss Cunningham promised.

She was soon to learn that what she sought could not be reliant on spontaneous giving. The purchase from John Augustine Washington was not to be accomplished until she had formed a dedicated group of co-workers, The Mount Vernon Ladies Association, and secured the renowned

Bostonian Edward Everett as a decisively influential publicist and money-raiser for the project. Everett contributed fees from lectures and articles totaling about $70,000, or over a third of the $200,000 purchase price in the contract John Augustine Washington signed April 6, 1858. All the necessary additional money, having been raised and paid over, he gave physical possession of the place February 22, 1860. Whereupon Ann Pamela Cunningham and a secretary obtained from New York, Sarah Tracy, to do the MVLA paperwork, moved in to observe personally the restoration begun by a Virginian, Upton H. Herbert. When war came to Virginia in 1861, Miss Cunningham was in South Carolina on a visit, and she had to remain there till 1865. Meanwhile Herbert and Miss Tracy, who was joined by a Miss McMakin from Philadelphia, took care of Mount Vernon. It was to the credit of both Confederate and Union soldiers that they did not have to deal with any marauders or looters of the mansion.

The subsequent story of Mount Vernon, during the years it became the most visited residence in America, is the subject of a succession of books; besides that by Messrs. Johnson and Wall, the best modern ones have been *Mount Vernon on the Potomac*, by Grace King, and *Mount Vernon Is Ours*, by Elswyth Thane (Mrs. William Beebe).

Mount Vernon has remained the responsibility of the Mount Vernon Ladies' Association, with admission fees and voluntary donations the only source for meeting maintenance costs. The regents of MVLA are unpaid; the reward of members is the satisfaction of having fulfilled Miss Cunningham's goal: "Such a monument of love and patriotism as never has been reared to mortal man."

The mansion in 1858, with scantlings bracing up the sagging veranda roof. The figure standing near the door may have been John Augustine Washington. (Photograph in the collection of the author.)

ACKNOWLEDGEMENTS

This volume owes practically everything except the author's mistakes to unstinted cooperation of numerous institutions, organizations and individuals; specifically:

The Library of Congress, The National Archives, Metropolitan Museum of Art, Corcoran Gallery of Art, Colonial Williamsburg and Hugh De Samper, The New-York Historical Society, The Mount Vernon Ladies Association of the Union, The New York Public Library, King Features Syndicate, National Society Daughters of the American Revolution, Sons of the American Revolution in the State of New York, Washington Headquarters Association (New York), Ulster County Historical Society (Kingston, N.Y.), Princeton University Library, Mr. and Mrs. John Whelchel Finger, Captain Andrew S. Hickey, U.S. Navy (Ret.), Mr. Hoffman Nickerson, Dr. Edward Pinckney, Mr. John Wolter, Mr. Herbert Bender, Mr. Ralph Hollenbeck, Mr. Don Ward, Mr. Al Lichtenberg, Mrs. Bente Hamann, Joseph N. Corcoran, Anne MacGuire Lewis.

In every instance, responsibility for errors of commission or omission rests solely on the author. Consideration will be given to any criticisms and suggestions from readers in revisions for subsequent editions.

Special thanks is due to Mr. Walter Wendell Frese of Hastings House, for prolonged, extraordinary encouragement and patience above and beyond the duty of a publisher; and to Marian Gosnell Kinnaird for her understanding tolerance during long periods of devotion by her husband to search for illustrations and data for the volume, and to writing of the text.

REFERENCES

George Washington: A Biography, by Douglas Southall Freeman, six volumes; New York, 1948-1954, with a seventh volume completed by John Alexander Carroll and Mary Wells Ashworth, 1957. This author does not represent himself as anything except a cursory examiner of the Freeman magnum opus. An estimate of the time that would be required for going through all the texts, proliferations of footnotes and appendices matched the time Mr. Freeman and his able associates were engaged in writing these: seven years.

Dictionary of American History, edited by James Truslow Adams, six volumes. New York: 1946.

Appleton's Cyclopedia of American Biography. New York: 1886-89.

The Spirit of Seventy-Six, by Henry Steele Commager, with Richard B. Morris. New York: 1958.

Encyclopedia of American History, by Richard Morris. New York: 1953.

Basic Writings of George Washington, edited by Saxe Commins, New York: 1948. Note: this work is derivative of *The Writings of George Washington from the Original Manuscript Source*, 1745-1799, in 39 volumes, 1931-44. I did not consult the latter work, but recourse was made to the separately published John C. Fitzpatrick volumes. *The Diaries of George Washington 1748-1799*, Boston: 1925.

Diary of the American Revolution, by Frank Moore. New York: 1858.

The Story of American Journalism, by Willard G. Bleyer, Cambridge, Mass.: 1927.

Pictorial Field History of the American Revolution, by Benson J. Lossing. New York: 1850-52.

Mount Vernon and Its Associations, by Benson J. Lossing. New York: 1858.

Mount Vernon Is Ours, by Elswyth Thane. New York: 1965.

Original Portraits of Washington, by Elizabeth Bryant Johnson. Boston: 1882.

Portraits of Washington, by Gustavus Eisen. New York: 1932.

Engraved Portraits of Washington: Catalogue of Sale of Hampton L. Carson Collection. Philadelphia: 1909.

The Oxford History of the American People, by Samuel Eliot Morison. New York: 1965.

Washington and the American Revolution, by Esmond Wright. New York: 1962.

The War of the Revolution, by Christopher Ward. New York: 1952.

The Story of the Declaration of Independence, by Dumas Malone, Hirst Mulhollen and Milton Kaplan. New York, 1954.

Washington: Commander-in-Chief, by Thomas G. Frothingham. Boston, 1930.

Washington, by Joseph Dillaway Sawyer, two volumes. New York, 1927.

Mount Vernon: The Story of a Shrine, by Gerald W. Johnson and Charles Cecil Wall. New York, 1953.

The Life of Washington, by Mason L. Weems, edited by Marcus Cunliffe. Cambridge, Mass., 1962.

The Story-Life of Washington, by Wayne Whipple. Philadelphia, 1911.

Narrative and Critical History of America, by Justin Winsor. Boston: 1884-89.

Washington's Farewell Address, by Victor Hugo Paltsits: published by New York Public Library in an edition of 500: 1935. This has transliterations of all the drafts of Washington, Madison and Hamilton, together with pertinent correspondence of the three.

Washington Speaks for Himself, by Lucretia Perry Osborn. New York: 1927.

The True George Washington, by Paul Leicester Ford. New York: 1896.

Harvard Guide to American History, by Oscar Hamlin. Cambridge, Mass.: 1854.

Who Was Who 1607-1896. Chicago: 1963.

The Life of George Washington, by Washington Irving. New York: 1855. Valuable for its engravings. As are:

Washington and His Generals, by Joel Tyler Headley. New York: 1847.

The Life of George Washington, by John Marshall. New York: 1804-1807.

Encyclopedia of the American Revolution, by Mark Mayo Boatner III, published 1966, was invaluable in proof-reading.

Other references are cited in the text.

WASHINGTON CHRONOLOGY*

Wherever it appears in the chronology, "GW" means George Washington; Mary Ball Washington, his mother, is referred to as Mary W; Augustine Washington as Augustine W; Martha Washington as Martha W.

Items in italics are pertinent events in the Colonies during the same years.

1731
Martha Dandridge born, June 2.

1732
GW born Feb. 11 (O.S.) at Pope's Creek, Westmoreland County, to Augustine Washington, aged 38, and Mary Ball, aged about 24. The parents were wed March 6, 1731.

1733
GW's sister, Betty, born, June 20. GW had been taken to Lancaster, Pa., on a Mary W visit to her uncle, James Ball, and had learned to walk.

1734
GW's brother, Samuel, born, Nov. 16.

1735
Augustine W moved his family to the Hunting Creek plantation, Epsewasson, but kept ownership at Pope's Creek.

1736
Mary W's fourth child, John Augustine, born, Jan. 24 (N.S.).
The Virginia Gazette started at Williamsburg. It was to be a part of GW's schooling.

1737
Augustine W visited England where GW's half-brothers, Lawrence and Augustine, were attending school.

1738
Mary W bore GW another brother, Charles, May 2.
GW's half-brother, Lawrence, returned from England, aged 20.

1739
Augustine W's family moved again, to newly purchased property on the Rappahannock, near Fredericksburg, called Ferry Farm.
GW's sister, Mildred, born June 21. (She died in 1740.)

1740
The Hunting Creek plantation deeded to Lawrence W, who absented himself 1741-2 with a Virginia regiment in a Cartagena expedition with British Navy.

*This chronology is a condensation of an original, comprehensive compilation made especially for this book. It is covered by copyright and must not be reproduced in any form, nor used in whole or in part in publication, phonograph, radio broadcasting, or television without the written permission of the publisher. The whole compilation will be made available to legitimate researchers.

GW's earliest known signature made in title page of a book of sermons given at London.

1741

GW, previously tutored by servants, had schooling at Fredericksburg. He wrote a poem to Richard Henry Lee.

1742

GW's half-brother, Augustine, Jr. ("Austin") returned from school in England.

1743

GW's father died. GW began to live with Austin, at Pope's Creek and with Lawrence at Mt. Vernon, alternately, away from his mother.

Lawrence W married Anne Fairfax of Belvoir.

1744

GW met, at Belvoir, Lord Fairfax and latter's son, George William, brother-in-law of Lawrence W, who became GW's closest friend and husband of Sally Cary, whom GW much admired.

1745

GW kept his geometry lessons in a copybook that survives. He competed in sports.

Whist, introduced from England, popular in the Colonies among both men and women. (GW and Martha W were to become players.)

1746

Mary W opposed GW's becoming a cadet in British Navy and was sustained by her brother.

1747

During this period GW read *The Young Man's Companion*, adapted his penmanship to its model, and transcribed its "Rules of Civility and Decent Behaviour" into a copybook.

GW, possessing surveying instruments that had belonged to his father, took lessons and, aged 15, began practice in this profession.

1748

GW's circle of "girl friends" included Mary Cary, Mary Bland, Betsy Fauntleroy, Lucy Grymes, Frances Alexander. He composed an acrostic to Frances.

Item in GW's account book: "To cash pd ye Musick Master for my Entrance 3/9."

Earliest known diary of GW begun Mar. 11, as he went on first surveying expedition, in Shenandoah Valley.

GW's first recorded illness: "Ague and fever, which I had to extremity."

1749

Martha Dandridge married Daniel Parke Custis in a June wedding.

GW appointed surveyor for Culpepper County, with a commission as surveyor from William & Mary College. He laid out Alexandria townsite.

1750

As surveyor, GW acquired land in Shenandoah Valley.

While swimming two girls ran off with clothing he had left on bank. GW had them arrested (a member of the family recorded).

Ohio Land Company obtained large tract on upper Ohio. Christopher Gist sent to explore it . . . Population of 13 Colonies: 1,207,-000.

1751

GW made his only trip abroad, to Barbadoes with the ailing Lawrence W.

1752

GW returned in Jan. to Virginia, Lawrence W following him. Lawrence died, leaving GW as executor and residuary heir in the event of the death of LW's daughter, Sarah. The latter died two months later.

GW initiated into Masonry, Nov. 4.

GW appointed district adjutant-general of Virginia militia with rank of major, at salary of £150 a year, Nov. 6.

1753

Major GW sent by Gov. Dinwiddie with message to French at Fort Le Beouf, demanding retirement from Ohio Valley territory claimed by England. Left Williamsburg Oct. 31. At Le Beouf Dec. 1.

1754

GW returned Jan. 16, with French reply. Dinwiddie had GW's journal of the expedition published. "There intervened but one day between my arrival in Williamsburg . . . for me to prepare and transcribe from the rough minutes had taken of my travels, this Journal."

GW commissioned lieutenant-colonel of Virginia regiment; sent Mar. 15 with two companies to complete fort at Forks of Ohio.

Fought first battle with French detachment, May 28 — beginning of French and Indian War.

GW gave up "Fort Necessity," which he had thrown up in Great Meadows, Penna. Led his troops back to Virginia under terms of capitulation.

Franklin's "Join or Die" cartoon started becoming a Colonial symbol . . . Gen. Edward Braddock arrived with troops to be C.-in-C. in America.

1755

GW, invited to join Braddock's expedition, left Mt. Vernon, Apr. 23.

Braddock's force surprised July 9; Braddock killed. French drove English from Forks of Ohio and erected Fort Duquesne.

GW made colonel-in-chief of Virginia forces for protection of the frontier.

GW defeated for House of Burgesses from Frederick County, running third.

1756

GW made trip to Boston, to report to British C.-in-C. in America, Gov. William Shirley.

Returning via New York, he met Mary Philipse, whom he wanted to marry.

1757

GW sent to Philadelphia to attend a conference of Colonial governors and aides.

GW out of army, with "bloody flux" (dysentery and fever). The 1½-story Mount Vernon manor house enlarged.

1758

GW elected to House of Burgesses, from Frederick County.

GW met the widow Martha Dandridge Custis at Williamsburg,

Feb. Became engaged to her, May.

GW joined Gen. John Forbes and Lieut. Col. Henry Bouquet expedition against Fort Duquesne in command of Virginia regiment.

GW resigned his commission, Dec.

1759

GW married Martha Dandridge Custis, Jan. 6 in New Kent County, Va., and spent honeymoon at Williamsburg, where he attended the Burgesses from Frederick County.

GW, his bride and her two surviving children, Martha and John, took up residence at Mt. Vernon in May.

1760

GW justice of peace for Fairfax County, 1760-74, holding court at Alexandria.

Earliest known description of GW written by George Mercer. (see page 1).

George III became king.

1761

GW seriously ill of malarial fever.

GW reelected to House of Burgesses.

GW acted as steward at horse races at Alexandria. "Let my people go to the races," was repeated entry in diary.

Strong Colonial opposition to English rule started with James Otis' oration in Boston against Writs of Assistance.

1762

GW chosen vestryman of Truro Parish, Fairfax, County.

GW attended March and November sessions of Burgesses from Frederick County.

1763

GW made two journeys to Dismal Swamp, May and Oct., having formed a company to drain and utilize the rich swamp land. (See 1766).

GW became warden of Pohick Church of Truro Parish.

Mason's and Dixon's Line surveyed. . . . War of Pontiac's Conspiracy broke out.

1764

GW attended sessions of Burgesses.

He had begun practicing medicine, to attend servants who were hurt or fell ill, after securing medical books and medicines from London.

1765

GW's first election to House of Burgesses from Fairfax County. He was present when Patrick Henry introduced resolution against Stamp Tax. . . . "If this be treason," etc.

Parliament passed the Stamp Act . . . Isaac Barre applied the name Sons of Liberty to American patriots . . . Stamp Act Congress held in New York.

1766

GW visited Dismal Swamp repeatedly to inspect operations. The company had accumulated 40,000 acres of the area.

Stamp Act repealed.

1768

GW re-elected burgess for Fairfax County.

GW raced his horses at Accotink.

1769

Gov. Norborne Botetourt ordered the House of Burgesses dissolved after it adopted the Virginia Resolves. GW met with other burgesses at Raleigh Tavern, Williamsburg, where GW introduced the Non-Importation Agreement.

GW re-elected burgess for Fairfax County.

GW went to Bath (Berkeley Springs) in western Virginia with Mrs. W and "Patsy" Custis in hope of benefiting the latter's health. She had a form of epilepsy complicated by tb.

1770

GW visited the Ohio region to select land for grants to Virginia veterans of French and Indian War.

GW rebuilt his Dogue Creek water mill. His flour was in demand in the export market. The plantation also baked biscuit for export. He licensed a fishery in the Potomac at Mt. Vernon.

GW chosen a trustee, or alderman, of Alexandria.

1771

GW re-elected burgess for Fairfax County.

1772

C. W. Peale painted his first portraits of GW, Martha W, John and "Patsy" Custis.

British revenue sloop Gaspee burned by patriots at Providence.

1773

GW's dearest friends, George William Fairfax and wife, went to England, leaving the estate, Belvoir, in GW's care.

"Patsy" Custis died at Mt. Vernon, aged 17, of tb. She bequeathed her share of the Custis estate to GW.

Christ Church, Alexandria, completed. GW bought a pew for himself and family.

GW went to New York, to place his step-son, John, in King's College (Columbia).

Intercolonial committees of correspondence formed . . . Boston Tea Party.

1774

GW bought a sloop for increasing Mt. Vernon crop shipments.

He presided over a county convention that adopted the Fairfax County Resolves. He offered to raise and equip troops and lead them to the relief of Boston. Made a member of the First Virginia Provincial Convention. Subsequently attended Continental Congress at Philadelphia, with Peyton Randolph presiding.

John Parke Custis married Eleanor Calvert, a descendant of Lord Baltimore.

Boston Port Bill enacted . . . A general congress met in Philadelphia in September.

1775

GW left Mt. Vernon May 4 for Second Continental Congress in Philadelphia. He was chosen C.-in-C. of United Colonies forces, June 15. On June 14 Congress authorized enlistment of regiments of riflemen — beginning of U.S. Army.

First engraved portrait of GW published in London, attributed to Alexander Campbell.

Naval auxiliaries instituted by GW for Continental Army. . . . John Manley's *Lee* captured British brig *Nancy*, Nov., with 4000 muskets and ammunition.

First town named for GW:

Washington, N.C., in June. First baby: son of Mr. and Mrs. John Morton, Basking Ridge, N.J.

Martha W began spending every winter at Army hq.

GW welcomed enlistment of Negroes in the Army.

Estimated population of the 13 Colonies: 2,300,000, exclusive of Indians. Largest States (in order) Virginia, Pennsylvania, Massachusetts. An estimated ⅔ of the people opposed the Revolution and remained loyal to British rule; some 40,000 entered British fighting forces.

1776

GW raised Grand Union flag at Cambridge, Jan. 2.

From Orderly Book 3/9: "The General (GW) lost one of his pistols yesterday in Dorcester. Whoever will bring it to him shall receive two dollars reward and no questions asked."

Howe evacuated Boston, March 17. "St. Patrick" was countersign of GW's army that night.

Proceeding from Cambridge, GW took up position at New York, with half of army on Manhattan, half on Long Island.

Thomas Hickey of GW Life Guard exposed by Phoebe Fraunces, June 21, as conspirator to kidnap GW for British. Hickey hanged June 28.

Lord Howe landed 10,000 British augmented by newly arrived Hessian mercenaries at N.Y., Aug. 22 . . . Battle of Long Island, Aug. 27 . . . GW withdrew forces to Manhattan, Aug. 29-30 . . . Battle of Kip's Bay, Sept. 15 . . . GW withdrew from Manhattan, Sept. 14-15 . . . Battle of Harlem Heights, Sept. 16 . . . Nathan Hale executed by British as a spy, Sept. 22 . . . Battle of White Plains, Oct. 28 . . . Fort Washington fell, Nov. 16 . . . Fort Lee given up Nov. 18 and march through Jerseys began.

GW crossed Delaware into Pennsylvania, Dec. 8 . . . GW recrossed Delaware, Dec. 25, and next morning won Battle of Trenton.

Congress moved from Philadelphia to Baltimore . . . Other temporary capitals before 1784: Lancaster, Pa.; York, Pa.; Princeton, Annapolis, Trenton.

1777

GW defeated British at Princeton, Jan. 3. In winter quarters at Morristown, N.J. till May.

GW proclamation that individuals take oaths of allegiance to U.S. or withdraw within British lines brought protests from State governments. Each asserted the right to outlaw those who refused oath to that State.

GW defeated by British at Brandywine, Sept. 11. LaFayette wounded . . . Lord Howe took possession of Philadelphia, Sept. 27; established his winter quarters . . . GW repulsed at Germantown, Oct. 4.

Brig. Gen. Thomas Conway's "cabal" against GW exposed, Nov.

First biography of GW published in London: *A Compendius History of General Washington, Commander-in-Chief of the Americans.*

Johann Kalb commissioned a major-general . . . Marquis de laFayette, Kalb's traveling companion to America, also commissioned a major-general, and attached to GW's personal staff.

John Burgoyne captured Fort Ticonderoga, July 5. "I have beat them! Beat all the Americans!" George III exclaimed when he received this news.

Battle of Saratoga, Oct. 7. Burgoyne surrendered, Oct. 14 to Horatio Gates . . . Lottery conducted by Congress to try to raise $5,000,000 . . . Articles of Confederation adopted, Nov. 15 . . . "Battle of the Kegs," Dec.

Army in winter quarters, Valley Forge, Dec. 18.

1778

France recognized U.S. Feb. 6.

GW turned Battle of Monmouth Court House, Freehold, N.J., into a victory, June 28, despite disobedience of Charles Lee. Lee courtmartialed and suspended from Army for a year.

Northern army in winter quarters in cantonments scattered from Danbury, Conn., to Elizabethtown, N.J. GW at Middlebrook, on Raritan River.

George Rogers Clark captured Kaskaskia and Vincennes . . . French forces arrived at Newport, R.I., under D'Estaing . . . A return of the Adjutant General showed 755

Negroes in Continental Army. Approx. 3000 Negroes served in the war.

1779

GW's h.q. during summer and autumn at New Windsor and West Point, N.Y.; moved in Dec. to Morristown, N.J., for six months.

Richmond made capital of Virginia . . . $35, $45, $55 currency issued.

1780

French army landed at Newport. GW met with De Rochambeau at Hartford.

GW's winter h.q. at New Windsor, N.Y.

Benjamin Lincoln surrendered Charleston. Horatio Gates sent by Congress to replace Lincoln as C.-in-C. in the South . . . Arnold conspired with Andre. He escaped. Andre caught and executed, Oct. 2 . . . Gates defeated in Battle of Camden, S.C., Aug. 16 . . . Nathanael Greene superseded Gates Dec. 2 in command in the South . . . Patrick Ferguson's Tory militia crushed at King's Mountain, S.C. by Carolina, Tennessee and Kentucky patriot forces.

1781

GW's birthday was first observed outside the family when Count de Rochambeau ordered special honors on the occasion to the C.-in-C. of the combined forces.

U.S. and French forces under GW started Aug. 19 from Hudson River to bottle up Cornwallis at Yorktown . . . Siege of Yorktown begun, Sept. 2 . . . Cornwallis surrendered, Oct. 19 . . .

GW in winter quarters at Morristown. The Pennsylvania line mutinied over lack of pay, food, clothes and marched toward Philadelphia to demand redress from Congress. Intercepted and placated at Trenton. Mutiny of New Jersey troops quelled.

First American diplomatic mission sent to Russia: Francis Dana and secretary (14-year-old J. Q. Adams).

1782

After GW rejoined army at Newburgh, it paraded for first time in full uniform.

GW created Purple Heart badge of military merit.

GW profile on 1¢ coin of Confederation.

Washington College chartered at Chestertown, Md. Washington College named at Lexington, Va.

Netherlands recognized independence of U.S. . . . . Preliminary articles of peace signed at Paris, Nov. 30 . . . French army departed from U.S. for Haiti, Dec.

1783

GW proposed to Congress a peacetime training of all men 18 to 25.

An anonymous circular distributed at Newburgh aroused men to press claims on Congress. GW, in an admirable address, met the critical situation and obtained a declaration of confidence in Congress.

Commissioned officers of Continental Army banded themselves into Society of Cincinnati; GW elected first president-general, June 19.

GW made a tour of Hudson and Mohawk regions with Gov. George Clinton, observing the possibilities of Mohawk navigation — the future Erie Canal route — and became Clinton's partner in land holdings.

British evacuated New York, Nov. 25, whereupon GW and Gov. Clinton entered it amid cheers . . . GW bade farewell to his officers at Fraunce's Tavern, New York . . .

GW celebrated Christmas at Mt. Vernon with Mrs. W, first time since 1774.

Congress ordered army disbanded, except for a custodian force.

1784

GW wrote to Congress for permission to retain (the parchment of) his original commission — the only personal request he ever made of the government.

GW inspected his properties beyond the Alleghenies on a 700-mile tour.

GW wrote Dr. James Craik, "Any memoirs of my life, distinct and connected with the general history of the war, would rather hurt my feelings than tickle my pride whilst I lived."

1785

Potomac Navigation Co. organized, May, with GW as president. Some understanding became necessary between Virginia and Maryland regarding navigation on the Potomac. Commissioners met in conference at Mt. Vernon. "From this seed sprang the Federal Constitution," it is stated.

1786

GW enlarged Mt. Vernon again.

GW urged "some plan by which slavery . . . may be abolished by law."

The Shays' Rebellion in Massachusetts, Oct. 1786-Jan. 1787.

1787

GW went as a Virginia delegate to Constitutional Convention in Philadelphia, and presided over it, May-Sept. 11.

Court actions for taxes on GW land holdings docketed thrice at Greensburg, Pa.

John Augustine W died. GW wrote with grief of "my beloved brother."

Publication of *The Federalist Papers* begun in New York to persuade ratification of the Constitution. GW wrote a friend: "The merits and defects of the proposed Constitution have been largely and ably discussed. For myself, I was ready to have embraced any tolerable compromise that was competent to save us from impending ruin."

Delaware the first State to ratify, followed by Pennsylvania, New Jersey . . .

1788

A turkey cookery recipe originated at Mt. Vernon: braising with a sauce of Spanish wine, Jamaica rum and spices.

1789

GW, chosen President, borrowed £600 from Richard Conway for traveling expenses and setting up a household at New York.

GW refused to accept a salary, only expenses. Congress voted him $25,000 a year.

GW, who once went five nights in succession to a Williamsburg theater where a red-haired actress was the attraction, used Presiden-

tial box at John St. Theater, N.Y. to see *The School for Scandal*.

GW made first Presidential tour, going into New England, Oct.-Nov. Ill on trip.

GW's mother died at Fredericksburg, Aug. 25.

First law of Congress approved by GW as President was an act to "regulate the time and manner of taking certain oaths."

1790

GW's Message to Congress, Jan. 8, had enduring phrase, "To be prepared for war is one of the most effectual means of preserving peace."

GW visited Rhode Island, Aug. 15-22, by sea.

He appointed first woman employe of federal government: Mary K. Goddard, postmistress at Baltimore.

GW moved his household to new capital, in Philadelphia, Aug. 30, ahead of Congress.

GW seriously ill of pneumonia, believed near death.

First U.S. Census taken. Total: 3,929,214. Center of population 23 miles s.w. of Baltimore. . . . Josiah Harmar defeated near Fort Wayne, as five-year Indian war began. ("I expected little from the moment I heard he was a drunkard," said GW.) . . . GW appointees to the Supreme Court held first session: John Jay (N.Y.), James Wilson (Pa.), Wm. Cushing (Mass.), John Blair (Va.), James Iredell (N.C.). Later GW appointees to the Court: John Rutledge, Thos. Johnson (Md.), Wm. Paterson (N.J.), Samuel Chase (Md.), Oliver Ellsworth (Conn.).

1791

Governor-General of Canada sent envoy to GW to determine if U.S. would remain neutral in impending war of Britain and Spain. (Britain wanted to transport forces through U.S.).

Boundaries of Federal District proclaimed Mar. 20. Commissioners named it Territory of Columbia and the capital city Washington. (GW himself modestly avoided referring to it as other than "The Federal City.")

GW toured Southern states.

Vermont admitted to Union as 14th State. . . . Indians surprised and defeated Gen. Arthur St. Clair's expedition in Ohio.

1792

GW named Anthony Wayne C.-in-C. of forces sent against northwest Indians.

GW vetoed an apportionment-of-representation bill, his first of two vetoes.

GW laid cornerstone of Executive Mansion at the Federal City.

Presidential electors re-elected GW and John Adams, Dec. 5.... Political parties had emerged, largely because of Hamilton's policies and the rivalry of Hamilton and Jefferson.

Kentucky admitted to Union as 15th State.... U.S. coinage authorized under a decimal system and U.S. Mint established by Congress. First silver coins struck from silver plate given by GW.... Cotton gin invented by Eli Whitney.

1793

GW inaugurated for second term, March 4.

GW met chief department heads at Mount Vernon Feb. 25 — the earliest "Cabinet" session.

GW issued proclamation of neutrality in war of France and England. Jefferson retired as GW's Secretary of State.

GW attended Rickett's Circus — which featured acts irresistible to an ardent horseman. Rickett interrupted his act to drink a toast to "The Man of the People." Jefferson noted in his diary that "a great deal of disapprobation appeared in the audience. Many put on their hats and went out." John Dunlap's American *Daily Advertiser* declared it "operated like electricity in producing general applause."

Cornerstone of the new Capitol at Washington laid by GW, Sept. 18.

1794

Armed resistance to internal revenue taxes broke out in Pennsylvania, July. GW issued a proclamation against the insurgents, Aug. 7. On Sept. 2, he called out militia of Pennsylvania, Virginia, Maryland to deal with the rebels. Sept. 30-Oct. 27, GW visited Pennsylvania, Maryland and Virginia during gathering of the militia, and at Bedford, Pa., ordered an advance, Oct. 23, against the insurgents. The trouble ended without an armed clash.

GW sent John Jay as special envoy to England, April 16. Jay effected a contentious treaty, Nov. 19.

Edmund Randolph appointed Jefferson's successor as Secretary of State.... Congress authorized six ships of war, in a revival of the regular navy.... Maj. Gen. Anthony Wayne won Battle of Fallen Timbers.

1795

GW wrote, Jan. 16, a classic letter of advice on love to his adopted daughter, Eleanor Parke Custis, with admonition, "*You,* as others have done, may find, perhaps, that the passions of your sex are easier raised than allayed...."

GW named Timothy Pickering Secretary of War, in place of Henry Knox, later in year made him Edmund Randolph's replacement when Randolph had to resign as Secretary of State amid charges of improper conduct in connection with Jay Treaty. The treaty was ratified by the Senate, Aug. 18, after strong opposition, led by James Madison.

GW wrote Patrick Henry "My ardent desire is to comply strictly with *all* our engagements, foreign and domestic, but to keep the United States free from political connexions with every other country, to see them independent of *all* and under the influence of none." (The term "entangling alliances" is attributed to Washington erroneously.)

Hamilton resigned as Secretary of Treasury; Oliver Wolcott appointed.

Senate approved treaty signed by GW, binding U.S. to pay annual tribute of $83,000 to Bey of Algiers for protection of U.S. merchant ships from Algerian pirates. Senate refused to ratify GW's appointment of John Rutledge as Chief Justice.

Congress passed stringent Naturalization Act.... Treaty effected with Spain, opening Mississippi River to American flatboats and other craft.

1796

GW's Farewell Address, published, Sept. 17.

Third presidential election, Nov. John Adams elected President; Thomas Jefferson, Vice-President.

Tennessee admitted to Union as 16th State.... Last frontier post, Mackinac, given up by British under Jay Treaty.

1797

GW vetoed reduction of army bill, Feb. 28.

GW retired from office, March 4, and returned to Mt. Vernon, March 15.

Senate expelled a member, William Blount of Tennessee.

1798

GW named C.-in-C. of provisional army raised for war with France, July 2.

GW made trip to Philadelphia to confer on military matters. It was his last journey.

Alien and Sedition Acts passed. ... Naval war with France began.

1799

Nelly Custis married Lawrence Lewis on GW's last birthday. Lewises' first child born, Dec. 1, at Mt. Vernon; thus GW lived to see Martha W's great-grandchild.

Dec. 10 he sent an adv. to Alexandria paper asking that "claims of every kind be brought by the first of January, that I may wipe them off and begin anew...."

Taken ill Dec. 12. Dec. 13, wrote last letter, to James Anderson, concerning improvement of cattle care at GW's farms. Died Dec. 14. Buried Dec. 18.

Rev. M. L. Weems began a biography before GW's death. Initial version, printed Jan. 1800, was to expand through some 90 editions.

INDEX

MONTREAL, 80
MORGAN, Daniel P., 123, 133, 163, 174-178
MORRIS, Gouverneur, 226-227
MORRIS, Richard, quoted, 234
MORRIS, Robert, 202, 225, 226-227
MORRIS, Mrs. Roger, (nee Mary Philipse), 33, 36
MORRIS, Roger, 33, 34
MORRISTOWN, N.J., 114, 118, 133
MOUNT Vernon Ladies Association of the Union, 16, 200, 252-254
Mount Vernon, The Story of a Shrine, 253
MOUNT Vernon, Va., 6, 9, 11, 14, 17, 24, 38, 39-43, 48-49, 54, 179, 199, 200, 201, 202, 206-207, 211, 228, 229, 233, 237-238, 245-254, 257-261
MUHLENBERG, Frederick, 214
MULLIGAN, Hercules, 191
MUTINIES, 259-260

N

NAPOLEON, Bonaparte, 235, 249
NATIONAL Gallery of Art, 44
"NECESSITY, Fort", 31, 257
NEGROES in Washington's Army, 258, 259
NELSON, Thomas, Jr., 181
NEW Brunswick, N.J., 118
NEWBURGH, N.Y., 185-186, 241, 259
NEW London, Conn., 169
NEW Windsor, N.Y., 179
NEW York City, 85, 94-101, 118, 179, 209-225, 260
NEW-YORK Historical Society, 211, 228
NEW York Public Library, 233
NICHOLA, Lewis, 187
NORTH, Sir Frederick, 2nd Earl of Guilford, 65, 157

O

OATHS of Allegiance, 259
O'BRIEN, Jeremiah, 81
OGDEN, Aaron, 171-172
O'HARA, Charles, 183
OHIO Company of Virginia, The, 24, 25, 26
ORDINANCES 1784, 1785 and 1787, 198
OTIS, James, 58, 59, 258

P

PADOVER, Saul K., 207
PAINE, Thomas, 86-87
PALMER, John W., 96
PALTSITS, Victor Hugo, 233
PARKER, Hyde, Jr., 173
PATERSON, William, 260
PAWTUCKET, R.I., 230
PEALE, Charles Willson, 134-136, 142, 144, 156
PEALE, James, 142, 147
PEALE, Raphaelle, 142, 147
PEALE, Rembrandt, 142, 156
PENDLETON, Edmund, 55
Pennsylvania Gazette, 84-85, 91, 133
Pennsylvania Packet, 135
PENNSYLVANIA, Historical Society of, 16, 136, 140, 164-165
PETTIT, Charles, 114
PHILADELPHIA, Pa., 86, 87-91, 158, 225, 260
PHILIPSE, Frederick II, 33
PHILIPSE, Mary. See Mrs. Roger Morris

PICKENS, Andrew, 174
PICKERING, Timothy, 73, 261
PINCKNEY, Charles Cotesworth, 237
PINE, Robert Edge, 18, 19, 136, 156
PITCAIRN, John, 70
"PITCHER, Molly" (see Mary Ludwig Hays)
PITT, Fort, 38, 54
PITT, William, 41
PITTSBURGH, see Forks of Ohio, Fort Du Quesne, Fort Pitt
POLK, Charles Peale, 156
PONTIGIBAUD, Chevalier de, 241
POPE, Nathaniel 2, 4
POTOMAC Company and Potomac Navigation Company, 248, 260
POWELL, Samuel, Mrs., 243
PRESQUE Isle, 26
PRESTWICH, Sir John, 93
PRINCETON, as Capital, 259
PRINCETON, Battle of, 112-113
PRINCETON (College of New Jersey), 135, 194
PULASKI, Casimir, 125, 131
PURPLE Heart (decoration), 260
PUTNAM, Israel, 70, 72, 76
PUTNAM, Rufus, 223

Q

QUARTERING Act, 69
QUEBEC, 80
QUINCY, Josiah, Co-defender with John Adams of "Boston Massacre" accused, 66-67

R

RALL (Rahl), Johann, 110
RAMAGE (Rammage), John, 152
RANDOLPH, Edmund, 228, 261
RANDOLPH, Peyton, 55, 258
READ, Thomas, 112, 113
RED Jacket, Seneca Chief, 229
REED, Joseph, 84, 85, 114, 136
REVERE, Paul, 64, 65, 66-67, 211
REVOLUTION, Sons of, 188
RICHARDSON, Ebenezer, 66-67
RICHMOND, Va., 156
RINGO'S (Ringoes), N.J., 102-103
RIVINGTON, James, 191
ROBERTSON, Archibald, 138, 150, 151
ROBINSON, Beverly, 33
ROCHAMBEAU, Jean Baptiste Vimeur, Comte de, 169, 179, 223
ROCKEFELLER, John D., Jr., 5, 58
RODNEY, Caesar, 88-91
ROE, Austin, 191
ROSENTHAL, Max, 136
Rules of Civility and Decent Behaviour, 11, 12, 14, 257
RUMSEY, James, 206, 231
RUSH, Benjamin, 87, 93
RUTLEDGE, John, 55, 58, 260, 261

S

ST. CLAIR, Arthur, 223, 261
SAINT-MEMIN, Charles de, 152-153, 156
SALOMON, Haym, 226-227
SARATOGA, Battles of, 119, 166
SAVAGE, Edward, 44, 147, 152, 218
SAVANNAH, Ga., 176-177
SCAMMELL, Alexander, 215
SCHENCK, John, 102-103
SCHUYLER, Philip, 54, 76, 84, 221

SHARPLES (Sharpless), James, 156
SHELDON, Elisha, 133
SHERMAN, Roger, 88-91
SHIPPEN, Margaret ("Peggy") see Mrs. Benedict Arnold
SHIRLEY, William, 33, 257
SILHOUETTES, 148-149
SIMITIERE, Eugene Pierre du, 93, 156
SLATER, Samuel, 230
SLAVES, VI, 246-248
SMITH, Francis, 69
SMITH, Samuel, 122
SNIDER, Christopher, 66-67
SONS of Liberty, 61, 62, 63
SPAIN, in America, 223, 260
SPARKS, Jared, 48
SPEARING, Ann, 31
SPENCER, Joseph, 76, 94
SPOONER, Dr. Shearas-jahub, 18
STAMP ACT, British, 54, 62, 63-65
STANSBURY, Joseph, 167
STEPHEN, Adam, 119
STEUBEN, Friedrich Wilhelm Von, 125-126, 129
STEWART, Alexander, 176
"STIRLING, Lord" (see William Alexander)
STOCKTON, Mrs. Richard, 241
STONY Point, N.Y., 122
STUART, Gilbert, 132, 141-144, 240-241
SULGRAVE MANOR, England, 2, 3
SULLIVAN, John, 76
SULLIVAN, William, 242
SULLY, Thomas, 108, 109
SUMTER, Thomas, 176-177
SUPREME Court, U.S., Washington appointees, 260

T

TALLMADGE, Benjamin, 191
TAPPAN Zee, N.Y., 160
TARLETON, Banastre, 174
THACHER, Dr. James, 161
THANKSGIVING, 218, 220-221
THAYER, Simeon, 123
THOMAS, Isaiah, 85
THOMAS, John, 76
THOMSON, Charles, 83
TICONDEROGA, Fort, 74, 75, 80, 99, 102, 259
TOWNSEND, Charles, 161
TOWNSEND, Robert, 191
TRACY, Sarah, 254
TRENT, William, 26, 28, 29
TRENTON, N.J. and Battle of, 103, 110-112, 241, 259
TRUMBULL, John, 135, 144-146, 152, 223
TRUMBULL, Jonathan ("Brother Jonathan"), 146
TUPPER, Benjamin, 160
Turtle (submarine), 85-86

U

ULSTER County Historical Society, 128
UNIFORMS, 76, 123, 174, 259
UNION Flag, Great (Grand), 82-85, 259

V

VALLEY Forge, Pa., 124-127, 259
VAN BRAAM, Jacob, 26, 29
VARICK, Richard, 209
VARNUM, James M., 158
VAUGHAN, Samuel, 140-141
VERGENNES, Comte de, 116

VERMONT (New Connecticut), 260
VERNON, Edward, 11
VETO (Washington's first), 261
VINCENNES, Ind., 162
Virginia Gazette, The, 26, 256
Vulture, H.M.S., 167

W

"WAKEFIELD," 5, 6, 7, 8, 9, 10
WALL, Charles Cecil, and Gerald W. Johnson, quoted, 253
WARD, Artemas, 72, 74, 76
WARD, John Q. A., I.
WARNER, Augustine, 4
WARNER, Seth
WASHINGTON, Anne Fairfax 9, 22, 23, 39
WASHINGTON, Anne Pope, 2, 4
WASHINGTON, Augustine ("Gus"), 2, 4, 6, 8, 9, 10
WASHINGTON, Bushrod, 201, 241, 248
WASHINGTON, Charles, 9, 10, 52, 256
WASHINGTON, Elizabeth ("Betty"), Mrs. Fielding Lewis, 9, 52, 256
WASHINGTON, Harriot, 201
WASHINGTON, George:
Ancestry, 2, 3, 4, 6
As Youth, VI, 8, 9, 10, 11, 12, 13, 14, 15, 16-20, 21, 22, 23, 24, 53, 256-257
Cherry Tree Myth, IV
Eye-witness Descriptions, 1, 2, 14, 48, 209-210, 239-241
As Soldier, 2, 4, 26, 36, 72, 77-78, 85, 94-97, 99-101, 102-113, 116-119, 122-131, 156-161, 176-184, 235, 257-260
Religion, 46-49
As President, 17, 18, 209-223, 226-233, 260-261
Quoted, 1, 2, 16-18, 22-23, 26-27, 29, 31, 38, 39, 46, 49, 50, 53, 54, 55, 77, 99, 102, 132, 133-134, 135, 136-137, 159, 163, 168, 174, 179-184, 184-185, 186, 196-197, 199, 201, 202-203, 206, 209, 210, 214, 215, 218, 221, 229, 233, 237, 239-244, 245, 246, 248, 257-261
As Farmer and Businessman, 39-43, 50, 54, 199-205, 206-208, 235, 237-245, 257-261

Portraits and Representations, I, 22, 25, 27, 34, 42, 44-45, 52, 132, 133-156, 183, 228, 240
Book-plate, III
Signatures, 12
Death and Memorials, 245-253
Last Will and Testament, 246-248
Biography, first, 259
Birthday, first observed, 259
Memoirs, attitude toward, 260
WASHINGTON, Jane Butler, 4, 6
WASHINGTON, John, 2, 4
WASHINGTON, John Augustine ("Austin"), 6, 10, 11, 24, 29, 201-202, 239, 256, 260
WASHINGTON, John Augustine, Jr., 248, 251, 253-254
WASHINGTON, Lawrence (G.W's grandfather), 4
WASHINGTON, Lawrence (GW's half brother), 4, 6, 9, 11, 14, 16, 21, 22
WASHINGTON, Lawrence (of Sulgrave), 2
WASHINGTON, Rev. Lawrence (of Purleigh), 2
WASHINGTON, Martha Dandridge Custis, 36, 37, 38, 39, 41, 44-45, 50, 113, 132, 135, 143, 199, 211, 215-217, 221, 233, 240-243, 245-246, 248, 251, 256
WASHINGTON, Mary Ball, 2, 4, 6, 8, 9, 11, 14, 16, 17, 18, 19, 202-203, 223
WASHINGTON, Mildred Warner (later Mrs. George Gale), 4, 256
WASHINGTON, Mildred (GW's sister), 9, 256
WASHINGTON, Samuel, 9, 10, 52, 201-202, 256
WASHINGTON, Sarah, 24, 257
WASHINGTON, William Augustine,
WASHINGTON, William (soldier), 174-177
WASHINGTON, W. Lanier, 18
WASHINGTON, D.C., 260, 261
WASHINGTON, FORT (New York), 101, 102
WASHINGTON, FORT (Ohio), 223
WASHINGTON Headquarters Association (N.Y.), 34

WASHINGTON AND LEE UNIVERSITY, 136, 260
WASHINGTON MONUMENT (D.C.), 251-253
WAYNE, Anthony, 119, 161, 163, 238, 261
WEBSTER, Noah, 240
WEEMS, Mason Locke, 261
WELD, Isaac, 242-244
WERNER, Alfred, quoted, 136
WERTMULLER, Adolph, 151
WEST Point, N.Y., 161, 163, 198
WHIPPLE, Wayne, 240
WHIST (card game), 257
"WHISKEY Insurrection", 231, 261
WHITNEY, Eli, 229, 230-231
WIGNELL, Thomas, 239
WILKINSON, James, 173
WILLIAMS, William, 152
WILLIAMSBURG, Va., 25, 26, 55, 56-57, 58, 239, 257-258
WILLIAM AND MARY College, 20, 28
WILLIS, Henry, 6
WILLS Creek (Cumberland, Md.), 26, 28
WILSON, James, 88, 201, 248, 260
WILSON, Robert, 186
WINCHESTER, Va., 229
WINSOR, Justin, 152
WOLCOTT, Oliver, 230, 261
WOLLASTON, John, 16, 18, 36, 37, 135
WOODBRIDGE, N.J., 209
WOODHULL, Abraham, 191
WOOSTER, David, 76
WREN, Sir Christopher, 56-57
WRIGHT, Joseph, 155, 156
WRIGHT, Mrs. Patience Lovell, 155
WYNKOOP, Henry, 214
WYTHE, George, 87, 88-91

Y

YANKEE (Yankey) *DOODLE*, 28, 72
YORK, PA., 259
YORKTOWN, Va., 83, 173, 179-184
YOUNG Man's Companion, 11, 12, 14, 257